TOPGUN
DAYS

TOPGUN
DAYS

DOGFIGHTING, CHEATING DEATH,
AND HOLLYWOOD GLORY
AS ONE OF AMERICA'S BEST FIGHTER JOCKS

DAVE "BIO" BARANEK

Skyhorse Publishing

Skyhorse Publishing books may be purchased in bulk at special discounts for sales promotion, corporate gifts, fund-raising, or educational purposes. Special editions can also be created to specifications. For details, contact the Special Sales Department, Skyhorse Publishing, 555 Eighth Avenue, Suite 903, New York, NY 10018 or info@skyhorsepublishing.com.

www.skyhorsepublishing.com

10 9 8 7 6 5 4 3 2 1

Library of Congress Cataloging-in-Publication Data

Baranek, Dave.
  Topgun days : dogfighting, cheating death, and Hollywood glory as one of America's best fighter jocks / Dave "Bio" Baranek.
     p. cm.
  Includes index.
  ISBN 978-1-61608-005-1 (hardcover : alk. paper)
  1. Baranek, Dave. 2. Fighter pilots--United States--Biography. 3. United States. Navy--Officers--Biography. 4. Navy Fighter Weapons School (U.S.) 5. Air pilots, Military--Training of--United States. 6. Tomcat (Jet fighter plane) 7. Top Gun (Motion picture) I. Title.
  UG626.2.B275A3 2010
  359.0092--dc22
  [B]
                                        2010010098

Printed in the United States of America

This book is dedicated to
my lovely wife, Laura,
who encouraged and assisted me
every step along the way.

Contents

Introduction

This is a story about an ordinary guy in extraordinary circumstances. In 1980 the U.S. Navy designated 451 Naval Flight Officers. Four years later only one of them became a Topgun instructor. That was me.

In the pages ahead you will experience events that are relatively rare, even in the universe of jet fighters, such as surviving the life-or-death experience of ejecting from an F-14 Tomcat during a crash, attending the Topgun class as a student, and returning to Topgun two years later as an instructor.

Before becoming an instructor at Topgun I flew in hundreds of dogfights, which usually lasted about two minutes each, and logged more than a thousand hours of flying time in the F-14 Tomcat, the Navy's premiere fighter and at the time one of the world's most capable aircraft. As a radar intercept officer, my seat was six feet behind the pilot's, so I got the same ride as he did and I was critical to our mission. I launched real missiles at targets, escorted Russian bombers probing our ship's defenses (they were our nemesis then), regularly flew only a few feet from other aircraft to accomplish aerial refueling, and made hundreds of head-snapping catapult launches and arrested landings on aircraft carriers—day and night. I flew at speeds of more than 1,000 mph . . . and occasionally less than 200 mph, which can be equally thrilling in the midst of a dogfight. Like my fighter squadron brethren, I did these things on a regular basis, and they make for great stories.

As a Topgun instructor I had to be an expert in American weapons and tactics so I could teach them in the classroom, and then man-up a sleek F-5 Tiger II fighter and fly like an enemy to present a challenging and realistic adversary for air combat flight training. For a guy who grew up dreaming about fighters, simply being a part of this world was a fantastic dream come true. Having to study and practice to achieve the highest level of expertise—Topgun's standard—was the icing on the cake. And when I thought it couldn't get any better, I was among the real Navy personnel who assisted Paramount Pictures when they made the movie *Top Gun* in 1985. Getting a behind-the-scenes look at this fantastic project was a thrill, as was meeting Tom Cruise, Anthony Edwards, and other Hollywood luminaries and being a part of something that still draws an audience more than two decades later.

Along the way I never lost my fascination with the sensory or technical aspects of the fighter business, and I experienced things that never occurred to me as a teenager: enduring camaraderie, personal growth, and the sense of

contributing to a worthwhile enterprise, which is both satisfying and humbling.

To help you understand the Navy fighter adventure I offer
brief explanations for technical terms and a **glossary** for easy
reference. In several places I provide Intel Briefs (short for
intelligence briefings) covering significant concepts that are
more complicated than could be explained within the narra-
tive. And I've included several dozen photos (eye candy)
to show some of the amazing sights Navy aviators see on a
regular basis.

Put your helmet and gloves on and strap into your ejection seat—your Topgun days are about to start!

ONE

Faceoff at 700 MPH

It's a hot, clear late-afternoon in August with plenty of time left before sunset . . . a good day for a dogfight.

Our jets are powered up, but our canopies are still open as we wait for the go-ahead to move onto our runways. I slip down the shaded visor of my helmet against the glare of the steel hangars shimmering in the air across the hot concrete. Hoping for a breeze, I settle back in my seat with my oxygen mask loose, my gloved hands hanging over the sides of the cockpit. My flight suit is a sun-absorbing black, uncomfortably hot during these few minutes on the ground.

My aircraft is a flat black, like burned paper, as are the three other fighter jets in my flight, waiting beside me. The only color appears on the tails of our jets and on our helmets—a red star in a yellow circle. It is a symbol few people recognize, but after today and for years to come, it will be seen by millions of people around the world.

Of the four black jets, only one, the flight lead, is a two-seat configuration. I sit in its rear cockpit, behind the pilot. From here I will process a blur of information in the form of green dots and codes and merge it with everything I see around me in the sky, struggling to stay mentally ahead of aircraft slashing past each other at near-supersonic speeds. I will also be the voice of our communications.

All this falls under the heading of **situational awareness**. Characteristically, American pilots have reduced all of this to a two-letter acronym: SA. It is a term fighter pilots of all nations have learned to appreciate.

Though I'm in the lead jet for the black flight, the mission will ultimately be directed by men in the white plane streaking down the runway and into the air ahead of us. It is an American-made Learjet, the type an executive or celebrity might own, though this one has been stripped of luxuries and specially modified for this unusual mission. The gleaming, state-of-the-art Learjet 25 is painted a glossy white with accent stripes and, as a high-end civilian jet, has been the focus of considerably more of the military ground crew's attention than our four black fighters.

Once the Lear is airborne, tower comes up on the radio telling us we are cleared to move into position for takeoff. To the control tower we are one unit, four sets of wheels leaving the ground simultaneously, but we refer to ourselves according to our position in the formation. Since mine is the lead aircraft for the flight, it is designated Dash One. My wingman is Dash Two, and the remaining pair are Dash Three and Four.

Dash One taxies in formation with our wingman across the yellow hold-short boundary line and onto the scorched concrete of the runway. Dash Three and Dash Four cross the near runway with us, then continue across a short dividing area to take up position on the left runway. The four crews turn instinctively to look at each other's aircraft, then we close our canopies simultaneously, reaching up to grab the metal frames, pulling them down, then pushing folding hand-grips forward until the canopy warning light goes out. Each runway now has two black fighters waiting wingtip to wingtip.

I clip my oxygen mask in place, the rubber refreshingly cool against my face. It brings that peculiarly clean, metallic smell of bottled air. In my student aviator days, it was the hardest part of flying to get used to; now the first breath always brings back the fresh excitement of flying, as if it were a cold, stinging taste of the earth's atmosphere at high altitude.

My pilot and I check the caution and advisory lights in our cockpit and confirm there are no problems. We look over our right shoulders, making one last visual check of our wingman. All surface panels on his jet are closed, there are no visible leaks or smoke, so we give him a thumbs-up signal. He gives our fighter a final look and returns the same thumbs-up.

On the other runway, Dash Three and Four have mirrored the ritual, completing their cockpit checks and visuals. We look over to see the swift upward arm motion from Dash Three that even from five hundred feet away can only be interpreted as a good-to-go.

Our mission is to fly head-on in opposition to the best-trained fighter pilots America has to offer, so the world can see whether they are really as good as they claim. Also among the best-trained pilots, we have been selected to represent the enemy. Our jets are much smaller than the thundering F-14 Tomcats, but we have our tricks, and we are a smart, seasoned, determined adversary. Within the next hour, we will be flying circles around them.

Air traffic control has opened the sky for us, and now tower comes over my headset to give us its final instructions before handing us off to departure control.

"Topgun 47 flight cleared for takeoff, switch Departure."

⚜

The no-worries accent of the native Southern Californian in the tower snaps me out of a momentary fantasy. Microbreak over, back to work. A little daydreaming on the job is only natural, but strapping on a fighter jet for a living requires a constant respect for the reality of one's situation. We're about to begin the portion of our job that can get us killed.

Pretending to be the bad guy is part of my regular duty. Those of us flying the black jets are full-time military officers, instructors at the Navy Fighter Weapons School based at Naval Air Station Miramar, just north of San Diego, where the U.S. Navy's best aviators are put through advanced training. Our school, a squadron of aircraft and the men and women who operate them, is known as Topgun.

As instructors, every day we dodge, parry, challenge, confront—and often beat—accomplished professional dogfighters flying the world's most advanced fighter jets. We do our best to simulate the skills of the best fighter pilots of an unfriendly nation as we fly small, nimble **A-4 Skyhawks** and **F-5 Tiger II** fighters. Being a worthy adversary sometimes requires a peculiarly divided frame of mind, and beating the Navy's front line fighters always requires the best efforts of proficient pilots. Being good is how every one of the instructors got to Topgun.

I don't often think like a "comrade," but today's flight is different. Hollywood has come to Miramar. Somewhere up our chain of command, the brass has decided to assist the producers of a Paramount Pictures drama loosely based on the real Topgun program. So they have come to one of the Navy's main fighter bases to capture realistic scenes with rows of fighters and functional hangars, a ready-made set. The Navy has operated at Miramar for decades, and Topgun has been training fighter crews here for more than fifteen years. This ambience would be difficult to duplicate.

The script calls for the hero, a Navy **F-14 Tomcat** pilot (call sign Maverick), to have a close encounter with enemy fighter jets making provocative feints at his aircraft carrier, a common occurrence for those of us who actually flew from carriers on contested seas. To set up the hero's romance with a female intelligence analyst, the enemy fighter he is to encounter would be a new, advanced type the West had never seen close-up before: a fictional MiG-28. The pointy-nosed F-5 had a sinister look, the director decided, so it was cast as the **MiG**, with a flat-black paint job to add to its menace. Topgun's paint shop was drawn into the stagecraft, supplying the black paint and Soviet-style graphics on short notice.

Today's Topgun mission was to fly those MiG-28s, and my black jet was the lead enemy aircraft.

Dash One's pilot—my pilot—is Bob Willard, the executive officer of the Topgun squadron, who goes by the call sign

Rat. There's a Hollywood connection here, too: he started flying F-14s in the mid 1970s, a few years after the horror movie *Willard* was released. It was the story of a maladjusted young man whose only friend was a rat, and though there's nothing rat-like about him, he decided the tough-guy sound of it might give him an edge within the competitive fraternity of fighter jocks. It's turned out to have the opposite result. Most of us who've spent time with him have come to associate "Rat" with "nice guy."

❦

With our clearance to take off, Rat tilts his head forward, presses extra hard on his brakes, and with his left hand advances his throttles to near-maximum power. The pilots in Dash Two, Three, and Four similarly hold their brakes and advance their throttles. In every cockpit, needles on a cluster of gauges move clockwise in unison as the engines run up. In my cockpit the sound increases a little, but our F-5s have relatively small engines, so through my helmet the noise is little more than a background rumble. Rat raises his head as he releases his brakes, and the other three pilots, following his signal, release theirs. The four jets begin to roll; the four pilots work their throttles to stay in formation as we smoothly accelerate down the runways. Rat is focused on the world outside, so I read off the airspeed to him.

"Off the peg . . . 60 **knots** . . . 100 knots." (100 knots is 115 mph.) At 160 knots the pilots smoothly pull back on their control sticks, and at 170 knots (196 mph) all four jets levitate off the runways together. From brake release to takeoff, a little more than twenty seconds have passed.

Airborne. As the lead, Rat makes another exaggerated head nod. He tilts his head forward and pauses. When he raises his head all four pilots raise their landing gear. We start tightening up the formation. Dash Two gets a little closer on our right side, and the other pair moves in over the grass between the runways to close in on our left. Several hundred feet off the ground, still flying above the eleven-foot main runway, Rat makes a smooth right turn from the runway heading of 240 degrees to a heading of 300. Speed increasing, he nods again to signal flaps up. The jets change from the high-lift takeoff configuration to clean vehicles capable of supersonic flight. The formation is tight now. In just a few seconds we level off at the standard departure altitude of two thousand feet and make a slight left turn back to 280 degrees to fly out to the coast; the turns keep us from flying directly over residential neighborhoods.

Miramar Road passes beneath us, packed with rush hour traffic. Below are several small shopping centers and warehouses, and then the I-805 and I-5 freeways, also jammed with commuters. I almost feel like a commuter, too. In my normal duties as an instructor I fly this route five or six times during a good week, heading out for training sessions with fighters, and I always enjoy the view and the freedom from being stuck in traffic. We fly above the brief line of cliffs and the narrow beach of Torrey Pines state park, and then we're out over the Pacific. We watch for civilian airplanes that may be close to our altitude, our eyes constantly scanning the sky.

I check in with San Diego departure control. My three wingmen and I listen to the Learjet already talking to departure control. We can tell the Lear is only a few miles ahead of us. For expediency, I request permission from our air traffic controller to join the Lear in close formation. This makes the controller's job easier and permission is granted quickly. Now we will fly as a single unit to our operating area, sixty miles out over the Pacific.

Every flight begins with a briefing in the squadron's ready room—a brief in the shorthand language of fighter crews—and today's brief, like those of the previous day, was notable for the presence of Topgun's guests: air-racing legend Clay Lacy, who will be piloting the camera plane, and the film's British-born director, Tony Scott, who will be riding along with his cameraman and technicians in Lacy's shiny Lear.

Scott arrived at the ready room each day with a stack of hand-drawn storyboards depicting the precise camera angles he wanted, based more on the story's cinematic requirements than on actual maneuvers fighter jets could be expected to accomplish safely. Rat then worked with Tony to transform his vision into a practical flight plan, illustrating the concepts using 1/72/scale models of aircraft mounted on sticks.

Then Lacy took the floor to stress the limited field of view of the camera and coach those of us flying the smaller F-5 how to make dynamic-looking maneuvers without actually moving much through the sky—roll the plane a lot, but don't pull on the control stick. Or, as Lacy put it, "Use a lot of bank, not a lot of yank." Today was the second day of movie-filming flights, and lessons like this were restated for the newcomers.

At the end of the brief, I introduced myself to Clay and told him that as a teenager I read about him winning the National Championship Air Race at Reno in 1970. He seemed pleasantly surprised to be recognized.

⚜

Forty miles ahead of us wait the two F-14 Tomcats representing the hero's jet and that of his wingman. With greater fuel capacity than our small F-5s, they launched well before us and have been leisurely cruising in a circle, tracking us on radar as we approached. The Tomcat crews each consist of a pilot and a radar intercept officer (RIO, in the rear cockpits), chosen from regular Navy fighter squadrons for their skill and experience but, like us, merely extras on the set today. The aircraft will be the stars in these scenes.

In a moment we're alongside the Lear, headed west above the Pacific. We're used to seeing fighters, and it's fascinating to fly formation on a sleek white Lear, as if we're motorcycle cops escorting a limo. Lacy has no trouble with the airspeeds we're used to; his Learjet is a hot number. We fly through clear skies above a layer of thin haze, the low afternoon sun providing dramatic lighting, with the gray-blue Pacific a dark backdrop below us. I get on the inter cockpit com and casually mention to Rat that this would make a cool photo.

With almost a decade of F-14 experience, Rat is one of the most respected pilots on the entire base, and not just because of his flying skill. He's a remarkably mellow, centered person (his passion for surfing might have something to do with it), always willing to take time to explain details or think through a problem when most of us would lose our patience. It's a quality that's made him an increasingly valuable liaison between the Paramount team and the Navy in the past few weeks.

Rat is well aware of my photography hobby, and he takes the hint. With a quick hand signal, he passes the lead to Dash Two, then adds power and pulls back on the stick. We climb about fifty feet above the other three F-5s. Rat banks slightly left, and we slide outside the group while Dash Two snuggles up to the Lear. I take a few snapshots of the black fighters cruising alongside the sunlit executive jet before we get down to business.

In a moment the Lear rolls into a left turn to head south and climbs to eighteen thousand feet. We all switch our radios to the area control frequency and listen as the Lear pilot checks in to identify us as a flight of five.

The F-14s are holding inside a rectangle roughly forty miles long and fifteen miles wide that's supervised by Navy air traffic controllers. Normally this and the adjoining areas are reserved for air combat maneuvering (ACM in Navy parlance). A training scenario that sets one fighter versus one adversary is called a 1v1, two fighters versus three adversaries is a 2v3, and so on. Fighters are always listed first, adversaries after the v.

Today it's a 2v4, with a Learjet on the side—seven high-tech jets wheeling around in a tight piece of airspace as if it were a huge soundstage.

❧

There are cameras behind an extra-large picture window in Lacy's Learjet and several periscope cameras looking above and below, as well as in external pods on one F-14 to show the good guys' point of view, and in our two-seat F-5F's cockpit to show the enemy's. Even with this coverage, filming the aerial swordplay of fighter jets has proven to be more challenging than expected. The footage shot from the Lear the previous day has turned out to be relentlessly undramatic. In the daily "rushes" (we've quickly adopted the Hollywood lingo), the crucial passes between the black-painted bandits and the American Tomcats looked about as exciting as a bunch of flies buzzing across a blue screen. There was just too much airspace between the jets to fit them into the same frame. It presented the kind of challenge Rat is drawn to, so he sat down with the two-star admiral in charge of fighter operations on the West Coast, who eventually agreed to make a one-time exception to the rules requiring five-hundred-foot clearance between aircraft during training maneuvers, provided the aviators themselves feel comfortable with the arrangements. The admiral has also made it clear the slightest mishap will result in a shut-down of the movie production.

The plan for today is to reshoot the head-on pass in several takes, starting with the five hundred feet of clearance we're accustomed to and gradually closing the separation between the black F-5s and the oncoming F-14s.

❧

As we approach the area, the F-14s report they have radar contact on us, a good start. Systems are working, people are where they are supposed to be, we're on track. As usual there is little talk. We stick to the bare essentials for coordination and avoid idle chatter. We go over the parameters for the first pass as we fly into position.

The two F-14s start on one station, their assigned holding point; our five aircraft, the four F-5s, and the Lear, are on another, ten miles away. As the mission commander, Rat makes a radio call, and the two teams turn toward each other. The wingmen in each group use standardized visual cues to help them stay in formation; the F-5 pilots align the nose of the next aircraft's missile with a corner of its canopy frame. The two opposing formations see each other as specks in the distance that grow progressively larger as the seconds pass. As the distance diminishes, I begin to wonder if we've talked-through these opposing formations thoroughly enough.

For this scene we're all going slow, only three hundred knots. If this were a normal training flight, the opposing sides would each be flying between four hundred to six hundred knots, sometimes buffeting each other with supersonic shockwaves.

Inside of a mile, both lead pilots make adjustments to avoid collision. Wingmen also adjust slightly to hold their formations. At our current speed it takes six seconds to close from one mile to the merge, the point when the formations will pass each other. Priority for the wingmen is to maintain position relative to their leads, but when we see the oncoming aircraft in our peripheral vision, the natural instinct is to touch the stick to avoid a collision. It would be exceedingly dangerous if six fighters gave in to impulsive reflex, so we concentrate on flying formation and trust physics and military discipline to see us through.

An instant later, the two Tomcats streak past the black flight and the camera plane, and fly out behind us.

While the formations fly away from each other to the set-up distance, everyone has the same thought: We need to fine-tune this. It takes a lot of discipline for everyone to stay off the radios with their own suggestions. After a moment, Rat suggests that on the next pass the F-14s refrain from making any flight adjustments once we're inside five miles, leaving it to the black F-5s to prevent collision. This makes sense to the Tomcats. The F-14 lead could have asked the same thing of the F-5s, but the Tomcats are bigger and easier to see coming. We also tweak the formations to give the wingmen a little more confidence they won't get sideswiped. Then both groups make 180-degree turns and set up for a second pass.

The Lear paces our F-5s, but with an offset. Clay Lacy, a former fighter pilot himself, has made a thriving business selling executive jets and wrangling aerial cinematography projects like this one. There are ten exceptional jet fighter jocks working this airspace, but I find myself admiring the way Lacy tweaks his course to stay in sync with the action. The clipped professionalism of his radio calls reveals his extensive flying experience. What impresses me most is that he still enjoys flying, when he could be sitting behind an expensive desk.

The second pass is similar to the first only much tighter—the F-14s streak past much closer than the five-hundred-foot separation I'm used to—but the real-time refinements give me some comfort. This tiny piece of sky is now as congested as rush hour traffic: four enemy F-5s, two American F-14s, and a white Learjet.

With the close pass accomplished, a feeling of satisfaction settles over me. We've shown these Hollywood types some of the snappy flying they came to see, and we've also shown them that military types can be flexible as well as bold, making real-time adjustments to a set plan. The unusually close pass had provided just enough adrenaline to make this a memorable afternoon.

Then movie director Tony Scott comes on the radio. "That's better fellas, much better. But can we do it one more time, only a bit closer?" His excited English accent is a sharp contrast to Clay Lacy's cool radio calls, but he is, after all, an artist. Those storyboards that seemed so impressive compared to the chalkboard diagrams we're accustomed to were his own handiwork; we had watched him dash off new visualizations during the brief.

⊰✻⊱

"A bit closer." The radio comes alive with an on-the-fly debrief of the last pass as we swing around to our stations like boxers returning to their corners before the next round. Rat communicates with the lead of the F-14 flight, asking if the second pass was comfortable enough for them to try a closer run and coming up with further refinements for executing an even tighter pass. Once the F-14 lead is satisfied, Rat goes over the details of the formations to satisfy everyone. No one objects, so it looks like a plan.

By now, we're like actors willing to take a little more risk for the sake of the audience, rather than just sticking to our normal five-hundred-foot separation. We've gotten a feel for the pace of filming and the director's requirements, and hearing words like "action" and "cut" on our radios has lost its novelty. As the Tomcats make their turn, we're pretty sure we've got it all figured out. This time, we're determined to be tight enough in the camera's frame to be recognizable aircraft: Navy-gray Tomcats and ominous black bandits, not just specks against the sky.

We again steady-up headed roughly west. Rat calls "tally-ho" over the radio, signaling that he sees the Tomcats.

Over his shoulder, I can just make them out as tiny dots in the late afternoon sky. I feel Rat making adjustments to our flight path. Our wingmen are tight and serious about staying there, bobbing slightly with each course adjustment. The Lear cruises alongside, perched outside our familiar formation. The only voice on the radio now is the lead Tomcat's RIO calling the distance every two miles—every twelve seconds.

When you're riding a jet, sitting a couple feet above screaming turbines and cocooned in a helmet and headphones, it's unusual to hear anything other than your own aircraft, your own breathing. In the final few seconds, the Tomcats quickly grow into discernible objects, then jets, and then in another second they're on us, blasting by suddenly like semi trucks on a narrow two-lane highway. I can actually hear them, a sudden *whoomp*!, before they recede into the sky behind us. It's genuinely scary, one of those things that will take a moment to put into words back at the Officers' Club.

The English accent comes up on the radio. "That's great, gents! Super!" Tony Scott's voice is elated. "Now if you don't mind, I'd like to set up for the MiGs chasing Maverick."

Clay Lacy radios, "Lear coming left to a heading of 070." Rat gives directions to our flight, and the Tomcats call in with their intentions. Next up is a dogfight scene, with our enemy jets threatening an American Tomcat. I steel myself for more thrills as we prepare to stage a dynamic event in a controlled space—like five motorcyclists in a cage. I hope that between the thorough flight brief and real-time adjustments we will both satisfy the director and bring the jets back in the same condition we signed for them.

Intel brief: What's in a Name?

Naval aviation lingo is a verbal shorthand that allows "those who know" to communicate efficiently, and also separates them a little more from everyone else. Most terms are related to the aircraft or the mission, but some refer to people.

The term "aviator," for example, might be thought of as anyone who flies, whether pilot or crewman. But when both words are capitalized—"Naval Aviator"—it's a designation that specifically means a *pilot*, the person who operates the stick, throttle, and rudder pedals.

The designation of non pilots can be more complex. The most general category is Naval Flight Officer (**NFO**), which refers to any officer who flies but is not a pilot. An NFO who flew in an F-14 Tomcat fighter was called a RIO, for Radar Intercept Officer. Those who flew in other aircraft were known by other terms according to their crew responsibilities.

For this book, I'll use the word aviator (lower case "a") to refer to pilots and RIOs.

TWO

Joining the Fighting Renegades

That head-on flight for the movie *Top Gun* took place six years after I graduated from college. By that time I was an instructor at the Navy Fighter Weapons School (Topgun), a squadron of hand-picked fighter pilots and RIOs—backseaters—flying hot aggressor aircraft to give Navy and Marine Corps aviators the best training they could get short of combat.

Being a Topgun instructor was more than a dream; it was the satisfying sequel to my dream of becoming an F-14 RIO. There had been many hurdles to clear along the way, and at times it seemed I might not make it to the next level. One time it seemed I might not make it to my next meal.

The path started at the Naval Air Station (NAS) in Pensacola, Florida, which is where every Navy and Marine Corps aviator starts, whether pilot or naval flight officer. Committed to flying the F-14 Tomcat, I arrived a month after graduating from Georgia Tech and joined a group that ran the full spectrum of interest and knowledge. Some didn't know a Tomcat from a Hawkeye, while others were like me, firmly committed to what they wanted to fly, whether it was a P-3 Orion maritime patrol aircraft, A-6 Intruder medium bomber, helicopter, or another in the variety of Navy aircraft.

In Pensacola, I trained as a naval flight officer. Yes, I had dreamed of being a *pilot*, but my vision deteriorated during college from twenty twenty to about twenty seventy. Rather than abandon my love of aircraft I revised my goal to becoming a radar intercept officer, the back seater in the F-14 Tomcat fighter. Some friends who faced the same choice decided they didn't want to fly if they couldn't be pilots, so they decided not to join the military or went to other assignments, such as operating ships. But I would rather fly than float.

As I progressed through training the group I was in gradually shrank, mostly due to people peeling off to go to different training pipelines, though a few left the program because of poor performance or a change of heart. Ultimately, however, several friends from my earliest days ended up in the same squadrons, and I worked more than five years with three in particular: Paul Rumberger, Steve Jacobsmeyer, and Gary Darby. Paul graduated from the University of Florida and was managing a grocery store when he decided he wanted more adventure. Steve graduated from the University of California at Davis and held several jobs before visiting a Navy recruiter on a dare. Gary, who graduated from the University of Texas and sold title insurance for several years, was a mature and friendly guy who didn't know much about airplanes or the Navy, but was in it with all his heart.

As proof of the saying, "it's not how many times you fall, but how many times you get back up," several episodes tested my commitment during my training. I got airsick on my first flight and a few flights after that, but it turned out that dynamic maneuvering was something I could get used to. I got a failing grade during one of my training flights in Pensacola and went before a progress review board that could have dropped me from flight school, but I bounced back and took steps toward self-improvement, such as keeping a notebook of areas to improve. I was waterboarded in survival school, too, but that wasn't anything personal: Many of us were exposed to that training opportunity.

In any case, the balance sheet was heavily tilted toward positive experiences and gradual improvement, exactly the way the program was designed.

After one year in Pensacola I progressed to Miramar, which had a very different ambience. Yes, we had flown jets in Pensacola but it was a training base and they were training jets—Miramar was the real world. I spent nine months in another training squadron, but it was the training squadron for the F-14 fighter and a *combat* squadron was adjacent to us in the hangar. We were that close. The F-14s, F-4s, and RF-8s we saw flying were a purposeful gray instead of the safety-painted white and orange trainers we were used to. These fighters were louder, and sometimes carried missiles and bombs. And there weren't a lot of young ensigns running around the base—we were now outnumbered by seasoned lieutenants, lieutenant commanders, and higher-ups in the food chain who had been on long overseas deployments, intercepted Soviet bombers trying to sneak up on our carriers, shot missiles, had friends who had died in plane crashes, and escaped death themselves. Almost everyone on Miramar had great stories, and I aspired to start on stories of my own.

These officers also had **call signs**, the essential nicknames by which aviators have been known since the earth cooled. Our Pensacola instructors had call signs, but we just called them "sir," so their nicknames were not as familiar. Now, however, we took our first step into the tight camaraderie of a regular squadron and call signs were everywhere: Crush, Snake, Pistols, Ripple, Hatch, Boom, Spock, Metro, Jimmy Mac, Barney, Drifty, and dozens more, each representing a colorful incident or characteristic, or maybe just a play on the owner's name. Every aviator who made it to the fleet got a call sign. Very few students had them yet, but our time was coming. The F-14 training squadron itself had a nickname, the **RAG**, from a decades old system known as the readiness air group. The Navy had final training squadrons for each type of aircraft, and they had changed the term for them to "fleet replacement squadron," but everyone still called them RAGs.

Arrival at Miramar meant that I was now a radar intercept officer (**RIO**), a specialized category of naval flight officer who worked closely with the pilot to fully accomplish the Tomcat's missions. As I approached assignment to a front-line Navy fighter squadron, a fleet squadron, I left behind the theory and basics of Pensacola and learned about the Tomcat, its missions, and my role. I had already discerned that the F-14 was big for a fighter, at nearly sixty-three feet long and typically weighing over sixty thousand pounds, it was larger than the popular F-4 Phantom it was replacing. But with powerful engines, innovative aerodynamics, and wings that swept forward for low speeds and back for high speeds, an F-14 could outmaneuver almost any fighter that came before it.

In our classes, simulators, and flights, however, the most important concept we learned was not technical but profound: the impressive specifications in our manuals were worthless without a crew—pilot and RIO—who were well-trained and flew their aircraft to its utmost, according to the assigned mission. (Additional details on the F-14's missions and the RIO's role are found in the sidebar, "Why the F-14 Had a RIO.")

In addition to other RIO friends from Pensacola, my F-14 training class included a pilot named Sandy Winnefeld, who graduated from Georgia Tech and Navy ROTC the year before I did. We were in the same class now because pilot training took roughly a year longer than NFO training, in part because pilots had to accomplish demanding carrier landings while they were students. It was great to have a fellow Georgia Tech alumnus in my class, and you will hear a lot more about Sandy.

There was no ceremony when my class finished the F-14 training squadron, despite the fact that it was a significant milestone that could be compared to finishing medical school—our formal training was done and we commenced our lives in an operational fighter squadron. I had fifty-eight F-14 flights and 91.2 F-14 hours in my logbook. I was in the fleet. I could go into combat. That did not appear especially likely in April 1981, but you never know. For some, the goal of flying fighters was only a few years old, but I had dreamed, hoped, and prayed for this since my grade school days.

I was assigned to Fighter Squadron Twenty Four. That bureaucratic name was reserved for official documents; we always called it VF-24 or used its nickname, the Fighting Renegades. And I was not going alone, as Gary Darby, Paul Rumberger, and Sandy Winnefeld were also assigned to VF-24, along with several other new pals from F-14 training. Steve Jacobsmeyer and other friends were assigned to VF-211, which deployed on the same aircraft carrier, so I would see them regularly for the next few years.

VF-24 operated out of Hangar Four at Miramar, a large cinderblock building with no air-conditioning that housed four F-14 squadrons: VF-114 Aardvarks, VF-213 Black Lions, VF-211 Checkmates, and VF-24 Renegades. Nicknames of the Navy's roughly two dozen Tomcat squadrons spanned the spectrum from menacing to humorous.

Each Tomcat squadron had about two hundred enlisted men and thirty officers. (Women were not assigned to fleet squadrons at the time, although that changed a few years later.) Most of the officers were pilots and RIOs, but several non-flying officers worked in the maintenance department, or handled intelligence and security matters. Most of the enlisted men were assigned to the maintenance department to care for the aircraft, engines, and systems, while others worked in the administrative and personnel departments or performed other duties throughout the squadron.

Paul and I reported the same day and stuck together most of the day. Everywhere we went we heard, "So, you're the new guys," followed by a pause just begging for a wisecrack.

We were shown around the squadron, including the ready room, administrative offices, and finally the maintenance spaces, where we would both work.

All Navy fliers have an important "ground job" in addition to flying their aircraft, which makes the squadron self-contained. My first ground job was typical for a new officer, I had some responsibility for the young sailors who maintained the weapons system of VF-24's Tomcats. Designated "Aviation Fire Control Technicians," they were AQs in the Navy's arcane classification system, so I was the AQ branch officer. I say I had "some responsibility" for them because they were really supervised by Chief Clifford McColley, who had proven his abilities and risen through the ranks. In addition to riding herd on two dozen eighteen to twenty-two year-old sailors, Chief McColley also had to teach me how to be a branch officer. He'd done it before, for my predecessor, and he would train the guy who followed me. Training new officers was just another burden the Navy's senior enlisted carried, and proudly.

So I didn't just zoom around the sky and read tactics manuals all day. I also got to know these young men from a variety of backgrounds, ethnic groups, and dispositions. I didn't plan or supervise their day-to-day work, but I was responsible for reviewing training programs, records, and other paperwork. I also enjoyed just hanging out with them, hearing about their girlfriends and their cars, talking about movies and music. The ground job added a lot of texture to the experience of being in a Navy fighter squadron. My ground job was something I had not given any prior thought to, yet being the branch officer for these sailors became a matter of personal pride.

The most common question Paul and I heard in our first days around the squadron was, "What are your call signs?"

We knew about call signs, but coming out of the RAG most of us just didn't have one. It is useless to ask a new guy what his call sign is, because he'll say Shark, Killer, Tiger, or (after the movie came out) Maverick, Iceman, or something similar. To the seasoned members of a fighter squadron, new guys fresh out of the RAG look more like Dopey, Meat, Tool, or Sand (as in, "This guy is about as useful as two hundred pounds of sand"). But still they asked us, and throughout my career squadrons continued to ask new guys their call signs.

VF-24 in those days had a typical range of call signs. Many were based on last names. Fred Hollinger was Holly, Chris Berg was Ice, and John Sill was Window. We had a Tex and a Cowboy. Many squadrons had one or both of these, usually from Texas. We also had Magic, Dragon, Okie, Drifty, Hatch, Frenchy, Gatsby, and dozens more.

A few guys tried to shake their call signs. Chumley kept pushing for J. D. but never got us to make the change. Another guy earned the call sign Buf—an acronym common in aviation, "Big Ugly F***er." But Chumley and Buf were good guys and both became successful businessmen after their time in the Navy, so a call sign definitely does not indicate the course of one's life.

Knowing that the question would come up, I had started thinking about my call sign before I left the RAG. I thought, "Baranek rhymes with bionic, so I'll be Bionic." I sought the counsel of Steve "Superman" Jones, a helpful RIO instructor who generously said Bionic sounded good to him. Unfortunately, at 6-foot-2 and 165 pounds, I didn't seem very bionic.

Plus it didn't sound good on the radio. A few weeks after I arrived at VF-24, my pilot John Boy shortened it to Bio and it stuck. Not very menacing, but at least it wasn't offensive.

For many of my RAG classmates who went to VF-24, call signs were also based on last names. Paul Rumberger became Rums, Gary Darby was Darbs, and "Sandy" Winnefeld's initials were J. A.W. so he became Jaws. Next door at VF-211, Steve Jacobsmeyer was Jake. But guys got call signs for other reasons, too. Bob Thompson was a tennis player who dressed better than most of us, so he was Preppy. Glenn McCormick kept Monk, his nickname from the Naval Academy. Chris Welty got his initials, C. J. We would very soon begin calling each other by these names almost exclusively. Once in a while someone would comment that he had to think for a moment to recall someone's real first name. This was only a slight exaggeration.

Two days after I started work at my new squadron the duty officer told me I had been added to the flight schedule for an 11:00 AM brief. My first flight in the fleet, it was scheduled as two jets to the surface-to-air threat simulation range at China Lake, California, 210 miles north of Miramar. A flight to China Lake was not in the RAG syllabus, so this would be something new for me. I was flying with Bullet, an experienced pilot, and we were assigned as the wingmen in a flight of two aircraft. The Navy calls two aircraft flying together a **section**. Holly was the lead pilot, with Ice as his RIO. They had both been in the squadron two years. The brief started with the navigation plan, radio frequencies we would use, expected fuel levels at various times throughout the flight, and other administrative items.

We then discussed tactical considerations. Our section was to fly through a range that had radars and computers to simulate enemy surface-to-air weapons, while technicians would make calls over the radio describing simulated missile launches or gun firings. Warning equipment in our Tomcats would provide information about the threats, and our pilots would maneuver our aircraft to try to defeat the missiles and guns. This may sound like a shaky proposition, but combat experience showed that in most cases a fighter could defeat a missile if he saw it and reacted correctly.

The brief covered the essential information and lasted about thirty minutes, shorter than I was used to . . . but I was no longer in a training environment being graded, I was in the fleet.

I walked out to a jet with Bullet, preflighted, strapped in, and started up. By this time I was comfortable operating from Miramar.

Shortly after takeoff, while climbing to our assigned cruising altitude, Ice started having problems with his radio as he talked to the air traffic controllers. His transmissions became scratchy and difficult to understand. As usual for this stage of the flight we were in a tight formation so I could easily see him gesture to indicate his frustration. Using the other radio, Holly said, "We're having radio problems. We can hear, but Ice can't transmit. You've got the lead."

Bullet said, "I've got the lead," to clearly acknowledge the change in responsibilities. He added power to our jet while Holly let his jet slide back, so they were now flying slightly aft of our aircraft. Then just to make sure I didn't miss the point, Bullet said over the intercom system (**ICS**), "OK, you've got the comms."

Gulp.

This change was significant, since I had to pick up the navigation and communication responsibilities. With my head spinning in the brief because of all the new details for me, I had taken comfort in the prospect of being the wingman. I planned to just tag along while the other three experienced people in the flight led the way. But that was not to be. I didn't have the option of saying, "I'll be ready in a few minutes," as we climbed through seven thousand feet on the way to our clearance altitude of sixteen thousand. I pulled out my navigation chart and checked our position. I started switching radio frequencies and doing the other things I had been trained for.

Bullet helped me along the way, and our section made it to the China Lake area.

As we approached, Bullet gave me a quick orientation to what was known as the **Echo Range**. (Electronic Warfare is EW, "Echo Whiskey" using the **phonetic alphabet**. We just called it the Echo Range.) The range is a distinct valley running east-west, about thirty-five miles long and seven to ten miles wide. The valley floor is 2,200 feet above sea level and the surrounding mountains reach 5,500 feet or more. The radars that simulate the enemy are located at three sites within the valley, small white buildings and radar antennas easily visible against the brown desert.

I switched from air traffic control frequency to Echo Range control, checking that our wingman also made the switch. Range control directed us to the western end of the valley. Bullet and I completed a checklist to set up aircraft systems for the event, so I turned on my radar warning equipment. Holly and Ice did the same and moved out to about two miles from us, a relatively loose formation so we could maneuver independently but still easily keep sight of each other. We were flying at sixteen thousand feet, 350 knots.

Range control said, "Commence the exercise," and exercise it was. My radar warning equipment immediately began to transmit warbling tones through the headphones in my helmet, lights flashed on the "threat warning" panel, and one of my three video screens switched from a navigation display to show a strobe indicating the direction to the threat radar.

A controller said, "Missile launch from site one, guiding on the northern F-14." That was Bullet and me. The radio call substituted for an actual missile launch; over enemy territory we would have received warnings from our equipment and watched for the missile launch. If in combat, we would launch small flares or chaff (packets of tiny metallized strips) to decoy a missile while our jamming equipment began its automatic operation, and the pilot would maneuver the aircraft like crazy, which is called jinking. But on this day we did not use the jamming equipment or chaff, we only jinked our way through the range. Bullet went to maximum **afterburner** and pulled the aircraft into a steep climb, then seconds later rolled inverted and put us into a dive. A few seconds after that, he rolled upright again and we were climbing. Using afterburner increased our engines' power, but at a great cost in fuel.

"Still guiding on the northern F-14, fifteen seconds to impact. Missile launch from site two, guiding on the southern F-14. Second missile from site one, guiding on the southern F-14." Minutes ago we were cruising over Los Angeles and now our two fighters had three simulated missiles heading our way. Holly and Ice began gyrations similar to ours as the controller announced even more missiles.

This was all new to me, and the blue sky and brown desert were soon smeared across my vision as we jinked through the sky above the Echo Range. Bullet did a great job of telling me what he was doing, and every few seconds I looked to the south to find our wingman. Sometimes this was to my right (if we were flying upright) and sometimes south was to my left (if we were inverted). I usually managed to catch a glimpse of their aircraft, though it could have been the Goodyear blimp for all I could tell. I just saw something flying near us. Prioritizing my mental resources in this confusing environment, I made a point to keep tabs on our fuel and our altitude as the world swirled around me. It took a long time to reach the other end of the range, since we were weren't zooming through in a straight line but were zig-zagging in three dimensions.

At the end of the first run Bullet said, "Bullet's got 10.9," meaning we had 10,900 pounds of fuel remaining. The reply was, "Holly's got 10.3." That was plenty for another run, so we told range control we were coming back, this time from east to west. They didn't mind since we had time left on our scheduled period. So we flew back through the range and got shot at. Again. A lot.

We then made a third run through the range, forgoing the afterburner in order to save fuel. This resulted in lower speed and made us easy pickings for the skilled technicians operating the simulated enemy systems. My brain was scrambled and I was soaked in sweat. But when we got back to Miramar I felt relatively good. I had handled the sudden change and assumed lead RIO duties. I had been to the Echo Range. I did not get airsick (this was still a minor concern).

I was definitely "in the fleet."

I would return to China Lake many times in the next few years, and the flights would get better.

The next event for VF-24 and me started the very next day, when we went aboard the aircraft carrier USS *Constellation* for refresher qualifications and training operations. Being able to conduct combat operations from an aircraft carrier day and night, in almost any weather, on any of the world's oceans, is what sets U.S. Naval Aviation apart. A handful of countries operate aircraft carriers, but none have as many as the United States (currently eleven), and no foreign carrier brings as many tactical aircraft to the fight as an American carrier. I was about to become part of this capability.

Up to this point, I had made ten carrier landings when I was in the RAG, fortunately in the backseat behind an experienced pilot because the activities and the pace seemed incredibly fast and confusing. I could barely keep up and wondered how I would ever become proficient at my profession, but I would soon find that a month of experience made a big difference.

THREE

A Pulse-Pounding
Carrier Landing

The aircraft carrier USS *Constellation* (CV-64) was scheduled to leave its homeport of NAS North Island on a Thursday morning for two weeks of training in the Pacific Ocean off Southern California and Northern Mexico. Connie, as we usually called her, would take her nine-squadron air wing along, as well as several smaller ships. Being a very junior member of the squadron, I had to be aboard the ship before it sailed at 7:00 AM, along with all of the enlisted sailors and a handful of other pilots and RIOs like me. The sixteen most-senior officers of VF-24 flew eight of our jets aboard later on Thursday.

I didn't want to deal with morning rush hour traffic so I packed my gear and some clothes, drove to the ship the night before, and got settled aboard. I can admit this now: I packed a lot of "civilian clothes." I took shorts, jeans, golf shirts, tennis shoes—as if I were going on a vacation! The ship had no plans to stop anywhere. We were going out for two weeks of operating to train the squadrons and the ship's crew, but I didn't know any better. I would spend most of the time in a flight suit, which we usually called a **bag**; the rest of the time I would be in my khaki uniform. So I walked aboard with two suitcases, when I needed one gym bag. Luckily I arrived at the ship late at night, stowed my luggage without being seen, and quietly unloaded it two weeks later. I never made that mistake again.

The other new guys and I enjoyed a free harbor tour of beautiful San Diego early Thursday as Connie majestically departed, assisted by several tugboats. Dry land soon faded in the haze on the horizon, so we went to the Renegade ready room. Each of the nine squadrons assigned to the air wing had a ready room, each ready room had a number based on its location, and VF-24 was in **Ready 6**. Renegade colors were black and red, so Ready 6 had red tile on the deck (floor), while the overhead (ceiling) was painted black. With fluorescent lights and overstuffed vinyl-covered reclining chairs, it looked like a gaudy cave, but I thought it had "Navy fighter squadron" ambience. I would spend many hours in Ready 6 over the next few years.

The squadron executive officer (**XO**) was the most senior VF-24 person aboard. This was Commander Bill Bertsch, who was second in command to the commanding officer (**CO** or Skipper), Commander Bill Switzer. Both of them had call signs from their earlier flying days, but we always called them XO and Skipper. In their late thirties, with the rank of commander and combat experience, the Skipper and XO seemed unbelievably wise and experienced to me, all of twenty-two and only an ensign, the lowest officer rank.

The next-senior VF-24 person aboard Connie at this time was an experienced lieutenant who was the squadron duty officer (**SDO**), assigned to make sure things ran smoothly. Pilots and RIOs like Buf, John Boy, or Ice, who had been in the squadron a year or more and knew how everything worked, were prime candidates to be SDO for the first day or two of carrier qualifications. The SDO job was assigned to a different officer each day, but in every Navy squadron of any type, the SDO is key to making the squadron run smoothly

The XO and the SDO monitored the flight schedule that organized when our jets were supposed to fly out from Miramar and land on the ship. The fly-on pilots would land and immediately taxi to the catapult for launch, then come back to land again, anywhere from two to six times to qualify, based on how long it had been since their last carrier landing. Once a pilot had his day landing qualification (day qual), he would get out of the jet and a new pilot and RIO would man-up, refuel the jet, taxi to the catapult, and launch to start the new pilot's day qual.

As a new RIO, I was scheduled to fly with the XO. RIOs didn't need quals like pilots, but the squadron tracked our flights to keep us roughly equal.

As soon as the ship was a requisite distance from land, air wing aircraft started working the carrier qualification pattern. The Tomcats came out in the afternoon, so I had lunch and returned to Ready 6 to wait. At about one o'clock the SDO got a phone call that Renegade jets were overhead, so the XO and I put on our flight gear and walked to Flight

Deck Control, a small and very busy "office" at the base of the tower structure, right on the carrier's flight deck.

Looking through round windows of thick glass, the XO and I watched the Tomcats land. Before leaving the ready room we learned that 210 was the first VF-24 aircraft in the pattern and its pilot would likely be the first one qualified. We waited about fifteen minutes as 210 worked the deck, then instead of taxiing to the catapult it was directed to an area for hot-switch and refueling. The pilot was day-qualled and we were going to use the jet for the XO's qual.

We opened the metal door of Flight Deck Control and walked out to face the constant 25-knot wind of the flight deck. A steady wind like that gets your attention. You have to walk as if moving through molasses, and if you get off-balance it can knock you over. Apart from the wind, the main sensation I perceived was the roaring whine of jet engines, so loud that our helmets merely dulled it below the level of pain. We walked between the tightly packed aircraft, always watching out for the blast from engines, the huge propellers of the E-2, fuel hoses, electrical cables, wingtips, and hurrying sailors. It was a three-dimensional minefield. I followed in the XO's footsteps as he confidently navigated the dangers.

Renegade 210 was being secured to the flight deck with chains as we approached. The pilot and RIO saw us, waved, and flashed us the thumbs-up. When given the signal by their yellow-shirted flight deck director, they shut down the left engine and raised the canopy. The RIO climbed out of 210 first and came directly down the ladder, then the pilot set the parking brake, unstrapped, got out of the cockpit, and walked back to the flat surface above the left engine intake. The XO climbed up the ladder and got directly into the cockpit, after which the departing pilot stepped forward and stood on the small foldout panel near the front cockpit and yelled into the XO's helmet, telling him about peculiarities of the aircraft that were of interest.

Meanwhile, down on the flight deck, the departing RIO yelled to the side of my helmet: "It's got a good nav system and good radar! The fuel totalizer display is two hundred pounds low! Should be fine for quals!" Since it was daytime, the weather was nice, we were close to land, and we did not have any reason to use weapons, our requirements for 210 were minimal: two good engines and essential systems such as electrical power and hydraulics. If there had been a significant problem with the plane, the crew would have radioed ahead.

So I climbed up, strapped in and plugged in, and the plane captain (**PC**) climbed down the ladder and re-stowed it.

On the intercom the XO used the common phrase to see if I was plugged in and could hear him. "How do you read me?" I heard his voice surprisingly clear in my helmet despite the howling engine noise and wind.

"Loud and clear."

He said, "Clear for the canopy," and I moved the lever forward to lower the twelve-foot-long, titanium-framed Plexiglas canopy. Once settled onto its frame, it jolted forward to latch securely, and the canopy warning light went out. The wind was gone and so was much of the noise, but we experienced eye-watering engine exhaust fumes taken in by our air conditioner and pumped into the cockpit.

Coordinating with the PC through hand signals, the XO started the left engine and shut down the right so it was safe to refuel. A sailor wearing a purple jersey attached a large, heavy hose to the ground-refueling fixture on the right side of the aircraft, buttons were pushed, and fuel flowed into our jet.

Every few minutes I heard the muffled roar of other Tomcats landing. I would see a jet seven hundred feet away at the back of the ship, then seconds later watch it lurch to a stop a few dozen feet from me. The scale of an aircraft carrier is truly amazing. On roughly the same schedule, I felt the powerful rumble of a jet going to **military power** before launching from the catapult, a hundred feet or so forward of our refueling spot.

The cat shots and arrested landings by other aircraft were something I felt more than heard.

Inside the cockpit we had a brief period of relative solitude while two thousand gallons of jet fuel was pumped into our aircraft. Fighter guys measure fuel in pounds not gallons, so to us this upload was about thirteen thousand pounds on top of what we had. I checked the navigation system, and it seemed accurate. The XO and I got settled in, then just waited. After a few minutes the stinging exhaust fumes were gone, as aircraft on the flight deck moved and the wind direction changed a little.

At this point I was halfway through my fourth day in a fleet Tomcat squadron and loving it. I expected to be here for about three years.

Refueling stopped automatically when our tanks were full. The PC and other ground crew had been taking a micro-break, and suddenly became very active again. The refueling crew unplugged the hose and the PC gave signals for the XO to start the right engine. Once it was running we rechecked our cockpit switches, methodically progressing from left to right turning on everything we would use during this flight.

Over the radio, I told the air boss in Connie's control tower, "Boss, 210 up and ready, gross five-eight thousand, pilot Bertsch." This meant that the jet was good for flight, we were ready to taxi, and that we weighed fifty-eight thousand pounds. The weight report would be used to cross-check the setting of the steam catapult. It also confirmed to those tracking the day's events that the pilot was VF-24 XO Commander Bill Bertsch. Carrier quals were dynamic, so it was important to confirm who was in which jet and getting qualified.

When the air boss relayed my up-and-ready report to the flight deck, a sailor wearing a yellow jersey ran toward our plane and stopped about fifteen feet away, eyes locked on the XO. This was one of the flight deck directors. He held up both hands in tightly clenched fists, the signal for "Pilot, hold the brakes." Then he looked at the PC and gave a "clean-off" signal by wiping his hands down the sleeves of his jersey, so the PC ran around to the tie-down chains and unfastened them, then scurried away with the heavy chains draped over both shoulders. Our flight deck director used signals to tell the XO to release the aircraft brakes and then directed us very precisely around the flight deck to the catapult.

Aircraft are parked so close together on a carrier flight deck that precise direction is essential. This placed a great deal of responsibility on the yellow-shirted director, who not only had to keep us from bumping into things, but also had to coordinate our path with other aircraft movements so the deck didn't become locked-up. In addition, he had to be mindful of the landing area, where every minute or so someone would decelerate from 130 knots to a complete stop, only to be quickly directed clear so the next plane could land. Unchained and taxiing, we became part of this intricate coordinated traffic pattern.

My head was on a swivel as I watched our wingtip clearance while we taxied on the deck. Even though I had only been on a carrier flight deck for my initial qual, the importance of the RIO's scan was drilled into me in all of my preparatory classes and squadron briefings in VF-24. The flight deck crew is exceptionally skilled, but I also had a role in protecting our aircraft from damage. Mistakes are rare. Our first director taxied us out of his area and handed us off to another director.

Once we started moving, I came up on the ICS and started the challenge and reply takeoff checklist.

"Brakes."

"Brakes check good," the XO replied. "Accumulator pressure is up. Spoiler brakes de-selected."

"Fuel," I said. "I'm showing 16-0."

"Normal feed, auto transfer, dump is off, transfer checked," the XO said. "Total is actually 16-2. Wings two thousand and two thousand, tapes even at six thousand, feed tanks full. Bingo set at 4.5."

Continuing my safety scan while watching movement on the flight deck outside the aircraft and listening for updates on the radio, I completed nine checklist items. Seven items remained uncompleted until we neared the catapult. Even though in my career I probably went through the F-14 takeoff checklist two thousand times, I always opened my kneeboard reference booklet to the page and ran down it with my finger on the next item.

As we approached the catapult a sailor ran toward our aircraft, stopped twenty feet from our nose, made eye contact with me, and with both hands held up a large box with changeable numerals on its face. I could see his intent expression. He was showing me the weight board, the final check for setting the catapult to provide the correct amount of force to launch our aircraft. The weight of any aircraft can vary by thousands of pounds depending on fuel load, equipment, and other configuration options. Verifying the number shown on the weight board was the final step in a series of weight checks and another indication of the aircrew's ultimate responsibility. If the catapult were set too low, it might not give us enough speed to fly. A high setting would cause excessive stress on the aircraft. Again, mistakes are rare, but that is because of the system of multiple checks, and simple standard hand signals allowed the RIO to make corrections if necessary.

The weight board read fifty-eight thousand—correct. I gave an emphatic thumbs-up and the sailor ran over to show the board to another nineteen-year-old assigned to set a valve that controlled the powerful steam catapult.

Near the catapult we were no longer in a crowd of jets, and our taxi director signaled for the wings to be swept forward. The XO said, "Wings are coming," and paused a second.

I quickly looked left and right and said, "Clear both sides," so he moved the wingsweep switch to "auto," allowing the wings to sweep forward.

Once our wings swept forward, which took four seconds, the XO lowered the flaps and slats, and I resumed the takeoff checklist to complete the seven items held in abeyance. I said, "Wings."

The XO said, twenty degrees, auto, both lights out."

We proceeded through the checklist to configure the jet for launch while a director gave the XO very precise signals to taxi us into place to attach the catapult to the nose landing gear. When the catapult was fired, it would pull us forward and, combined with our engines, accelerate us to flying speed after a run of roughly three hundred feet.

Once we were in position things happened at an even quicker pace. On signal, the catapult moved forward a few inches and engaged our nose landing gear with a perceptible thud that indicated a solid hook-up. This is called taking tension. A sailor scrambled up to inspect the hook-up, then ran back to his assigned staging area, showing an unambiguous thumbs-up. The director signaled for run-up to military power, so the XO advanced both throttles and watched engine instruments climb and stabilize. We would not use afterburners this time since our weight was less than sixty thousand pounds.

The "mil power" signal also cued a pilot to perform a control wipeout to move the stick to the extremes of its range and ensure it has no restrictions. As the XO performed the wipeout I quickly turned my head to visually observe movement of the flaps, spoilers, and rudders. Flight deck crewmen stationed around the jet also confirmed that everything worked and gave thumbs-up signals. The director then handed us off to the shooter, the only officer in the sequence of flight deck controllers.

While the shooter waved two fingers of his left hand above his head, the signal to keep the engines at military power, we both checked that we didn't have any caution lights lit. Over the ICS, the XO said, "Looks good up here, no lights. Ready to go?"

"Yes, sir!"

When the XO sharply saluted the shooter, the standard signal that we were ready for launch, the shooter visually swept the flight deck to ensure it was clear, and with a dramatic sweep of his arm leaned forward and touched the flight deck. In response, a sailor in the walkway on the edge of the flight deck turned his head left and right to check clearance yet again, then pushed a lighted red button on a dirty gray control panel. Complex and powerful machinery was activated, and after a delay of about a second, the catapult fired.

With a head-snapping initial jolt followed by almost unbelievable force, our twenty-nine-ton fighter was hurled forward. I heard and felt a metallic sound and vibration like a train on tracks, which rose in frequency as we accelerated. It took great effort for me to look at the airspeed indicator. In my peripheral vision the flight deck environment blurred. Visually I could just discern a horizon. We reached the end of the track and received another jolt as we were flung into the air. We were accelerating through 150 knots and climbing.

The cat shot lasted two seconds. The entire sequence from when the catapult took tension until we were airborne was less than twenty seconds.

In a few seconds we leveled off at our fly-out altitude of six hundred feet and flew ahead of the carrier. This was smooth and quiet compared to the flight deck, and I felt much more aware and competent than I had when I landed aboard a carrier in the RAG. Of course I still had a lot to learn, and I would improve in increments large or small with every flight.

It was a long afternoon of both flying and waiting on deck. The XO and I were in our jet fighter for more than three hours. It started with "comfort time," about fifteen minutes of free-flying in clear airspace to allow a pilot to become comfortable in the jet before he starts his qual. Then we checked in with *Constellation*'s air traffic controllers and entered the carrier qualification game plan. We could have been called down immediately, but on that day we weren't. We started in high holding at sixteen thousand feet, flying lazy circles ten miles in diameter, sometimes alone, sometimes with other Tomcats. Once in a while a specific jet would be called down so its pilot could get his day qual.

Since the purpose of this flight was to get our carrier landing quals, the XO had already put our **tailhook** down. The tailhook created almost no drag, and by convention pilots lowered their hooks as soon as they began to prepare for landing.

The aircraft holding below us descended for their landings, so we took their place in low holding at two thousand feet and flew circles five miles in diameter. We continued to fly at the sedate airspeed of 225 knots to conserve fuel. From two thousand feet we could clearly see every movement on the flight deck and developed a sense of how the qualification period was going.

The air boss came up on the radio, "Tomcats in low holding, Charlie now." Charlie is the unclassified code word to descend for a carrier landing. We had another VF-24 Tomcat as our wingman, flying on our right side. We had been in low holding about twenty minutes, and it had been more than an hour since we launched.

Suddenly our activity level went from almost serene to full speed. The XO continued to fly a circle until we were off the carrier's left side headed in the opposite direction—

"abeam the ship" in Navy talk. From this point we descended again. We had been conservative with our fuel, so we actually had to dump a few thousand pounds to get under the maximum landing weight of the F-14. Fuel streamed from a three-inch wide pipe at the tail of our aircraft, becoming a wispy white trail that quickly fell out of the sky.

As we descended, the XO held his right hand above the canopy rail so the wingman could see it, and moved it backwards twice, the signal to be ready to sweep the wings aft. He tilted his head forward, and when he raised his head he set the wingsweep button to the "aft" position. Cued by the hand signal and head nod, our wingman set his wingsweep button at the same time and the wings of both Tomcats swept from twenty degrees to sixty-eight degrees. With our wings swept we looked like the supersonic Navy jet fighters that we truly were.

We descended to six hundred feet above the ocean and accelerated to about 450 knots as we flew behind *Constellation*, above the light gray ship's wake that scarred the ocean for miles. At this speed we felt some g-forces as we made the hard left turn to fly toward the carrier.

Level at six hundred feet, we flew toward the carrier from a few miles aft. The turbulence that inspires nervousness in airline passengers is a normal phenomenon, and it adds another element of interest to flying close formation in jet fighters. Our wingman bobbed alongside us as if on a giant bungee. It was through the constant effort of a skilled pilot that they did not either drift out of formation or bump into us.

As we passed over the ship the XO gave an exaggerated "kiss-off" sign to the wingman, then rolled our jet ninety degrees left and pulled hard on the stick to create 6 g of force as he reduced the throttles. This is called the **break**, and it's the quickest way to return to a ship or airfield for landing. Because of the laws of aerodynamics, aircraft decelerate quickly under g-loading, and manually sweeping the F-14's wings back increased the effect. So we went from 450 knots to our landing speed of precisely 134 knots in less than twenty seconds as we completed the 180-degree turn.

Our wingman flew straight ahead and kept checking our position, then timed his break turn to get the desired interval between aircraft. This way we could land and clear the flight deck landing area before his landing.

When we passed 250 knots decelerating in the turn the XO selected "auto" on the wingsweep button and the wings swept to their full-forward twenty degree position. He then lowered the landing gear, flaps, and slats. When done correctly, the break turn results in an aircraft being in the correct starting position for a carrier landing: one and quarter miles away from the oncoming carrier, six hundred feet above the ocean, at the correct landing speed, and configured for landing. We usually met these numbers within a few percent every time.

While the XO was flying the jet, making rapid changes in airspeed, and moving switches and levers to get ready for landing, I was backing him up by checking altitude and airspeed. As the wings swept forward, I started the landing checklist by saying, "Wings." The XO said, "twenty degrees, auto, both lights out."

I said, "Gear," and he said, "Three down and locked, transition light out." As he said this I looked over his left shoulder and verified the landing gear indication on *his* instrument panel, since the RIO did not have a landing gear position indicator. We went through the nine items on the checklist to set up the jet for landing.

The carrier landing is part hand-eye coordination, part physics, part magic, and a measure of suppressing the urge to say, "This is crazy, let's go to a runway!" Good training and a lot of practice gave me the ability to suppress that urge; I never had the feeling that it was "risky," although, of course, I was aware of the various potential unpleasant outcomes. In my earliest landings, the first thirty or so, this was probably because of confidence in the experienced pilots with whom I flew, as well as naïveté. As I became more accustomed to the environment and more capable, I was able to verify that things were going well or participate as a crew and make them right.

Seconds after we passed abeam the carrier, the XO started a turn by rolling into a twenty-seven degree angle of bank. We crossed the ship's wake at an altitude of 450 feet, continuing the left turn at twenty-seven degrees angle of bank, with a rate of descent of three hundred feet per minute—a textbook setup—then soon saw the optical landing system's bright light, which from a mile looks like a yellow dot (and is called the meatball or just the ball). Shortly after we crossed the wake we rolled wings-level on centerline and on altitude.

I rapidly checked my airspeed gauge and altimeter, then transitioned to the ball to determine whether we were on glide slope, the invisible sloping path that represents the proper angle of descent to landing. I also looked ahead at the carrier and flight deck less than a half-mile away. We were fifteen seconds from landing.

From the front cockpit the XO could see the ship well, but rather than eyeball the whole picture, he focused on key indicators. He picked up the ball as we crossed the ship's wake and that became his first priority. With discipline he shifted his attention to the wide stripe painted on the landing area centerline to determine our lineup, his second priority. His third priority was a gauge in the cockpit that showed **angle of attack**, which indicated optimum approach airspeed.

While I looked at the instruments available in front of me and gleaned as much as I could from looking forward over his shoulder, the XO kept up a disciplined scan of three things: the ball, our lineup, and the angle of attack gauge. Over and over, meatball, lineup, angle of attack. Meatball, line-up, angle of attack. It is one of the carrier pilot's mantras. Of course he was not just watching instruments, he was still flying the plane. It's an understatement to say that a carrier landing may be the most challenging task any pilot performs regularly.

I had two speaking parts. First, if we were more than one knot from the correct landing speed, I told the XO about it over the ICS: "three knots fast," or "two knots slow."

Second, once we rolled wings-level I reported to the landing signal officers (LSOs) on the flight deck, "Two-one-zero, Tomcat ball, 7.8, Bertsch." Two-one-zero referred to our aircraft side number, 210, while 7.8 was the amount of fuel we had —7,800 pounds.

Their reply was: "Roger ball, 7.8."

It takes much longer to describe than it does to fly.

We thudded onto the flight deck with another head-snapping jolt, which morphed into a strong deceleration as our tailhook caught one of the steel arresting cables. Four of them were stretched across the landing area, but any one will do the job. I was thrown against my locked harness while we went from 134 knots to zero in about two seconds and less than four hundred feet. The arrested landing is called a "trap," and in terms of physical sensations is kind of like a cat shot in reverse.

Under precise direction of the flight deck crew, we swept our wings back and taxied clear of the landing area. As we prepared for another cat shot, the air boss came up on the radio and told everyone, "Ship's in a turn." This meant *Constellation* had reached the edge of our assigned operating area and needed to turn around to reposition. We would not go to the cat just yet. The airplanes flying overhead continued to hold, while those of us on deck just sat.

The XO and I sat on deck for a full hour while *Constellation* repositioned herself in the assigned area and again turned into the wind. We then taxied to one of the catapults, swept the wings out, completed a takeoff checklist, and launched again. We climbed to six hundred feet and this time immediately made the 180-degree left turn, flew aft of the ship, and got another trap. The first cat and trap took more than an hour; the second one took less than five minutes.

Completing the second landing meant the XO was requalified for daytime carrier landings. But in another few minutes we got a third cat shot and trap as a bonus.

After the third trap we were directed to the hot switch area and another VF-24 pilot walked up to 210. It was Holly, and I noticed he didn't have an RIO with him, which meant I would be staying in the plane; fine with me. We shut down the left engine, raised the canopy, and repeated the pilot switch procedure, then the XO climbed down, I lowered the canopy, and Holly said hi. We had enough fuel to launch without refueling and the carrier qualification pattern was running smoothly, so Holly and I spent twenty-five minutes in the jet and got two cat shots and two traps. Holly was now requalified for day carrier landings.

My total time in aircraft 210 that afternoon was 3.7 hours. Most of the time had been spent just waiting, so I wasn't tired. After a quick dinner I briefed for the night qualification flight with one of the other senior pilots. That resulted in one night cat shot, one night trap, and another 0.9 hours of flight time. In most cases it only took one trap for a night qual.

The rest of the two-week at-sea period was unremarkable, as the purpose was basic refresher training for the aviators in all squadrons in the air wing as well as the ship's crew. I had seven more flights, an average of one every other day. Like Rums, Jake, Jaws, Monk, and the other new guys in VF-24 and VF-211, I learned a lot every day.

We quickly adapted to the typical schedule for aviators on a carrier. We stayed up until 1:00 or 2:00 AM most nights and generally skipped breakfast (sleeping in unless scheduled for an early flight), then ate lunch, dinner, and a meal at 11:00 PM. We were all pretty excited to finally be in fleet squadrons. We talked about flying all the time, especially at meals. The wardroom was loud with echoing voices recounting flight stories, describing lessons we learned or simple realizations, and always telling tales of mistakes made by others. Of course there were rough spots and unpleasant parts of the job. And there were always new things to learn, but two years out of college I was exactly where I wanted to be.

Intel Brief: Why the F-14 Had a RIO

The Radar Intercept Officer (RIO, always spoken as "rio," as in Rio Grande) gained a seat in U.S. Navy fighters as a result of mission requirements and hardware limitations, and proved his worth in training and combat missions.

A mission that made the F-14 Tomcat unique was fleet air defense—defending Navy aircraft carriers and other ships from raids by dozens of Soviet bombers. Though cumbersome themselves, the bombers could launch fast, long-range, high-flying cruise missiles, and their raids would be escorted by powerful radar jammers. These threats required a complex weapons system, a radar and missile combination that stretched the limits of technology when they were developed in the late 1960s. The F-14's weapons system, known as the AWG-9, included a more powerful radar and larger antenna than other fighters, giving it the ability to scan huge volumes of airspace and track up to twenty-four targets. The primary missile for fleet air defense was the AIM-54 Phoenix, which provided an unprecedented one-hundred mile range and included a small onboard radar to guide itself to the target during the final phase of flight. The AWG-9 could support up to six Phoenix missiles attacking six different targets simultaneously. They could also defeat radar jamming or attack the jamming aircraft itself.

Impressive as the equipment was, it required a skilled operator to optimize it in various stages of a mission. On patrol or searching for the enemy, the F-14 RIO selected the scan pattern of the radar from a dozen choices and ensured the antenna searched the correct portion of the sky. He selected from among four search radar modes, taking into consideration such factors as the environment and expected threat. When targets were detected, the RIO quickly analyzed the situation and advised the pilot where to fly to optimize radar performance and set up for an attack. The RIO examined the raw radar return for information that the AWG-9 computers might miss or misinterpret, in some cases activating radar or missile functions to counter specific threats. With his training, the RIO was an expert on these threats to carriers. Whether he pushed the red button in the rear cockpit to launch long-range missiles or the pilot squeezed the trigger on his control stick, a skilled RIO would be essential to defeating a Soviet bomber raid.

Some air defense fighters relied on a single pilot to operate the weapons system while flying, but they did not have capabilities comparable to the F-14. Other aircraft had already proved the value of a second crewman to aid the pilot during critical phases of the mission, from radar-equipped night fighters of World War II, to some of the F-14's immediate predecessors, such as the F-4 Phantom and F-101 Voodoo. And no contemporary aircraft, friendly or threat, could match the F-14 or its weapons system in mission capability.

While fleet air defense was important, the primary mission of the F-14 was as a fighter, participating in sweeping enemy fighters from hostile skies and protecting U.S. attack aircraft so they could reach their targets, according to the Navy and manufacturer Grumman Aerospace. This mission meant that exceptional maneuverability was essential, and when the F-14 was new its maneuvering was considered amazing despite the fact that the plane weighed thirty tons or more. In this traditional fighter role, the RIO again had to perform as an integrated part of a two-person crew for the mission to succeed.

In the fighter mission, the F-14 normally used the AIM-7 Sparrow missile or AIM-9 Sidewinder. The Sparrow was guided by radar and could be launched at targets at a range up to thirty miles; the Sidewinder homed in on heat emitted by targets out to five miles or so. The F-14 also had a gun that fired 20mm shells at a rate of one hundred per second, although it was normally fired in fifty-round bursts (a limit that was set before takeoff).

The F-14 could also perform reconnaissance, using a large camera pod attached to its belly. The typical aircraft carrier had two F-14 squadrons and only one of them was assigned the reconnaissance mission. Since VF-24 didn't have the mission it isn't addressed in this book.

The F-14's engines contributed to its capability as much as its radar and weapons. While the TF30 turbofans in the original F-14A had some teething problems, they also had impressive performance. At one end of the spectrum, they could be operated very efficiently so that an aircraft could stay aloft about three and a half hours on internal fuel alone, without aerial refueling. If the pilot wanted maximum power, however, he selected full **Zone** 5 afterburner and extra fuel would be injected into the engine tailpipe and ignited, providing greater thrust. Maximum afterburner burned fuel at up to two thousand pounds per minute, a rate that would consume all internal fuel in eight minutes and so had to be used sparingly.

United States forces have always flown very capable *single-seat* fighter and attack aircraft, and the debate about whether one or two seats is "better" can be relied upon to get lively whenever it comes up among aviators. But once the decision was made that F-14s would carry RIOs, its designers distributed the workload by placing almost all controls for its computer, radar, and electronic countermeasures in the rear cockpit. Certain flight-critical systems, such as radios and basic navigation, could be controlled from either cockpit. The pilot had the only stick and throttles, along with all other essential controls and instruments. Thus, "crew coordination" became a familiar term and basic skill of all F-14 crews. The F-14 flight manual provided a key to effective crew coordination by identifying crew responsibilities in various stages of flight. The pilot and RIO were jointly responsible for planning the mission and inspecting the aircraft preflight. Once in the aircraft, the RIO was responsible for communications and navigation, as well as prompting the pilot for certain checklists (the challenge and reply method). The RIO also performed copilot duties such as monitoring fuel state and aircraft altitude.

It must be noted that F-14 pilots were capable of flying, communicating, and navigating on their own, but the assignment of duties to RIOs was a useful starting point for crew coordination, which was taught in classrooms and practiced in simulators and flights. In fleet squadrons, most crews included a senior person with two years or more of experience and a junior person. Junior pilots were paired with senior RIOs, and vice versa. Crew coordination practices were refined and handed down in addition to being formally discussed during flight briefings and training meetings. Every aircraft accident or incident was also analyzed, and any lapse in crew coordination was identified and highlighted as a learning point for others.

The U.S. Navy continues to operate two-seat fighters. Today's aircraft carriers have four squadrons of Hornet or SuperHornet strike fighters, one of which flies the two-seat F/A-18F variant. But the back-seaters are called WSOs (Weapon Systems Officers), invariably pronounced as "wizzo." The Air Force also calls its F-15E fighter back-seaters WSOs.

Intel Brief: Training for Aerial Combat Without Paintball Missiles

If someone invented paintball-type missiles, aerial combat training would be a quieter event. That's because in the absence of a physical simulated missile—one that doesn't damage the target—aviators make radio calls to indicate launching a missile at another aircraft.

American fighters use the following terms:

Fox One: launched an AIM-7 Sparrow medium range radar-guided missile.

Fox Two: launched an AIM-9 Sidewinder short range heat-seeking missile

Guns: fired rounds from the gun.

Adversary pilots simulating the enemy use the unclassified code name for enemy weapons with similar capabilities. During the time of this story, these were "Apex" for a medium range radar-guided missile, "Atoll" for a short range heat-seeking missile, and "Guns."

The F-14's long-range AIM-54 Phoenix, rarely used in fighter vs. fighter scenarios during my time, was "Fox Three."

The radio call had to include the target aircraft type, altitude, and other information to help all aircraft discern who was targeted, such as: "Fox Two, A-4 left hand turn at sixteen thousand," or "Atoll, F-14 chasing the F-5 at twelve thousand."

When adversary pilots were in the fight, whether from Topgun or one of the Navy's other adversary squadrons, they usually made the determination whether a shot was a kill. If an F-14 was targeted, for example, and deployed chaff or flares countermeasures and made a good maneuver that would likely defeat a missile, the adversary pilot would radio, "Good break, continue," and the engagement would proceed.

If the shot was judged as a kill, the radio call would be "F-14, you're dead," or "That A-4 is dead." The dead aircraft then performed a roll and exited the engagement.

When we worked on the Tactical Aircrew Combat Training System (TACTS) Range, the system sounded a tone when a missile was launched, and a few seconds later indicated whether it was a kill. But we still needed a radio call to indicate who was targeted, and adversary pilots sometimes overrode the TACTS ruling, making their own kill determinations based on the training objectives of the flight.

Finally, we selected our weapons based on training objectives for the flight. If we wanted to practice close-in dogfight maneuvering, both the fighters and bogeys would simulate using less-capable missiles that would limit shot opportunities, rather than the state-of-the-art weapons F-14s would carry into real combat.

FOUR

Fight's On

CLR-LAT-NORTH-3-2-5-2-5-ENTER. CLR-LONG-WEST-1-1-7-0-8-5-ENTER. I pressed buttons on the keypad on the console to my left, entering the latitude and longitude of the VF-24 flight line at Miramar—32 degree 52.5' North, 117 degree 08.5' West—into my inertial navigation system. The buttons were big enough that I could use the keypad while wearing my gloves.

We had just started our engines.

It was a warm afternoon in July and I was flying with my regular pilot, Lieutenant John Alling, call sign John Boy (after a character on *The Waltons* TV series). John Boy and I were a standard crew for my first five months in VF-24. In F-14 squadrons the same pilot and RIO flew together most of the time to improve crew coordination and effectiveness.

John Boy had been in the Renegades about two years when I joined the squadron. He had completed a seven-and-half month deployment aboard Connie and had been through the five-week Topgun class with Ice as his RIO. (Holly and Buf had also been through the Topgun class.)

John Boy picked up several habits from his Topgun experience. For example, when we found ourselves airborne over the Pacific with a few spare minutes and extra fuel we would frequently practice maximum-performance turns. Flying a fighter well takes practice. If the pilot doesn't pull back hard enough on the stick the turn will not be as tight as intended, while too much pull will result in excessive stress on the aircraft (overstress) and could also lead to a stall or other undesirable results. Topgun emphasized precise aircraft control in its approach to fighter employment.

John Boy would ask if I was ready, then say something like, "Bio, check our heading, looks like 270 to me. Here comes a level turn to the left. Start your clock." So I would push a button to start the stopwatch function of the clock on my instrument panel as he engaged the afterburner, rolled the aircraft about 80 degrees left wing down, and pulled hard on the stick. We usually started these turns at fifteen thousand feet and 350 knots. G-forces built instantly, usually to about 6 g, and the plane shuddered as aerodynamic forces did battle with the laws of physics. The Tomcat had what I always considered ingenious aerodynamics. Although it was large for a fighter, a properly flown Tomcat could dominate smaller and lighter aircraft.

We would complete a 180-degree turn in twelve to fifteen seconds and John Boy would say either, "Well, that's what it's supposed to feel like every time!" or, "That wasn't very good," depending on how we performed compared to the Tomcat's maximum capability.

But on this day we would not practice turns; we were going head-to-head against two adversary jets in air combat maneuvering (**ACM**) above the empty desert southeast of Yuma, Arizona. John Boy and I had the flight lead, Cowboy was our wingman pilot, and Ice was his RIO. Two fighters against two adversaries or bogeys is a 2v2. (After the F-14 RAG and two months in VF-24 I'd made significant progress in my ability to appreciate and perform my duties in the dynamic ACM environment—so this is a good place to explain it in more detail.)

Our flight brief took about thirty minutes. As with my earlier flight on the Echo Range and all tactical mission flights, we quickly covered items such as route of flight and radio frequencies, then reviewed tactical considerations such as radar search plan to cover the airspace, radar lock options for likely bogey formations, maneuvering in the dogfight that we expected, and other combat training subjects. In the real world we might destroy enemy fighters with missiles before a tight dogfight was required, but today one of our objectives was to practice engaged maneuvering where two fighters (friendly aircraft) fought two **bogeys** (enemy aircraft), so we briefed the close-in fight. As required by safety rules, one of the bogey pilots attended our brief to cover some essential items, then he left for a detailed brief with his wingman in Miramar's Hangar 2.

Getting into my flight gear by then took just a few minutes. It had become a simple routine instead of the twenty-minute "sweat-ex" (sweating exercise) associated with my early flights in Pensacola. Though the G suit, harness, and survival gear weighed almost twenty pounds, by this time it all felt comfortable.

John Boy and I walked to the jet about forty minutes before our scheduled takeoff time. In the few minutes it took to walk past the fighters on our line we casually chatted, and he reminded me of a mistake I had made on a previous flight. I wanted to be a good RIO, and the criticism helped. I was still using the personal critique notebook I'd started in Pensacola and mentally recalled some of my own comments as we approached our assigned jet.

We conducted the preflight and climbed into our seats. After the PC assisted us with strapping in, he took up position on the right side of the jet. Many times when I was standing on the top of a jet during preflight, I thought back to the very first time Rums and I climbed onto an F-14 when we were in the RAG, standing there in my khaki uniform with my hands on my hips. That lasted only a moment and then I scrambled back down before I fell or did something stupid.

The steps involved in starting the jet were similar to what we went through aboard the ship, and required coordination using hand signals between John Boy and the PC. Once both engines were online I started the AWG-9 weapons control system, which turned on the radar in a standby mode and started the inertial navigation system. In a few seconds the nine-inch diameter tactical information display (**TID**) became active and I entered our latitude and longitude to tell the system where it was starting. It would track our position during the flight. I set up the cockpit while checking the small symbol slowly moving from left to right at the top of the TID, while the center of the screen showed progress of the onboard checkout routine. Sixteen abbreviations flashed as each system was checked: CAD, TCN, BCN, and more.

Seven minutes after engine start our system checks were complete and our navigation system was ready. We looked at Cowboy and Ice a few planes away and got a thumbs-up, so I called Miramar ground control for permission to taxi. The PC directed us out of our parking space, then we made our way without assistance along the taxiways. As we approached the hold short area I started the takeoff checklist, and at the hold short called Miramar Tower. We were quickly cleared and made a "flight leader separation" takeoff, in which the wingman started his takeoff roll five seconds after the lead.

For takeoff John Boy went to Zone 5 on the engines (maximum afterburner), which provided thirty-six thousand pounds of thrust; our jet weighed about sixty thousand pounds so initial acceleration was impressive if not eye-watering. It did not compare to the mind-boggling power of a catapult launch, but a burner launch in a Tomcat was significantly more exciting than what travelers experience in a commercial airliner. A Tomcat in full burner reaches takeoff speed less than fifteen seconds after brake release, using roughly two thousand feet of runway; a Boeing 737 airliner usually requires more than twice the distance and time.

Immediately after getting airborne John Boy pulled the throttles out of burner back to military power to comply with airspeed limits and noise-control rules around Miramar (as well as save fuel and allow Cowboy to join up and get in formation for the flight).

It took less than thirty minutes to cover the two hundred miles from Miramar to the range.

Like the Echo Range at China Lake, fliers had identified visual cues to mark the boundaries of the area above which we were cleared to fly. Small mountain ranges marked the east and west borders, with Interstate 8 on the north. The U.S.–Mexico international border was the southern boundary of the range, and we referred to various landmarks to keep from violating this limit. The terrain within these boundaries was a mix of dark brown desert and craggy hills. I especially liked flights over the desert because they seemed more realistic as combat training than those we flew over the water.

Aeronautical charts show this airspace as Restricted Area #2301 West, or R-2301W, but we all called it the **TACTS Range** because it was the site of a system that recorded in great detail what aircraft were doing—the Tactical Aircrew Combat Training System. Each aircraft carried a small pod that transmitted the necessary data to support the system, including airspeed, altitude, g-forces, a cue if we had a track on a target, and more. TACTS was the video debriefing system shown in the movie *Top Gun*, and I thought it was a cool gadget when I was first exposed to it. With experience, I appreciated its value even more.

Approaching the TACTS Range, each fighter completed the combat checklist. I checked in with our range controller and heard that the bogeys were ready. We started a left 360-degree holding turn while checking that our TACTS pods worked, which they did. John Boy said he was ready to start and I got a thumbs-up from Ice so I told the controller, "Fighters are ready."

"Tape recorders on. Fight's on, fight's on," the controller replied. "Your contact bears 117 degrees, thirty-seven miles."

In the time it took for that 360-degree turn we shifted from cruising along an airway to simulated combat.

As the RIO in the lead aircraft I analyzed the controller's initial report and called over the radio, "Fighters steady one-two-zero." Our section finished the turn and rolled wings-level heading 120 degrees. Ice and I knew the shape and orientation of the range, so we already had our radars pointed in the right direction as our pilots rolled-out. We were level at twenty-three thousand feet, accelerating through 350 knots, Cowboy a little more than a mile away to my right side. My radar swept back and forth. I was searching the high altitude block.

After a few seconds Ice called, "Contact, 115 degrees at thirty-five miles, fifteen thousand. Flight of two." He was searching below our altitude and detected both of the adversary aircraft, which were at fifteen thousand feet. In accordance with our brief, the first aircraft to detect the targets became the lead, so Ice directed us through the rest of the intercept.

His radar quickly calculated the bogeys' heading so he called, "Bogeys heading 310, come left to 100."

We continued to refine our approach as our radars tracked the simulated enemy, who were flying a profile based on the training objectives for this mission. At Ice's direction we adjusted our heading, speed, and altitude to arrive in an advantageous position. At the speeds we were flying and given the setup distance, the radar intercept took less than three minutes. Then all four aircraft were in the same piece of sky—the **merge**—and the dogfight began.

Four aircraft turned, rolled, climbed, and dived in that small piece of sky, rarely more than three miles from each other. During the engagement our speed varied from about

450 knots to as little as 100 knots. As our speed changed during the fight, our wings smoothly and automatically swept forward and back to provide optimum lift. We generally stayed between ten thousand and twenty thousand feet altitude. G-forces varied from less than 1 g to slightly more than 6 g. If you traced the paths of all aircraft throughout the fight it would look like a **furball**, which was one of our terms for an ACM engagement.

I was able to keep track of our wingman and both simulated enemy aircraft for most of the fight. John Boy was aware of all three with no problem, which is something experience brought him. Using the clock code that every schoolboy knows, he said, "Watch the A-4 at right five low, I've got the guy at eleven high."

"Got him," I replied, grabbing the handle above my instrument panel and twisting my upper body in my seat, straining against g-forces and my straps to maintain sight of the little adversary.

After two years of training I had a good sense of my RIO duties during an ACM engagement, which included helping the pilot keep track of everyone, occasionally operating the radar if a bogey was ahead of us, and looking behind us to ensure that no one became a threat. I also kept track of our location in the area, altitude, airspeed, fuel, and other essentials of flying a jet fighter. Knowing my duties was one thing; performing them well was still a work in progress.

In the front seat John Boy was doing many of the same things, *plus* making decisions every microsecond about exactly how best to fly our jet and trying to get a good shot at the simulated enemy. He operated the stick, throttles, and rudder pedals, and also used the small control switches mounted on the stick and throttles, such as a button to select which weapon would be fired if he took a shot, another to open and close the speed brakes, and more.

Air combat maneuvering is a full-brain task.

It's also physically demanding. I constantly twisted in my seat and repositioned myself to keep sight as the aircraft I was watching moved around the sky. Once I had a sense of his movement I looked away for a second to update our wingman's position, or check the guy John Boy was actively pursuing. Sometimes I even wrote notes on my kneeboard card that would help when we reconstructed the fight in the debrief. Many of my movements were in a high-g condition, which make everything feel like it weighs more than it really does. At 6 g, everything feels like it weighs six times as much as it does in normal gravity (1 g). A typical adult's head weighs almost fifteen pounds with a helmet and oxygen mask, so at 6 g it effectively weighs ninety pounds—a lot of weight to move around tracking bogeys in a dogfight. Say my arm normally weighs about ten pounds, then at 6 g I was trying to operate cockpit switches while moving sixty pounds of weight. It took some getting used to, but this was a part of every engagement. We felt g's whenever we made a turn. Higher speeds and tighter turns meant more g's.

During engagements like this, g-loading started at the merge with our turn to get into position to take a gun shot or rear-quarter missile shot. We pulled 6 g for ten seconds, but the bogey maneuvered, so John Boy reduced his turn and rolled the airplane to start a climb. The climb began with a 4-g pull for eight seconds, then reduced g-loading near the top when we were inverted and gravity began to pull us down the backside of the loop. It went on like this —6 g for twelve seconds, 1 g for five seconds, 4 g for eight seconds, 2.5 g for six seconds, 1 g for three seconds, 6 g for eighteen seconds—for anywhere from one to three minutes in a typical engagement. During that time several things likely would have happened to end the fight:

- Bogeys or fighters were "killed" by valid missile shots.
- The engagement reached a stalemate and was not worth additional time or fuel.
- We reached a pre-planned low fuel level (**bingo**) or ran out of range time.
- An aircraft violated one of the safety rules.

When any of these conditions were met, the engagement ended with a call of "knock it off" over the radio and all aircraft stopped maneuvering. This was repeated by every aircraft to ensure everyone got the message.

"Roger, knock it off."

Due to the physicality of moving around under high g-forces, the end of an engagement usually found everyone gasping for breath as if we had just finished a wrestling match.

The G suit that now felt so normal (which is really an anti-G suit) came into play every time we pulled more than about 2 g. A valve opened and air was pumped into the suit, squeezing my legs and lower abdomen to prevent blood from pooling there. This helped prevent blackout from lack of oxygen to my brain. It may seem simplistic, but it works.

On that July afternoon we completed three intercepts and subsequent engagements (dogfights). The third was a short setup of only twenty miles, to save fuel and time on the intercept that we could use on the engagement. We then left the range and returned to Miramar.

Our flight time was 1.4 hours.

As training progressed, all squadron members increased our flying discipline by reducing radio communication and using hand signals when we were in formation. For example, instead of making the radio transmission, "You've got the lead," a pilot would tap his helmet and point to the wingman. The new flight lead would then tap his helmet to acknowledge, "I've got the lead." To determine his wingman's fuel, the lead RIO did not ask over the radio. He extended his thumb from his fist and put it in front of his face in a drinking motion. The wingman responded with a hand signal of his fuel quantity. These and dozens of other signals were well established among fliers, and since we were preparing to deploy for potential combat operations, we used them.

A few months after I joined VF-24 it was time to update the names painted on the sides of the aircraft. On F-14s, names are painted on the canopy rails, the frame that holds the Plexiglas. The name on the jet has nothing to do with who actually flies it; jets are assigned based on what is available when the crews man-up, but having my name on an airplane was a meaningful reward for getting there. I guess it went back to my childhood, seeing airplanes with names on them and wondering, "Who are those guys?" Now I was one of them.

There is no official way to decide which names go on which jets but squadrons generally follow similar rules. It starts with the air wing commander, who has his name on the "-00" aircraft in all squadrons in the air wing. Names of the most senior members of the squadron are on the low-numbered aircraft starting with -01. In VF-24, Skipper Switzer and his RIO were on 201, the XO and his RIO were on 202, and so on. VF-24 had more aviators than aircraft, so the most junior of us had to be content with our names on only one side of the jet, and my name was in the most junior place it could be, on the right side of aircraft 214: LTJG Dave Baranek, with LT John Alling on the front canopy rail. I had recently been promoted from ensign to lieutenant (junior grade), so I was bursting with pride.

When my mom visited San Diego I took her to Miramar to show her my squadron. It was a quiet Saturday morning so we walked out to the flight line and found the jet with my name on it. I proudly pointed it out to my mom without saying anything. What words would be necessary when your name is on the side of an F-14?

My mom said, "Your name is David, not Dave!"

For the remainder of my time flying Navy fighters, I always made sure that my full name was painted on an aircraft.

With the ACM flights, trips to the carrier, cross-country flights, hanging out at the Officers' Club (O-Club), squadron parties, and now my name on a jet, I was getting pretty full of the "I fly fighters" attitude. Somehow I got the idea that everyone wanted to know that, and I thought of having a T-shirt made that read, I fly fighters! I mentioned this to Gary, which was one of the smartest things I could have done.

"If you do that, somebody's probably going to start a fight with you and kick your ass," he said. "That's pretty obnoxious. Everybody has to have a job, Dave, you just happen to like yours. Don't make a big deal out of it."

Gary was right, and I decided the T-shirt wasn't a good idea, but more important, I got another dose of perspective to go along with my mom's comment. I was fortunate that I enjoyed what I did, and I started to realize that it would not be the ideal job for everyone.

In my first six months with VF-24, before we started our long deployment, only one-fourth of my flights started and ended at Miramar. Though it was our squadron's home base, we traveled a lot, making five trips to the *Constellation* of two to four weeks each, plus a two-week trip to the remote Naval Air Station at Fallon, Nevada (east of Reno) for intensive training. I also took cross-country flights with pilots who wanted to go to Florida, Virginia, and Washington DC. I made a total of 105 flights in six months, of which only 26 started and ended at Miramar.

Those 105 flights equated to more than two hundred hours, a good rate of flying that provided me with a solid bank of experience. From careful preflights I began to know not only where each panel was, but also which fasteners were prone to problems. On some jets the edges of some panels were bent from being pried open or hammered closed during maintenance. I had been on missile launch exercises, where we fired actual missiles at target drones, and had flown chase to observe a Harpoon missile during a test event. I had helped handle emergencies in flight, using my training to bring the plane back safely to base. But most of the flight time was routine, flying to or from a training range or patrolling an assigned station waiting for a simulated enemy. Whether exciting or routine, every hour provided the opportunity to learn about my fighter and mission.

My experience was part of the preparation for **deployment**, the next big thing in the squadron's never-ending stream of events. This one began on Tuesday morning, October 20, 1981, when the USS *Constellation* battle group departed San Diego for a seven-and-half-month trip to the Western Pacific and Indian Ocean. The battle group included five surface ships (cruisers, destroyers, and frigates), a nuclear submarine or two, and of course the aircraft squadrons of the air wing. We never really knew how many submarines were with us.

The day of departure was similar to what I had experienced on the shorter carrier training trips. I was still so junior in the squadron that I walked aboard the night before, but this time I took a few pieces of luggage because we were scheduled to visit a half dozen ports. Air wing aircraft flew aboard over a two-day period and then we headed into the wide Pacific.

During deployment, I continued to fly thirty to forty hours a month and build experience, and most of the flights continued to fall into the "routine" category. While flying, I would look out and examine the upper surfaces of my jet, noting greasy footprints that marked the paths trod for repairs and preflights. I watched with fascination as the slats extended and the wing shuddered during high-g turns, accompanied on humid days by streams of vapor uncoiling from the wingtips for hundreds of feet and miniature clouds of atmospheric humidity condensing along the top of the wing.

I accumulated hours of gazing at other Tomcats from a distance of forty to sixty feet as we orbited the ship in section waiting for our turn to land. After years of looking at aircraft in books and airshows, I was now immersed in the world of a spectacular fighter. The F-14 was not just a large machine, it was a complex and ingenious design that revealed more details the more I looked at it. The vertical tails had a small rib on each side to control airflow. The horizontal tails were actually attached to bulged areas along the sides of the fuselage. I noticed dozens of other features that I had not previously suspected.

I would look at a wingman—the pilot moving the controls and the RIO operating the systems—and think how small were we men who commanded this magnificent sixty-three-foot, thirty-ton fighter. About that time my pilot would ask, "Can you get an update of his fuel state?" and I would be reminded that this was my job.

FIVE

Rocket Rider

Two weeks out of San Diego, after a short stop at Pearl Harbor, *Constellation* continued west, leaving the United States and moving far enough from land that personnel transfers would be logistical headaches, and they became rare. All of the new officers ordered to the squadron had reported, and those who had completed their assigned tours had been detached. From this point on, squadron composition remained stable for the duration of the seven-and-a-half-month deployment, so the leadership of VF-24 took the opportunity to reorganize the standard pilot and RIO pairings.

Under the new plan I was assigned to fly as RIO for the commanding officer, Commander Bill Switzer. I had become comfortable flying with John Boy, and when the new crews were announced I didn't look forward to the change, but as a junior Renegade I had no say in the matter. The whole squadron shifted, so we all had to adjust to new pilots or RIOs.

Skipper Switzer was, like Commander Bertsch the XO, in his late thirties and a veteran of more than a hundred combat missions in Vietnam. But he had been a member of the Navy's Blue Angels flight demonstration team, which meant he had flown their incredibly demanding performances routinely for several years.

He'd been laid back about flying as a young officer, just along for the ride, he told me once in his sharp West Virginia twang. And then one day when he was a junior lieutenant his own CO told him he could make something of himself if he took the job more seriously. He buckled down after that, the Blue Angel tour followed, and then positions of increasing responsibility that led to this command, riding herd over 250 men, some of them incredibly dedicated professionals, some of them barely more than homesick eighteen-year-olds.

Flying with the CO had good and bad aspects. As the senior pilot in the squadron, Skipper Switzer was the lead for most flights, so I received a lot of experience preparing for flights, briefing, debriefing, and leading. Also, the CO and I weren't often assigned overnight alert duty, sitting in a parked jet with nothing to do half the night. We did take a few of these shifts, just to be fair. OK, we took at least one. I remember sitting for hours and watching a sunrise over the Pacific from a cockpit. It wasn't bad duty.

For a junior officer like me, the worst moments of flying with the CO were the few occasions when he would want to correct the flying of other squadron members, all of them senior to me. By convention in the F-14, the RIO did almost all of the talking over the radio, acting as the aircraft's voice.

Skipper Switzer and I were sitting on the flight deck one day waiting to start engines, and we looked up to see three Renegade Tomcats in low holding. They didn't look quite right to him, so the Skipper said, "Bio, tell them to tighten their formation."

Squadrons were aware of the attention they got from crewmen when they were in eyeball range of a carrier, so flyers didn't mind having someone point out when they were drifting, but I was uncomfortable being the voice telling them to smarten up. What was I going to say? Options included telling the CO "It looks fine to me," or asking him, "Why don't you tell them?"

I came up on the VF-24 base frequency and said, "Overhead, check the formation. Dash Three looks a little wide."

Hours later, after I completed my own flight and was back on Connie, I made a point of running into members of the offending flight to let them know I was only conveying what the Skipper had said. They knew a junior guy like me wouldn't be criticizing their flying, but they made a big deal of letting me off the hook. Criticism was part of life in the squadron, and it went both ways. They let me get away with it this time.

That was about as bad as it got. The good outweighed the bad by a wide margin.

Skipper Switzer was amused by my photography hobby. He'd indulge me by spending time in formation in afterburner so I could get a good shot of the cones of flame or by ordering a turn so the afternoon sun fell just right on our wingman.

More significantly, he appreciated that I was serious about doing the RIO job well. During one exercise, I had a long-range radar contact on a U.S. Navy P-3 patrol plane simulating an enemy. Our approach angle precluded using the radar's normal long-range tracking, so I ran the entire one-hundred-mile intercept in search mode, constantly losing and having to reestablish contact. It was demanding work that took me back to those charts full of numbers I memorized in Pensacola. Eventually we intercepted the P-3, and I could tell the Skipper was impressed.

Soon Connie was near the Philippines, cruising through the exotic Western Pacific headed for the Indian Ocean. Our deployment was typical for the Navy in those days. After the showdown with Iran in 1980, all carriers spent some of their deployed time in the Indian Ocean near the Iranian coast. This was also during the Cold War, so on every flight we carried live missiles and our gun was loaded. We were in the real world, and the carrier battle group was a combat-ready force representing American interests.

To emphasize that fact, I escorted two Soviet reconnaissance aircraft that flew near the *Constellation*. The ship was operating in the South China Sea between the Philippines and Vietnam. In those days the Soviet Union used the air and naval base at Cam Ranh Bay, Vietnam, which once had been a U.S. base. Soviet aircraft and crews conducted rotation flights between their home bases and Cam Ranh Bay on an almost regular schedule, and whenever a U.S. carrier passed along their route they never missed a chance to wave.

The United States has a worldwide network of intelligence gathering sites, so we knew that two Soviet Tu-95 Bear aircraft were headed our way. They could easily have been cruise missile launchers, but these turned out to be reconnaissance and targeting platforms. I briefed at 5:45 AM, flying with Holly. After launch we headed out two hundred miles from the *Constellation* and orbited, our orders being to intercept the Bears within about twenty miles of this distance. Since the Bears were maintaining a constant airspeed and heading it was not a difficult intercept, and we accepted the range mandate as our small part of larger geo-political posturing.

Everything went smoothly. As we orbited on our station, I detected the Bears on radar more than one hundred miles from our jet. We took a few more orbits while they approached, then ran a radar intercept and completed the rendezvous. It was exciting for me to fly alongside a real enemy aircraft.

Originally designed in the 1950s as intercontinental bombers, Russian Bears are large aircraft, about the size of the Boeing 767. Holly had escorted them before, on the previous deployment, and gave me a tour as we joined on them. As we got close, we could actually hear their engines and large propellers and see a crewman in the small compartment at the tail, manning the guns and defensive radar. I wrote notes about the numbers painted on the aircraft, antennas, and other details to report to intelligence after we landed. Most of these flights were benign, but before takeoff the briefer always reminded everyone of dangerous incidents that happened occasionally, when Soviet crews would try to cause the escort to lose control by flying slowly and suddenly making a sharp turn in the direction of the fighter.

Most flights on deployment were more boring than intercepting enemy bombers. But the term "boring" is relative. Each flight started with a catapult launch, included aerial refueling, and ended with an arrested landing. In between these events we usually flew a mission called "**CAP**," for combat air patrol, but there was nothing "combat" about it, we orbited at an assigned station over the ocean.

Since approaches by Soviet aircraft were rare, the vast majority of CAP missions turned into low-intensity training in basic fighter ops. We would fly to our assigned station and check in with a controller from an E-2C Hawkeye radar aircraft, *Constellation*, or one of the other ships in the battle group. We then spent ninety minutes flying 1v1 radar intercepts against the Tomcat on the adjacent CAP station. We didn't have the fuel to fly much faster than max conserve (225 knots), so the intercepts were not very challenging and we didn't dogfight at the merge. Still, such flights filled several important purposes. Pilots practiced the difficult aspects of carrier ops such as aerial refueling and carrier landings. RIOs thoroughly checked the aircraft radar, missiles, and weapons system. Radar intercept controllers received valuable training. We flew CAP missions day and night, exercising many of the systems and processes we would use if the carrier saw combat.

Every few days I was scheduled on a multi-aircraft flight (which offered a greater challenge than the 1v1 I saw during CAP flights), or to escort a practice attack mission for which the fighters would coordinate with the A-6 or A-7 bombers, or a mission with planned ACM. These were welcome breaks from the routine, with the dogfighting of a planned ACM mission the ultimate prize.

Movies, meals, mail, training, ground job. It was an easy routine to settle into. Years later many people referred to deployments as *Groundhog Day*, after the 1993 movie in which Bill Murray is forced to relive the same day again and again.

On December 19, *Constellation* was near the middle of the Indian Ocean, 150 miles northeast of the island of Diego Garcia. I was not scheduled to fly that day, only to brief at 1:15 PM as a spare. We manned spares because if an aircraft broke in the close scheduling of carrier operations it was more efficient to have a replacement waiting to go. Duty as a spare wasn't a completely bad deal, for if the day went smoothly spares sometimes got launched for some bonus action.

Just as the brief started, the pilot who was supposed to lead our flight launched as a spare for the event before us, setting off a ripple effect through the roster. When the squadron duty officer looked at the day's schedule for a replacement pilot, he saw that Skipper Switzer was available, and when the Skipper arrived at the ready room he chose to fly with his regular RIO, me. No big deal, last minute substitutions happened all the time. As the new lead RIO, I suddenly became responsible for the flight brief. Fortunately, the flight was typical for the deployment, so I was able to pick up the brief almost in mid-sentence and take over the flight lead.

The flight was scheduled as a series of 2v2 radar intercepts, Tomcats against A-7 Corsairs. The goal was to concentrate on the radar intercept portion and then, at each merge, have short, easy engagements that were likely to be fun as well as good training. A-7s were tactical fighter-bombers and their pilots always enjoyed mixing it up.

Skipper Switzer and I manned Renegade 205, launched at 3:00 PM, and expected to be back in time for dinner. It was yet another perfect tropical day with a few small clouds.

Repetitious but remarkably beautiful. I enjoyed the controlled challenge of the 2v2 and the intercepts went well.

Soon after launch we were in low holding, watching the next event launch on the flight deck two thousand feet below, with Cowboy and Ice on our wing. A pair of Tomcats from VF-211 flew the opposite side of the circle, standard procedure for returning for daytime landings. As the last aircraft was set up in the catapult, our section was approaching the best point in the circle to start a descent for landing ahead of the VF-211 jets.

Instead of continuing the holding-pattern turn, Skipper Switzer steadied up and we flew aft of the carrier, with Cowboy in tight formation. We swept our wings back, descended, made the left turn, and passed over the ship at six hundred feet and five hundred knots. The Skipper gave Cowboy the kiss-off sign and we made our break turn to burn off airspeed as Cowboy and Ice continued ahead to establish their interval for landing.

Left break turn, throttles reduced to idle, wing-sweep mode to auto, and we continued our setup as I had done seventy-nine times before. We completed the landing checklist, made our left turn behind the carrier, and got ready for another landing. I noticed the time was 5:15 PM as we made visual contact with the ball that would guide the Skipper through the final approach. It was dinnertime and I thought about having a slider tonight, just before we slammed onto the flight deck.

My next conscious thought, a fraction of a second later, was that something was wrong. I should have been thrown forward into my shoulder straps by the sudden deceleration of the trap, but instead I was still sitting upright.

Anyone who's been involved in a fender bender has experienced time dilation, that odd awareness that your mind has shifted into another gear and your body hasn't caught up. Each sliver of time contains many thoughts, many perceptions, but the body, as if weighted down by g-forces, seems unnaturally sluggish and apart. I watched *Constellation*'s island, the towering structure that holds the ship's bridge and flight control facility, sweep by as we rolled through the landing area past other aircraft. I heard the rumble of the deck plates beneath our wheels, and a second of silence passed over the ICS while both of us processed the situation. My hands were on the lower ejection handle mounted on the front of the seat, and I knew without thinking that if I pulled that handle there would be no turning back—our seats would rocket us out of the plane.

We rolled along the deck. There was some resistance slowing us down, but nowhere near enough to bring Renegade 205 to a stop. In a normal trap, the arresting wire plays out like a fishing line under tension, and the rollout of several hundred feet of cable takes about two seconds. For those seconds my brain was registering that this could still be a minor oddity and there was still a chance we would come to a stop. Then there was one last feeble tug, but we continued rolling toward the end of the landing area. We were traveling about fifty knots—too fast to stop, too slow to fly.

Skipper Switzer called, "Eject! Eject!" His voice had taken on a new urgency, almost impatience—What are you waiting for? His hand was on the stick, still trying to fly, so it was my job to pull the handle that would eject both of us.

I reacted on his first syllable, yanking the yellow-and-black striped ejection handle. We were close to the edge of the performance envelope for successful ejection, but it didn't matter now. Once I pulled the handle, everything that followed was automatic.

My Martin-Baker GRU-7A ejection seat was in charge now, and it started running through its programming, doing some very smart things. I immediately saw gray smoke in the cockpit and knew this indicated ignition of the detonating cord that ran around the canopy seal. The explosive cord destroyed the powerful latches securing the canopy to the aircraft, and a very fast heartbeat later I felt a rush of wind as the metal-framed Plexiglas canopy flew free.

When the ejection sequence control mechanism determined the canopy had cleared the aircraft, the rocket in my seat fired. I instantaneously experienced an acceleration force of about 20 g—outside the recommended operating range of the human brain—and blacked out for a few seconds.

My next conscious thought was profoundly confused. I needed to know how old I was. My brain was rebooting, and this seemed to be a crucial index, the progress bar of my consciousness being reassembled. In a few more fractions of a second I remembered that I had ejected from an F-14, and then suddenly I was back in real time. I could hear the wind and feel myself flying through the air.

What the landing signal officers watching events from the flight deck saw was Renegade 205 disappear over the edge of the deck and then me, a moment later, ride my seat to roughly the height of the tailfins of planes parked along the flight deck. This meant I started descending, unconscious and with an unopened parachute, from about sixteen feet above the steel surface. I owe my life to the fact that our jet tilted to the left as it slipped over the edge, otherwise I would have free-fallen to the deck rather than splashing into the ocean.

The seat actually sensed this was a low-altitude ejection and went through its sequence quickly. It severed the straps that held me in place, and I felt myself being separated from the seat cushions. At the same instant, my parachute deployed and blossomed, and I felt a jerk as the nylon lines and harness attaching me to the chute took tension. I opened my eyes just in time to splash into the water.

To prevent pilot-RIO collisions during ejection, the rocket in the pilot's seat fired four-tenths of a second after the RIO's. This was enough time for Skipper Switzer to become impatient, and he reached for the ejection handle mounted on his headrest just as the automatic sequence I had set in motion launched his seat, an instant before 205 hit the water. The Tomcat had tilted more left-wing-down, so Commander Switzer was rocketed almost horizontally. The landing signal officers said he skipped several times across the surface of the ocean as he was flung away from the carrier, giving a new significance to the term "Skipper."

I splashed into the water and had been submerged for only a fraction of a second when a device, activated by salt water, fired and inflated my life vest. I bobbed to the surface aware and alert. With my head above water, I unclipped my oxygen mask. The time dilation effect had passed by now, and sounds and sensations came through in real time.

Only four or five seconds ago I had been sitting in the cockpit of a Tomcat landing on a flight deck, but that familiar reality was gone. I processed what I knew of this new reality.

I was bobbing in the Indian Ocean. It was daytime. The water was warm, about eighty-five degrees. I had landed just a few feet from the nose of Renegade 205, which I was amazed to discover was also floating. This unfamiliar view of a Tomcat took me a moment to process. The missing canopy gave the sleek plane a broken profile, and the twin tails rose above the surface of the ocean like gigantic fins.

A few feet beyond 205, just a hundred feet from me, *Constellation* skimmed past at twenty knots. My gaze ran up the huge, curved slabs of Connie's gray hull and I saw dozens of people looking down at me from the edge of the flight deck, six stories above. I could see their helmeted heads and goggled faces and I gave them a thumbs-up to make clear I was feeling good under the circumstances. Then I decided to get back to my own job.

Time in the water at this point, less than twenty seconds.

My primary task now was to detach myself from my parachute. From training I knew that a parachute does not float on the surface like a film of silk, but instead fills with water and sinks. An aviator could soon find himself attached to a bag of water weighing thousands of pounds that will drag him under despite the best flotation vest. I had read reports of aviators who ejected successfully only to meet tragic ends this way, and since Pensacola I had been put through the training several times, which included actually detaching from a parachute in the water.

I flung off my wet gloves with a flick of each wrist and released the fittings of my parachute harness, but discovered a new challenge: I was surrounded by my parachute, and knit up among its tough nylon lines. Moving in the water only entangled me more deeply. Not a problem, I had trained for this, too. Bobbing on the large swells and falling into the troughs spawned by the carrier, I calmly paddled backwards away from the chute. After only a few strokes, I could tell this procedure wasn't working like it had in the pool in Pensacola. I was only getting more tangled up. Daytime, warm water, and an inflated flotation vest were all factors on the plus side, but I was growing concerned about becoming trapped.

In a pocket on the right front of my survival-gear vest I had a razor-sharp folding knife, standard issue for cutting through parachute lines. But in all of my training I had been warned to cut lines only as a last resort. "Cut one line, and it becomes two lines," our trainers warned, a statement that seemed remarkably sensible at the time, and they urged us to try swimming out of the mess. But the school solution was not working, and I decided I had to cut my way out of those lines, to "**John Wayne** it" I would say later. I retrieved the orange-handled knife.

I tried to use the curved safety blade, but it didn't work at all, so I went for the four-inch straight blade. Once upon a time there had been a problem with the blades opening inadvertently, so the survival equipment riggers had a policy of duct-taping the blades closed. I smiled at the ridiculous situation I now found myself in, using my thumbnail to try to find the end of a strip of duct tape. I promised myself on the spot that for the rest of my flying days I would always fold over the end of the tape to create a little pull-tab, a vow I kept.

Eventually I peeled off the duct tape and opened the blade, then scooped together a loop of parachute lines with my left hand and sliced through it with my right. The straight blade succeeded where the curved blade failed, and the lines cut away cleanly.

Time in the water: less than a minute.

Still entangled in about half the rigging, I felt a sudden surge of relief as I was sprayed and buffeted by the rotor wash from the SH-3 Sea King rescue helicopter overhead. Rules required that a helicopter fly in close proximity to the carrier during all takeoffs and landings, but its presence was something you tended to forget as long as everything went smoothly. The chop of the big helicopter's rotors was a welcome sight now. In our case, helo pilot Lieutenant Commander Sam Taylor had been watching as 205 went over the side and was in the perfect position to get to us immediately.

I looked up to see a rescue crewman's face looking down from the open side door, less than fifty feet above me. Feeling comfortable—and happy to be alive—I gave him a big thumbs-up and a grin, but then I was startled to see the helicopter bank and fly away. I admit, I was so focused on my own situation, I had forgotten about Commander Switzer. Now I realized I wasn't the only one in harm's way.

Commander Switzer was about a hundred feet behind me and could see me struggling with my parachute lines. As soon as the helicopter arrived above him, he waved it back to me. When the chopper returned to my position less than a minute later, I was still sawing at lines and beginning to realize how true the trainers' warning had been. The tough nylon lines seemed to be multiplying.

Overhead, the helo lowered a rescue sling on a cable and was maneuvering it close to me. I thought again about those aviators dragged down by their chutes, and decided I didn't

⌃ In front of a TA-4 Skyhawk, a trainer version of the attack jet, at NAS Pensacola. The smile is because I had only one training flight left, and was on the verge of flying fighters.

⌃ The Skyhawk was widely used and loved by pilots who flew it in training and in combat. The white and orange paint job enhanced safety on this two-seat trainer version.

F-14 Tomcats looking sharp on the flight line of Fighter Squadron 24 (VF-24) at Naval Air Station (NAS) Miramar, outside San Diego. The squadron nickname was "The Fighting Renegades."

VF-24 F-14s over central California's Sierra Nevada mountains, transiting from Miramar to Fallon, Nevada, for two weeks of intense training.

⌃ Feeling cool, shortly after arrival at NAS Miramar. Reality would soon set in.

✿ Commander Bill Switzer, commanding officer of VF-24, promotes me to lieutenant (junior grade). Two years out of college, after 21 months of training, I was getting acclimated in my first real squadron.

✿ In front of the first F-14 to bear my name. That was a milestone but many challenges remained.

⚓ A VF-24 squadron plane captain directs an F-14 aircrew at NAS Miramar preparing to taxi for a training flight.

⚓ F-14 Tomcat with two F-4 Phantoms returning to Miramar after a training flight off Southern California.

⚹ A Tomcat climbs in zone 5 (maximum) afterburner above the central Pacific, bluish cones of flame roaring from its engines. The white missile is a live AIM-7 Sparrow.

⚹ VF-24 F-14 performs a roll above the Pacific Ocean off San Diego. Overall the Tomcat maneuvered well for such a large aircraft.

⚹ Self-photo showing the excellent visibility afforded by the F-14's canopy. RIOs grabbed the handle in the foreground to help turn around during dogfights. The striped handles above my head are for the ejection seat.

⚹ VF-24 Tomcat above the aircraft carrier USS Ranger.

⚞ Aircrews from VF-24 and VF-211 carry their bags across the flight deck shortly after flying out to USS Constellation for a month of training operations off the coast of Southern California.

⚞ "J. O. bunkroom" - typical accommodations for the most junior officers (J.O.s) aboard an aircraft carrier. Six officers lived in this one.

⊼ Lieutenant Bob "Preppy" Thompson briefing a routine training flight in VF-24's ready room aboard USS Constellation.

⊼ Airmen Howell and Brigham - two VF-24 plane captains (PCs), the junior enlisted men who were responsible for routine maintenance of our aircraft. Like most PCs, they were good guys who worked hard.

⚓ F-14 refueling from the tanker version of the A-6 Intruder medium bomber. Aerial refueling was a challenge for the pilot, and we did it almost every flight from the carrier.

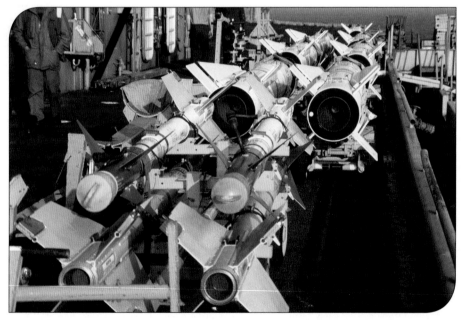

⚓ Stacks of live Sidewinder and Phoenix missiles wait on the carrier flight deck to be loaded on F-14s.

⌃ An F-14 escorts a Soviet Il-38 May patrol aircraft near USS Ranger in the Indian Ocean. We tried to stay between their plane and the carrier when they got close.

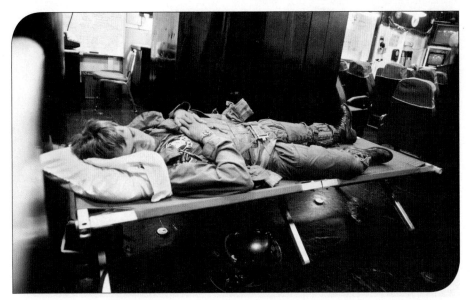

⌃ Gordo tries to sleep on a cot in the ready room, wearing all of his gear, while on overnight alert. Sometimes the pilot and RIO had to sit in the cockpit for hours, depending on the carrier's location and status.

⋆ Close-up of Monk and Tex in Renegade 212, the jet with their names on it. Aircrew flew what was available, regardless of the names, so it was a pleasant coincidence to fly "your" jet.

⋆ "Steel beach" - VF-24 pilots and RIOs relax near A-7 Corsair II attack jets during a non-flying day on USS Constellation. These breaks helped squadrons to catch up on aircraft maintenance and paperwork, but everyone would rather be flying.

⌃ Rums, me, and Monk enjoying our ration of two beers on "beer day," which was held after 45 continuous days at sea. During my second carrier deployment our continuous time at sea resulted in two beer days. No one wanted to go for a six-pack deployment.

⌃ Our wingman tightens the formation as we return to NAS Cubi Point, Republic of the Philippines, after a low-altitude training mission.

⚞ The officers of Fighter Squadron 24 (VF-24), the "Fighting Renegades," on the flight deck of USS Ranger in 1984.

⚞ A VF-24 F-14 cruises low and fast over the rough southern California desert. Training over land was a challenge for RIOs operating the AWG-9 radar in the F-14A, so these flights were among the most valuable.

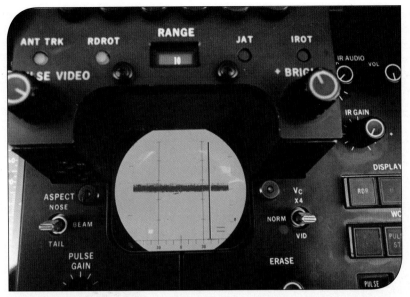

An F-14 radar scope. The thick horizontal line is the radar reflection of the ocean, and two small blips can just be seen below it, near the center. These are A-7 attack jets trying to sneak up on the carrier during an exercise. We intercepted them.

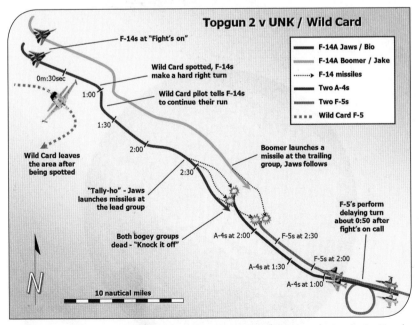

Diagram of a simple intercept and engagement from a flight as a student in the Topgun class — where the wild card tried to jump us.

⌃ Top to bottom: a two-seat F-5F Tiger II, a single-seat F-5E Tiger II, and an A-4F Skyhawk show the variety of camouflage patterns Topgun used. Both types were agile, while the F-5 had a higher top speed, and the A-4 had better maneuverability at low speeds.

⌃ The Topgun patch given to all students who completed the five-week course. They wore it proudly.

want to become another depressing case study. I stopped what I was doing and grabbed the rescue sling.

Lieutenant Commander Taylor put the sling in the water just a few feet from me and dragged it forward with surprising delicacy while I swam toward it. The blinding wind and pelting saltwater spray would have been almost painful in another situation, but at this moment they were comforting as I decided that, more than anything, I wanted to be attached to that helicopter. It was simple to wrap the sling around me and fasten it, and this time I gave a thumbs-up with enthusiasm. Beam me up, Scotty!

I was still heavily entangled, and as the crewman slowly raised me I reached down to grab another handful of nylon lines. They cut easily, but as I cleared the water I was still snagged on too many lines. The crewman lowered me to ease the weight of the rigging and I made another grab and slashed through the worst of the tangle. This time when the crewman raised me, the last few nylon lines slipped free of my gear and fell into the sea.

Determined to show that I had paid attention in training, I concentrated on my job of hugging the sling and allowed the rescue crewmen to do their jobs. They pulled me into the helo.

Safely inside the copter's cabin, I had my first opportunity to assess the situation, and I decided I was happy. I checked my watch and estimated I had been in the water about three minutes. I was fairly calm at this point, having focused almost all of my attention on the satisfaction of solving small problems. I went down a quick checklist of my body parts and realized how fortunate I was not to have any injuries or even discomfort. Despite the struggle with the parachute rigging, I hadn't had to fight for my life. It had been an assault on the senses, but the equipment worked, and I was prepared for every step of the way.

I turned now to look around at the rescue crew, and was startled to find I was looking at a familiar face I hadn't seen in years, Petty Officer Ernie Lashua. We had been in ROTC at different universities and had met on a four-week combined summer training exercise four years before.

"Ernie! What are you doing here?" It turned out we'd been together on *Constellation* for months and never crossed paths. Ernie had probably been on duty, watching from a Sea King helicopter identical to this one, during many of my landings. It had taken a small catastrophe to bring us face to face.

Our reunion was cut short when Ernie answered an intercom call from the helo pilot. The news was they'd lost visual contact with Commander Switzer. It was a jolt and my first thought was I waited too long to eject, that Skipper Switzer had paid for my mistake with his life. The anxious moments before the rescue crew spotted the Skipper seemed like an hour to me.

While the crew had been concentrating on getting me out of the water, Commander Switzer had drifted away from Connie. As we approached him now, I looked out the open door and saw him calmly floating in smooth water, his parachute bundled beside him in a comically small pile. It hadn't deployed, just spilled open on impact. The Skipper had come down the hard way. Even from this altitude, it was clear he was feeling under the weather.

This time the helicopter lowered a swimmer into the water to assist. Petty Officer Jeff Marshall checked the Skipper for injuries that might require the more formidable body rig the Sea King carried, and I was relieved to see him proceed with the simple sling. They rode up together on the cable.

When they pulled Commander Switzer into the helo, we shook hands. I shouted over the noise, "Did we do anything wrong?" He slowly shook his head no as he thought back over the last few confusing and harrowing minutes.

He reached up, grinning, and patted Lieutenant Commander Taylor and copilot Lieutenant Commander Jim Carlin on the shoulder. He told them, "Great job. Thanks!" I would have shouted the same, but it seemed redundant. I think they could read my gratitude in my face.

Connie was a mile or so away. As the helo approached for landing, I began to make out personnel clustered on the deck, and a dreadful thought came to me. I prepared myself for the possibility that this story might not have a happy ending after all. When a cable carrying enough tension to stop a fighter jet fails suddenly, all its energy is released and it becomes a massive bullwhip easily capable of cutting a man in two. Even less severe hits and despite the deck crew's safety gear a loose arresting wire can break bones and crush organs, even on less-severe hits and despite the deck crew's safety gear."

As we hovered above the deck, it became clear that tragedy had been averted on the flight deck of Connie, too. The clusters of people I had seen from a distance resolved into hundreds of crew members waiting for us. Our squadron XO, Commander Bertsch, was the first to greet us as we hopped down to the deck, and many others shook our hands and slapped our backs. Though they might not have known us personally, everyone on this floating airport understood the emotional significance of bringing endangered aviators onboard. We were people like them, doing a dangerous job. Jets can be replaced, people can't.

We walked to *Constellation's* medical ward, where squadron mates brought us dry flight suits, underwear, and socks. In the hours after the incident we received complete physicals with an emphasis on X-rays to spot spinal injuries. The docs discovered that Commander Switzer suffered a cracked vertebra, and they ordered him off the flight schedule for thirty days.

The Skipper claimed he got a lot of paperwork done during that month. I can testify he drove squadron duty officers crazy, spending more time than usual in Ready 6. He recovered fully, and the docs returned him to normal service after the thirty-day break.

In the hours and days that followed, we learned what caused the mishap.

There are four identical arresting wires on the flight deck, and a landing aircraft can catch any one of them to make a safe landing. Since aircraft weights vary considerably, the shock-absorbing machinery at each end of a wire—the valves and hydraulics that bleed away the energy of a speeding jet plane at a dramatic but measured rate—must be set to the weight of the incoming aircraft. Personnel in the tower and on the flight deck report aircraft type to the arresting gear crew, who then set the valves.

In our case, the crewman assigned to set the valves on the number four wire was new to the job, not yet fully qualified. When the crews for the other three wires reported they had set their valves, he made the same report but hadn't actually set anything. The number four wire was left at its previous setting of fourteen thousand pounds, far short of what was required to catch our fifty-two-thousand-pound Tomcat. By the time his supervisor noticed the mistake it was too late, and all of the sailors in the area were lucky to escape without serious injury when the equipment came apart.

There was a backup system using repeater gauges, but the gauges for the number four wire had not worked in some time. Normal ops continued, relying on the voice report from the arresting gear room.

On that day, Renegade 205's number came up, and it was four. Our tailhook hopped over the number three wire and engaged the fourth, whose fourteen thousand pounds of tension slowed us down a few knots. But then the cable played out freely down the length of landing area until the arresting gear mechanism was completely overwhelmed and the cable snapped. Fortunately the arresting cable broke free at both ends at the same moment, preventing a gigantic whiplash that would have caused havoc on the flight deck, and the Tomcat dragged the spent cable down the deck and harmlessly over the carrier's side into the ocean.

There was an investigation, of course, and conclusions were fed back into the live-and-learn system of naval aviation operations.

Skipper Switzer and I also learned about other corners of the event.

Given that they could see me flailing with my parachute and lines, it might have seemed prudent for the helicopter crew to put a swimmer in the water to help me. They skipped doing this, however, to get me onboard as quickly as possible. From their altitude, they could see that my chute was already starting to go underwater, sucked down in Connie's immense, swirling wake. This was something I hadn't even considered, and was glad I didn't know.

Renegade 205, known to the Navy as F-14A number 159623, floated for about three minutes before sinking, just about the time I was being hauled into the helicopter. The Navy did not attempt to recover the fighter, so you're welcome to look for it. Its location is 5 degree 26' South, 73 degree 39' East. It's on the bottom of the Indian Ocean, approximately fourteen thousand feet—two and a half miles—straight down.

Commander Switzer and I were the second and third Navy fliers, respectively, to use the new seawater-activated device that inflated our flotation vests. If the incident had happened a month earlier, it would have been necessary for me to activate my vest inflation valve manually, underwater, moments after I'd recovered consciousness from a 20-g event. The little seawater sensor significantly contributed to our survival, and I was happy that it became standard equipment.

As Skipper Switzer and I walked to medical that day after being delivered to the carrier, we passed Ready 6. Streak was standing in the doorway, and as we walked by he handed me a folded piece of paper. I opened it later as I sat shivering on an examination table. It read, "Welcome to the club." Streak had once ejected from an A-4 Skyhawk. A number of my Fighting Renegades brethren were also members of the club: Magic had ejected from an F-8 Crusader fighter; the XO and Drifty had made hasty exits from an A-4 and an F-14, respectively.

I suffered no injuries and was cleared to fly a few days later. My first flight after the ejection was with Magic, an experienced lieutenant commander, and as we were preflighting the jet he looked at me and said, "Now Bio, we probably won't have to eject on this flight." He was right.

I can't say I gained any spiritual insight from the experience or a new appreciation for life. Colleagues didn't treat me differently because of that one time I came back without my airplane. But for several years after I'd been fished out of the Indian Ocean, some moment of the experience came back to me at least once a day. Eventually, new experiences took its place, and then sometimes I'd realize I'd gone for days without thinking about it.

Over the remaining five months of the deployment I had eighty more "routinely exciting" flights typical of carrier-based operations. About a third of these were night missions.

A month before we completed the deployment I was on a night 2v4, two Renegade F-14s flying intercepts against four A-7s, with a starting distance of forty miles. Since it was night we didn't engage in air combat maneuvering after the merge, but the number of radar targets and their efforts to complicate our approach challenged us. I was the lead RIO, and Window was the wingman RIO. In my year with VF-24 I had flown a lot of intercepts. I did well at detecting and tracking targets using the radar, making the simulated missile launches, and directing my pilot and our wingman to an advantageous position at the merge. But even though I was the lead RIO on this flight, every time Window came on the radio it sounded like he was reading the bogeys' playbook. He contributed immensely to our situational awareness as he calmly and accurately described the A-7s' formation and maneuvers and added other essential information to fill-in what I missed.

In Ready 6 after we landed, I asked him, "How did you get to be so good?"

He was modest and replied that he'd been doing this for two years more than me. He said he didn't have any secrets, just experience. I knew that I could be better than I was, and I worked hard to continuously improve.

Near the end of the deployment VF-24's senior officers planned the squadron's training schedule for the fifteen months until the next deployment. Most of the training would consist of all-squadron events such as two weeks of air-to-air gunnery and periods of carrier-based training off the coast of California. In between there was a ramp-up of individual training such as high-speed low-level naviga-tion flights, the Echo Range, more ACM, and launching live missiles at targets. This is what I experienced when I joined VF-24 as an ensign, and now they were planning to train the next group of new guys. There were many other factors in the plan, such as the schedule for turning aircraft in for periodic overhaul and schools for our enlisted technicians.

One of the high-interest events on the schedule was five weeks as a student at the Navy Fighter Weapons School—Topgun. The choice of who attended was up to each squadron CO, and the announcement was eagerly anticipated in every Tomcat squadron. VF-24 decided to send Jaws and Bio.

I was going to Topgun.

SIX

The Topgun Way

My Topgun class started on a Monday morning in September 1982. I had about 680 Tomcat hours, which just met Topgun's minimum for RIOs. It would be difficult to determine the number of ACM engagements I had been in, but they totaled hundreds. I had a lot of experience and learned from my mistakes, and I was ready for the intense training Topgun offered.

Instead of driving to Hangar 4, I drove to Hangar 1 at the other end of the base. Gray and functional, Hangar 1 resembled the other hangars on Miramar, and Topgun shared it with two fleet Tomcat squadrons, VF-1 and VF-2. Inside, however, it was different, starting with the stairwell adorned with dozens of silhouettes of enemy aircraft shot down by Navy and Marine Corps pilots over Vietnam—the most recent war at the time and the conflict during which Topgun was born.

The upstairs hallway was adorned with gifts presented by previous classes: imaginative photos, action-filled drawings, and clever plaques with small models. One plaque even displayed an actual aircraft panel deformed by the air loads of a high-speed flight during the class.

I went into Classroom 1 with its worn blue carpet, dark wood paneling, chrome-legged tables with wood-grain laminate tops, and institutional chairs. The wall-mounted air conditioner was the most opulent feature, but the Navy Fighter Weapons School was not about furnishings. Classroom 2 was similar, but a little smaller.

Black-and-white photos of every Topgun class back to the first in 1969 adorned the walls of Classroom 1, mounted in inexpensive government supply system frames. Small aircraft symbols were pasted above a few of the graduates on some pictures, denoting those who had shot down enemy aircraft.

I arrived about ten minutes before the 7:15 AM start time. Jaws was already there. A few other students had arrived, and the rest soon trickled in. The Navy students wore khaki uniforms because there was no flying on the first day, only classes, but this would be the last time I wore my uniform for the next five weeks. From then on it was a flight suit every day. A few students got coffee in styrofoam cups from the little "coffee mess" next to the ready room. There were no doughnuts or bagels.

Our class was made up of eight fighters, four Navy F-14s and four Marine Corps F-4 Phantoms, so we had sixteen pilots and RIOs. We took up the front two rows of tables. Remaining seats were taken by intelligence officers and aviators who only attended the classes and did not fly, part of the Topgun Ground School. But I figured the class was about *us*, the eight fighter crews who came in with our skills and experience, listened to lectures, and then went out and fought our instructors.

Jaws and I were "Topgun Three." This would be our call sign for flying events for the next five weeks. We shared our table with "Topgun Four," Boomer and Jake from our sister squadron, VF-211. We knew them and had known we would be paired for the class, so we didn't need to go through introductions.

Topgun One and Two came from VF-51 and VF-111, two other Tomcat squadrons on Miramar, and I spent a few minutes saying hello. I also met Topgun Five through Eight, flying Marine Corps F-4 Phantoms. I was surprised to find a Navy Flight Surgeon—a board-certified doctor—as the pilot of one of these Marine Phantoms. The other seven pilots and RIOs of these venerable fighters were active duty or reserve Marines.

I would say we were not awed or intimidated to be at Topgun. Those in the class from Miramar had been exposed to Topgun all along, sitting next to their camouflaged aircraft while waiting to take off, and flying against them when they occasionally provided adversary services for the RAG or fleet squadrons. We were fighter guys anyway, not about to be impressed by other fighter guys, even if they were good.

A few minutes before the class got underway, one of the instructors walked to the front of the room, put a tape of rock music into a small player, and cranked up the volume. Conversations withered and we headed for our seats in anticipation of the start.

At precisely 7:15 AM the CO walked in, Commander Ernie Christensen, call sign Ratchet. He had flown combat missions in Vietnam and had been a Blue Angel twelve years earlier, as a lieutenant. He had already commanded an F-14 squadron. He was very well spoken, exuded confidence, and made us students feel welcome in his kingdom.

Class was in session.

Ratchet was followed into the room by about fifteen other officers, the rest of the Topgun instructors. They were wearing uniforms, khakis for the Navy officers, olive green trousers and khaki shirts for the Marines, and stood shoulder to shoulder across the back of Classroom 1. They were just a few years older than most of us, but they had an incredible presence as befit their role as Topgun instructors. They carried the somewhat conceptual responsibility of training Navy and Marine Corps pilots for combat, as well as the tangible responsibility of conducting complex and dangerous simulated-combat flights. In addition, with each lecture to fighter pilots and RIOs they put their personal reputations—and that of the organization—on the line. An audience of fighter guys is a tough crowd. These instructors inherited exceptionally high standards from men who were legends in the fighter community. They were becoming legends themselves, at least to the dozens of men they taught and trained, and some of them to the entire community of Navy fighters. They looked like they were enjoying themselves.

Ratchet turned the music off. He did not open with a joke. He made some brief remarks, then had the instructors introduce themselves.

"Hi, I'm Al Mullen, call sign Shoes. I've completed two deployments and have 1,200 flight hours in the F-14. I will be giving the Combat Section Tactics lecture."

"I'm Brian Flannery, call sign Beef. I've got 1,000 hours of F-14 time and two deployments. I'll be giving lectures on F-14 1v1 and Radar Missiles."

"I'm Steve Schallhorn, call sign Legs. I have 1,100 hours in the F-14 and I'll be giving the Course Rules lecture and **Division Tactics**."

Down the line it went. In a few minutes they were done and left the room. It was quite a display, and then we turned back around to the front of the room.

Ratchet continued his comments, addressing our class schedule, ground rules for lectures and flights, and other details. He told us nothing classified, nothing tactical, just important information to help us get through the next five weeks.

When Ratchet finished he turned on the music again and gave us a ten-minute break. We had been in the room forty-five minutes, but it seemed like five.

For the next five weeks classes started and finished on time and we took breaks every fifty minutes to an hour. Topgun classes were run very professionally. And all instructors played rock music during breaks.

More important, all instructors adhered to the high standards that I had noticed immediately. Even though some had earned impressive Navy awards and medals, they did not wear ribbons on their uniforms, only their Wings of Gold and Topgun nametag. Lectures lasted from one to two hours. No one used notes, yet each lecture was expertly coordinated with the rear-screen projection slides. Instructors stood confidently beside the podium, not behind it, and any explanations requiring drawing on the whiteboard were executed neatly and accurately. These guys were all ass-kicking fighter pilots and RIOs, yet their demeanor in front of the class personified not swagger and arrogance, but control, precision, and authority.

The first few classes were almost generic, but engaging because of the way the information was packaged and the incredible delivery.

- "Southeast Asia Box Score." After a break, Ratchet gave a short lecture that summarized aerial combat experiences in the Vietnam War, with emphasis on the lessons relevant to future fighter operations.
- "Fighter Performance Comparison" established ways to compare American and potential enemy aircraft based on objective measures. It sounds simple and wasn't even classified, yet it was insightful and imaginative, contributing to the foundation of knowledge on which later classes were based.
- "Teaching and Learning," in which Topgun's lecture techniques and high standards were spelled out for us to use when we returned to our squadrons, supported the concept of Topgun graduates becoming weapons and tactics leaders within their squadrons.

By Monday afternoon we had the first of the classified lectures that were the most interesting to the class. Lectures were classified because they presented the latest tactics American fighters would use in combat, technical explanations of how our weapons worked, and the most detailed information available on potential enemy tactics, aircraft, and weapons.

We took a short break in the afternoon to go outside and stand in two rows next to a green-and-tan camouflaged F-5E Tiger II for our class picture. In five weeks it would be hung on the wall of Classroom 1, but I'm sure none of us thought about that—our brains were rapidly filling from the Topgun firehose of information.

Many days began with a lecture at 7:00 AM. We had one or two lectures then briefed for the first hop. The lectures increased in complexity as the class progressed. After establishing our knowledge of American and enemy systems we moved into tactics, starting with detailed techniques for flying our own aircraft and progressing through 1v1 combat to section and division tactics.

Instructor after instructor maintained the same impressive delivery, the same enthusiasm, and the same apparently limitless knowledge of the subject. One of Topgun's basic principles was honest criticism, so we all had critique sheets. Try as I might to find flaws or to show my brilliance by suggesting improvements, almost all of my comments were simply, "Great lecture. Great delivery and information." There were about two dozen classes over the five weeks, front-loaded in the first few days.

Topgun was sometimes called a "graduate course in fighter tactics." My two years in Tomcats, in the RAG and time to date in VF-24, had been the undergrad work I needed to prepare me. The final step to this learning experience was to reinforce the lectures, concepts, tactics, and technical details by flying.

Jaws and I made our first Topgun flight on the second day, a Tuesday afternoon, flying in an assigned working area over the Pacific. It started with a scripted performance demonstration before we began the full-blown 1v1 ACM engagement. We had briefed the events in detail and I had them written on my kneeboard card, and I did what I had done in my early days flying with John Boy: punched my clock, made notes, and observed. It wasn't very demanding work for a RIO, but my time was coming.

"Three, two, one, go."

Spartan was calm on the radio. Calm and crisp. Topgun instructors sounded like that. In the cockpit of a single-seat F-5E lightweight fighter, he pushed his throttles forward, selecting afterburner on his two small engines. We were flying in a tight formation at 250 knots, and when he said, "Go," Jaws selected Zone 5 afterburner on our two big engines. As always happened when going to max burner from a slow speed, I felt the burner stages provide quick successive kicks. The powerful thrust was impressive. Holding altitude level at fifteen thousand feet, both jets surged forward through 300, 350, 450 knots.

In just a few seconds our Tomcat had pulled into the lead, and a few seconds later Spartan said, "Knock it off" as we approached supersonic speed (Mach 1, about 600 knots). We slowed rapidly when Jaws pulled his throttles out of afterburner. Spartan was a short distance behind us and quickly re-established the formation, taking the lead.

With a few more scripted maneuvers intended to highlight differences in our aircraft, we completed the performance demo. Some of the demonstrations reinforced lessons in aerodynamics from my days in Pensacola.

Spartan asked our fuel state over the radio then reiterated the start parameters for the 1v1, an unrestricted engagement. "Jaws, let's steady up on a heading of 270, eighteen thousand feet, 350 knots. Let me know when you're ready."

We flew a steady heading while Spartan moved out to one-and-half miles separation and matched our speed and altitude. In just a few seconds I called, "Jaws ready on the left."

"Spartan's ready, recorders on, fight's on."

The consistent pacing of his communication allowed Jaws to anticipate the final words, so our jet started moving the instant the fight started.

Jaws was as sharp as could be. He aggressively and precisely whipped our big jet through the sky. He rolled sharply to the right, then pulled hard to the 6.5-g limit. Although my G-suit inflated, my peripheral vision became gray as I strained to keep the small F-5 in the circle of useful vision that remained. After about ninety degrees of turn, Jaws eased the g, snap-rolled left, and pulled again. Spartan was fighting a smart fight. With hundreds of hours dogfighting against F-14s, he knew how to reduce our advantage and where he might intimidate us into making a mistake. Jaws tried to get a short-range Sidewinder missile shot on the first pass but it didn't happen. I anticipated a series of hard maneuvers until we could get into position for another shot.

Spartan flew his F-5 to its limits. Even though on paper it was inferior to the Tomcat in almost every category, a highly skilled pilot using the right tactics could stay alive and even take valid missile or gun shots (all simulated, of course). If the Tomcat crew made a mistake, the result could be a clear win for the F-5.

Jaws and Spartan, in their separate aircraft, continued to analyze dozens of bits of information that changed each fraction of a second in this dynamic environment. Each second they made dozens of decisions and corresponding adjustments: a small tweak of the trim button on top of the stick; a large deflection of the stick, rudders, or throttles; a change of flap position, weapon selector, or some other control. As in all tight 1v1 engagements, g-forces varied every few seconds, airspeed ranged from less than two hundred knots to more than four hundred, and altitude ranged thousands of feet as we shifted from horizontal turns to climb or dive depending on the situation.

And what did this RIO do in a Topgun 1v1? The same as when I was flying with John Boy, and what I expected I would do in combat: checked the F-5's position to back up Jaws and anticipate when to activate one of the scan-and-lock radar modes controlled by the RIO (called dogfight modes because they were most useful in dogfights). I twisted in my seat to look behind and around us for threatening aircraft, although during a 1v1 this was just practice for the multi-plane engagements ahead. I also checked things that could kill us or cost us the airplane, such as our altitude, fuel, and airspeed, as well as our position to make sure we had not spilled out of our assigned area.

As before, I actually made notes about the progress of the fight, either drawing simple diagrams or using a crude shorthand such as, "Bog nose low LT, ftr level RT 90, rev 180." That means, bogey nose-low left turn, fighter right turn for 90 degrees, then reverse for 180 degrees. I ran through this cycle every few seconds, frequently telling Jaws that I still had sight of the bogey, or reporting airspeed or fuel state, partly as a way of saying, "Even though you're doing the flying, I'm right here with you in the fight." I was always looking for information and a way to contribute.

After a few more turns Spartan was above us, but he was running out of airspeed. This meant he would have to descend and would have limited ability to maneuver. Jaws had maintained our airspeed and could use it to get into position for a Sidewinder shot, so we had the advantage.

Then Spartan used one of the tricks in the F-5's repertoire. Shoving the stick full to one side and stomping a rudder pedal, he pivoted the aircraft and came nose-on faster than expected. He called a shot, "Atoll, F-14 at twelve thousand feet," using the unclassified code name for a short-range missile carried by enemy aircraft.

Jaws had to discard his intended game plan to make a sharp defensive move known as a break turn, and called "flares!" over the radio to simulate dispensing countermeasures. Combat experience and test shots proved that, if properly executed, a combination of maneuvers and countermeasures could defeat many missiles.

"Good break, continue."

Spartan had deemed our response to his shot effective. We survived to continue the fight, but we had lost some airspeed and would have to work to regain an advantage and get into launch position. The fight progressed through more hard turns, then reached a point of relative stagnation where it would take a lot of time and fuel for either aircraft to develop an advantage, so Spartan called, "Knock it off."

I repeated the call, "Roger, knock it off. Jaws's state 8.8," adding our fuel state.

We had fought for more than two minutes, and I was panting from the exertion.

Spartan quickly provided instructions to set up for the next fight. Jaws started a gradual turn to the assigned heading and started a climb, then told me to keep an eye on Spartan so he could make a few notes of his own. We didn't talk much between engagements, we were busy. In a few seconds Jaws let me know he was done with his notes and had Spartan in sight.

"OK, tally right two o'clock. Fuel is 8.6, everything looks good up here."

After the second engagement we joined up and flew back to Miramar for the debrief.

I had been in many a debrief, one for every flight I'd ever made. Some I'd considered quite extensive, but none were like this. Spartan conducted an incredibly thorough review of the performance demo and 1v1 engagement we had just completed. He used diagrams on the whiteboard to provide a comprehensive and accurate scene-by-scene recreation of the dogfight. That was impressive enough from a technical aspect, but his emphasis on learning points was truly extraordinary. He supplemented the whiteboard diagrams with careful maneuvers of 1:72-scale plastic models of the F-14 and F-5 to illustrate important points. These models were mounted on wooden dowels about a foot long. Every squadron had a collection of them hanging on a wall of their ready room, but Spartan's expert use showed how valuable these seeming toys could be. In Topgun debriefs we never used our hands to simulate the aircraft; that was reserved for the O-Club, the beach, or anywhere else.

Whether using the models, the whiteboard, or simply talking, at every opportunity Spartan demonstrated exceptional knowledge of the F-14, gained through study, observation, and discussion, because as a Marine Corps F-4 pilot he had never flown it. He reiterated material presented in classroom lectures and showed how the "part-task training" of a sterile 1v1 fit into the bigger picture of U.S. fighters engaging in combat in support of a larger military mission.

The debrief was as long as the flight, more than an hour, which turned out to be typical of the Topgun experience. And unlike other debriefs, which sometimes seemed like a formality keeping me from dinner or the O-Club, this one was impressive and enjoyable in a professional sense from start to finish.

On Wednesday, our third day, classes again started at 7:00 AM. I arrived five minutes early. During the first break, Jaws made the suggestion, "Hey Bio, let's set a standard to help us succeed. Let's be fifteen minutes early for every event." He didn't need to talk me into this, it just made sense. For the rest of Topgun we were fifteen minutes early for everything. Making the commitment to be early was no more difficult than arriving on time, and it was a stress reducer as well as helping me to be more ready for classes and flight briefs.

We were scheduled for three 1v1 hops after the morning class, fighting against an A-4 Skyhawk, with all engagements on the TACTS Range near Yuma. The A-4 was designed as a light bomber, had no afterburner, and could not exceed the speed of sound. But Topgun's A-4s had the most powerful engines that the Navy could fit into them and had been stripped of most electronics and weapons system components, so they were very light. They were the devil in tight turning engagements. Like the F-5, the A-4 was inferior to an F-14 in most categories—on paper. But, also like the F-5, the Skyhawk had some tricky moves. For example, the A-4 had a phenomenal roll rate, which gave it the ability to reverse direction quickly and sometimes cause a Tomcat pilot to revise his entire game plan.

We briefed in Topgun classrooms for the first flight then drove to VF-24 to man-up. We taxied to the hold short and met our instructor for a flight leader separation takeoff. We flew on his wing for twenty minutes over Southern California mountains, farms, and desert, and into the range in South-western Arizona. We checked in with range control, got into position for a neutral start, and then heard, "Recorders on, fight's on."

Three 1v1 flights. We could expect nine or ten all-out engagements against this Topgun A-4. This was going to be a full day. Cool!

At the end of the first flight we landed at the Marine Corps Air Station in Yuma, just a few miles from the edge of the range, to debrief while our jet was refueled. We debriefed in a small room and then moved to the larger and better air-conditioned room with the big-screen TACTS system. The instructor did not rely on the all-seeing TACTS replay, but used it as a tool to supplement and illustrate his extensive debrief.

When we finished the debrief, Jaws felt he had been looking inside the cockpit too often at our airspeed during the fights. He knew that I was able to keep sight of the bogey and do all of the other things I was doing, but those actions did not contribute to our effectiveness in these

Topgun 1v1s. Airspeed was the most important information for him in these flights because it affected how tight we
turned and whether we could use climbing maneuvers, but
it was only one of the eight or ten things I covered in my
scan and reported to him. So he asked if I would read off
our airspeed every few seconds, essentially become a verbal
airspeed indicator.

A verbal airspeed indicator? I had four years of college!
Two years of flight training! A deployment! Hey, don't you
remember—I ejected!

Well, that's what I thought.

What I said was, "If that will help us win these fights,
you've got it."

We grabbed a quick lunch at the flight line café (just a
pack of peanut butter crackers and a soda for me, thanks)
then manned-up for the second hop of the day. It took less
than five minutes from takeoff until we were on the range.
We checked in and set up for the first engagement. Since we
had just taken off, our F-14 was nearly full of fuel and we
were limited to only 5.5 g, but three minutes of that was still
a workout.

My activities were more focused during this engagement than before. I did not forgo my crew responsibilities
for safety, such as monitoring altitude and fuel, but my
comments over the intercom system consisted almost exclusively of reporting airspeed.

"360 knots. 360. 350. 350. 340. 360. 370. 370."

And so it went, at about three to four second intervals
at first, and then eventually less frequently. At the knock-
it-off call Jaws said that was just about what he wanted, so I
figured I was contributing.

We were able to pull to 6.5 g for the second engagement because we had burned enough fuel. Jaws continued to fly a sharp and aggressive Tomcat, and we made a good showing against the A-4 in four engagements, then landed at Yuma to debrief, refuel, and brief for the final flight.

We launched in the mid-afternoon for another series of 1v1 engagements over the TACTS Range, with me as the verbal airspeed indicator. I was artificially focusing on one data point, but that's what my pilot wanted and it didn't compromise the plane or mission, so I would do it. We had three more good engagements and knocked it off with enough fuel for the flight back to Miramar.

We taxied the jet to VF-24, hopped out, and drove the mile to Topgun in my red '77 Trans Am. I figured I would enjoy another debrief watching the big screen in the TACTS facility at Miramar, which had a telemetry link to the range at Yuma and recorded all events, but the instructor wanted to just use a small room at Topgun.

"Bio, why don't you debrief the first engagement for us."

I'm sure I had a look of surprise as I headed for the white-board, but maybe surprise is not a strong enough word. By this time I had seen nine Topgun 1v1 engagements debriefed and was content to enjoy the show, nodding with all of the sagacity I could muster. Of course I had made notes as always during the fight, but I had become a little complacent focusing on my role as verbal airspeed indicator.

At the board I drew the side-by-side arrows depicting the start of a neutral 1v1, blue for the fighter and red for the bogey as always. I began to describe the action, but was interrupted by the instructor.

"Wait a minute, what was the fighter's game plan?"

"Of course, our game plan. The fighter planned a sustained-energy fight against a bogey with limited energy addition rate." I was able to complete a coherent sentence, and then add a few more thoughts.

In reply I got a look of, "Good break, continue." I had not done so badly that I was told to sit down, so the trial continued.

I had notes on most of the turns so I could draw at least a framework on the board and even use the models when appropriate. With help from Jaws and prodding from the instructor I was able to get through the debrief. It was a relief to finally come to, "And then we knocked it off."

Leading the debrief was a good remedial lesson on "crew concept," joint responsibility for our fighter and its operation. I didn't even need to write this one in my self-evaluation notebook. I expected to be accountable for our radar and intercept work, but I could not and did not want to abdicate involvement in our engaged maneuvering.

The rest of the debrief was exceptional only because it was a typical Topgun debrief. Our third day had started at 7:00 AM, and we finished about 6:30 PM.

By Thursday afternoon I had completed six flights in the Topgun syllabus.

Jaws and I had seen a range of game plans flown by A-4s and F-5s, including the smart fight, the intimidation fight, the conservative fight, the sucker fight, and more. Each bogey game plan offered us opportunities as well as risks. Dogfighting is a lot more than "max burner and pull for all you're worth." Instructors challenged us to intelligently evaluate the aircraft and pilot we were fighting, then select an appropriate game plan and execute it.

By the end of the week I was convinced Topgun debriefs met the same high standards as every other part of the school. For example, acknowledging that fighter pilots (and RIOs) were at the very least somewhat egotistical, Topgun attempted to remove the personal aspect from debriefs as much as possible by using the third person. Rather than, "I then performed a great maneuver and shot you," Topgun taught us to say, "Then the fighter pulled to max instantaneous turn rate, sacrificing airspeed for a valid AIM-9 shot. The A-4 did not react and was called a kill." This was not English-drawing-room formal in practice—we were, after all, wearing bags—but the effort added civility to the debriefs and forced us to examine our actions more objectively. This in turn contributed to the learning value of the flight and helped keep debriefs from degenerating into ego-fueled arguments.

Another hard requirement of Topgun debriefs was a summation listing of Goods and Others, aspects of the flight that went well for the fighters and aspects that did not go so well. So I would find myself at the end of a full day, after ten full-on, exhausting, kill-or-be-killed dogfights, helping to fill in a chart drawn on the whiteboard. It might look like this:

Goods:	Others:
Game plan	Bogey evaluation
Airspeed control	Fuel management
Weapons employment	
Engagement reconstruction	

We tried to have more items in the Goods column, but didn't always succeed.

In a remarkable bit of fortunate timing, the annual Tail-hook Association Reunion was held in Las Vegas the first weekend after my Topgun class started. Tailhook gained notoriety in American culture after the 1991 reunion, when a small number of participants acted irresponsibly or criminally and the situation spiraled out of control, landing the whole event in the headlines. For most years since the first reunion was held in 1956, however, Tailhook was a reasonably civil gathering of far-flung friends who shared the common bond of carrier-based aviation and gathered annually to tell stories, renew acquaintances, and see exhibits and panel discussions on naval aviation. When I went it was a big, boisterous party and Topgun attended in force.

The reunion was held at the Las Vegas Hilton, and just walking into the spectacular lobby I started seeing friends from Pensacola. I caught up on a lot of information, including deployments, missile shoots, ejections, marriages, new cars, and other things of interest to guys in their twenties.

Friday evening Jaws and I bumped into each other and over beers talked about our first week at Topgun. We both thought we were off to a good start. Jaws said he appreciated my reading airspeed, because it helped get the most out of the 1v1 flights. We then discussed "contracts" that specified our roles in the cockpit. This was similar to the crew responsibilities we had learned since our early days of flying, but was more specific.

The conversation eventually became a pact that we would be honest with each other as far as our performance in the plane, and would not be defensive about suggestions. "No personal defensiveness" was how it came out. It may not sound like much, but it set the right tone for the next four weeks. I had just turned twenty-four. I was looking forward immensely to the challenging flights ahead.

Intel Brief: Simulating Enemy Aircraft—Camouflage Paint is Just a Start

In its first two decades Topgun primarily used two aircraft to simulate the enemy: the A-4 Skyhawk and F-5 Tiger II.

The A-4 was designed as a light attack jet, had no afterburner, and could not exceed the speed of sound, but the basic design was very maneuverable. Topgun's A-4s were lighter than those flown by regular squadrons and had the most powerful engines possible, which improved their dogfighting performance. One of the A-4's attributes was its roll rate of 720 degrees per second, one of the highest for any aircraft. The A-4 usually simulated the MiG-17, a subsonic fighter from the 1950s whose weapons were guns and heat-seeking missiles of limited capability. MiG-17s were very maneuverable and used by dozens of unfriendly nations, so as a training opponent the MiG-17 had value. Several nations have continued flying MiG-17s in the twenty-first century.

The F-5 was designed from the start as a fighter, but it was a simple design intended for export to American allies, rather than a complex aircraft type normally operated by U.S. forces. As such, it was small, light, and maneuverable. With its sleek lines and two small afterburning engines, the F-5 was able to exceed the speed of sound. The F-5 usually stood in for the MiG-21, which is supersonic and carries a variety of missiles as well as a gun. Both the F-5 and MiG-21 have some moves that make them dangerous in a dogfight. The MiG-21 was also used by dozens of air forces, and hundreds of the aircraft remain in service. Topgun used the single-seat F-5E and two-seat F-5F.

The MiG-17 and MiG-21 were the most common opponents when I went through the Topgun class, but sometimes the A-4 and F-5 simulated other aircraft based on the training scenario.

Over the years, other aircraft have also served in Topgun. They are:

- T-38 Talon. A two-seat trainer used by the U.S. Air Force, the T-38 was the MiG-21 simulator in Topgun's early years. It resembled the F-5F but had less-powerful engines and lacked other refinements.
- F-16N Viper. A version of the front-line F-16 fighter simulating the more capable threats that emerged in the mid-1980s, such as MiG-29 and Su-27.
- F-14 Tomcat and F/A-18 Hornet. Starting in 1995, Topgun used these aircraft as adversaries while also adding a new role of flying "blue air," where an instructor-flown fighter operates with the student fighters going through the class.

An interesting aspect of all Topgun aircraft was their camouflage paint schemes. MiGs were designed in the Soviet Union but used by a variety of potential enemies worldwide, so Topgun painted its jets in a variety of schemes. Some were splotchy green and brown suitable for jungle environments, while others were various shades of tan for countries that expected to fight over a desert. American forces might fight anywhere, so the variety of camouflage schemes made sense for our training. Topgun also displayed interesting paint schemes of non-threat countries, such as Sweden's jagged green-and-gray pattern, which just looked cool.

Comparing the A-4 and F-5 with the F-14:

	A-4F	F-5E	F-14A
Length	40 ft, 3 in	47 ft, 5 in*	62 ft, 9 in
Wingspan	26 ft, 6 in	26 ft, 8 in	64 ft (spread), 38 ft (swept)
Typical takeoff weight	18,000 lbs	16,000 lbs	62,000 lbs
Internal fuel capacity	5,500 lbs	4,500 lbs	16,200 lbs
Maximum speed	580 knots (670 mph)	920 knots (1,060 mph)	1,340 knots (1,544 mph)
Service ceiling	42,000 ft	52,000 ft	50,000 ft

This is the length of an F-5E as used at Topgun, with the "shark nose" modification, and differs from information shown in some published sources.

SEVEN

Wild Card Bogeys

My return flight from the Tailhook convention left Las Vegas Sunday morning. I was re-immersed in Topgun by way of a 6:00 AM brief on Monday, but one of the great things about being a lieutenant is that 6:00 AM is doable, even on a Monday after a weekend in Vegas.

The intensity and pace established in Week One continued. Pay attention and try hard or get left behind. They never actually "failed" anyone or sent them home, but we didn't know that. Besides, I'm sure everyone in the class had coveted a seat in the Topgun class since their early days flying fighters (if not before). We all wanted to do well, and this was the best flying we'd seen.

The Topgun syllabus used a building block approach and progressed rapidly after the 1v1 flights through 1v2 (a real challenge), 2v1, and 2v2. The heart of the course was a series of 2vUNK flights—two fighters versus an unknown number of bogeys. We all said, "two-vee-unk." We eventually flew several complex 4vUNK flights and a giant 8vUNK simulated strike.

As the scenarios evolved, I expanded my sphere of tactical concern outward from my own cockpit, beyond the 1v1 space, to encompass several aircraft and consider our mission.

The 2vUNK is a realistic and valuable training scenario. On the fighter side, the basic unit for combat employment of Navy fighters is a section composed of lead and wingman. The value of a second fighter was borne out repeatedly, so the Navy almost never assigned a single fighter to a combat mission.

On the bogey side, in the real world you rarely knew for sure how many you were facing. Despite the quality of E-2 or ship-board radar controllers, despite the fighters' ability to sanitize airspace, despite the enemy aircraft you may kill before the merge, if you were over enemy territory and you were engaged, additional enemy fighters could show up at almost any time. This happened in combat, so Topgun trained us for it.

Unexpected enemy aircraft could appear while fighters were running an intercept, with the RIOs looking at their radars and pilots setting up a tactical formation, everyone thinking fifteen to thirty miles ahead. If a bogey got into firing position during the intercept it could land a sucker punch. To help pilots and RIOs be ready, Topgun used the "wild card," a bogey that could jump the fighters during their intercept, before the merge. (This is completely different from how the term is used in the movie, where a wild card is an undisciplined pilot. For example, Jester describes Maverick by saying, "He's a wild card, flies by the seat of his pants.")

After the wild card was introduced on the third section tactics flight, we had to be prepared for them on most flights, so Boomer, Jake, Jaws, and I worked them into our game plan.

After the 1v1 flights and 1v2, we flew with Boomer and Jake on every flight, taking turns as flight lead and wingman. Once an intercept developed, we could switch tactical lead and wingman roles based on factors such as one aircraft having a significantly better radar picture, or a change in our relative positions as we swept through the sky toward the merge. We briefed the ground rules for these changes and used radio calls to accomplish them. We soon became a close team of four instead of just two.

Jake and I already got along well, having known each other from Pensacola, which gave us three years of friendship including many evenings at O-Clubs and other social venues.

Jaws and Boomer didn't have a long personal history and were more competitive than Jake and me. Very talented pilots who showed true mutual respect, they also got into energetic discussions about fighter tactics and how our section should operate. But disagreements took place only when it was just the four of us. The instructors and other class fighters didn't see or hear any of it. Each of us knew that we would do better if we worked closely and smoothly together instead of one trying to rise above the others.

For me, it was impressive to watch the self control exhibited when we transitioned from "private" to "public" environment. The public mode included the classroom, briefing and debriefing, and any time in the aircraft. Even if we did not all agree on something, we were always calm and mutually supportive when others were around. It was a ground-based example of not leaving your wingman, to use a phrase emphasized in the movie

By Week Three our section was well sorted out, having gone through a lot of group dynamics in Week Two. All four of us knew our individual roles and we had honed our teamwork to a lethal level. Simulated lethality, of course.

On Wednesday morning of Week Three, a few minutes after 11:00 AM, we were holding west of the TACTS Range. Jaws and I had the lead, with Boomer and Jake as wingman. We were in loose formation at an altitude of twenty-two thousand feet, flying at max conserve airspeed waiting for another section of fighters to finish so we could take our turn on the range.

We had launched a few minutes early, but rather than just kill time waiting, we switched the front-seat radios in both jets to listen to the other section. I don't know if anyone else did this, but it was standard procedure for us. We heard the fighters ahead of us run intercepts, call missile shots, and get engaged at the merge. We sometimes heard their communications deteriorate into yelling because of frustration, anger, or both. Yelling on the radios sounded really bad. This experience, coming just moments before we were to enter the same arena, always proved valuable. It helped our section prepare mentally and gave us fresh incentive to remain calm and professional.

The other section knocked off their last fight and headed for Yuma to refuel and debrief. After what I heard on the radio, I wouldn't want to be in that little room. We reset our front-seat radios to the section tactical frequency, and on the backseat radio I called, "Topgun Three and Four at Telegraph Pass, ready for weapons checks." Telegraph Pass is a visual landmark at the northwest corner of the range, where the fighters usually waited. We coordinated with our controller to verify that our TACTS pods were working.

Our controller said, "Bogeys on station, ready."

Having done this about two dozen times in Topgun, our section was ready by this point so I replied, "Fighters are ready."

The controller immediately said, "Recorders on, fight's on. Bogeys 108 degrees at thirty-six miles, twenty-two thousand, headed northwest." Their altitude of twenty-two thousand feet would surely change as the bogeys used common tactics such as changing altitude to try to confuse us.

As we completed our left turn, Jake and I had both slewed our radars as far as possible to the side to point toward the threat. I was searching medium to high altitude, he was searching medium to low. For initial detection I used a long-range automatic mode and almost immediately saw radar contacts. I reported this as, "Jaws contact that call. Fighters steady one-zero-zero." On a mission like this we used the pilot's call sign for our aircraft. My directive call to the pilots (fly a heading of 100 degrees) was more important than the target location at this point. This was something all RIOs are told starting in Pensacola and graded on at the RAG. Now at Topgun it was hammered home—during the intercept the lead RIO has to *direct* the fighters.

The radar placed a small target symbol on the nine-inch TID in front of me. Jaws had the same picture on his screen, but he was not looking at it. We had talked about all of this in setting our contracts, including our lookout and information gathering responsibilities during portions of the intercept.

I took two seconds to look high over my left shoulder and then throw my head to look high over my right, scanning for a wild card. We were not pulling g's so it was easy to look around, but a wild card would be hard to see against the bright midday sun. Nothing up there. Jake was doing the same in his jet. I returned to my radar.

I noted bogey altitude, about the same as ours, and with my left hand reached up to push a square button on the panel in front of my face to switch the radar to a manual mode (pulse search, which showed objects at their bearing and range from our aircraft). With my right thumb on a small roller on the antenna control stick on the center console I set antenna elevation and adjusted other knobs to enhance the radar picture. These actions were subconscious by now. I leaned forward to squint at the other radar display in my cockpit, a four-inch wide scope in front of my face that displayed raw radar; the glowing green screen displayed black blobs representing mountains, and I discerned several well-defined black dots, which were aircraft. "Jaws, single group, 108 at 32," I estimated over the radio. It was still early in the intercept so I didn't have to be too accurate.

I reached up and switched back to the auto-track mode (track-while-scan, auto). I told Jaws about my radar mode switches. If I was having problems, he would suggest a possible solution, but this run was going fine so far.

"Boomer same," Jake said. He saw the targets that the controller and I called and had no additional bogeys in his altitude block.

We were flying about 350 knots, the bogeys about the same, for a closing speed of 700 knots. This was the slow part of the intercept.

It was now thirty seconds after the fight's on call.

"Jaws, 112 at 30, 22 thousand, heading west, speed 350." My radar was automatically tracking one target and occasionally showed another symbol, but it couldn't yet distinguish the additional targets. I didn't need any new directive calls at this time. We were headed roughly east (100 degrees), accelerating through 400 knots, with Boomer and Jake on our left side about one-and-half miles away. Every few seconds I looked for a wild card.

On the ICS I told Jaws, "I see additional targets in pulse, but they're just a gaggle."

"Roger."

I looked up and left again, then right, then said on the radio, "Jaws, hard right, tally, right five high!"

I'd spotted a bogey—a wild card—about ten thousand feet above us, just beginning his attack.

Jaws added power and pulled our jet into a 4-g turn to the right, abandoning the intercept to deal with the immediate threat. Boomer did the same and started to go nose low so both fighters were not in the same piece of sky. Four sets of eyeballs looked high and to the right.

After thirty to forty degrees of turn we heard over the radios, "Fighters continue."

Yes! That was the instructor in the wild card jet. We had seen him early enough to meet the training objective, so now we could turn our attention back to the intercept.

Over the radio I said, "Jaws left, steady 110." Estimating we were about twenty-five miles from the bogeys, I wanted to get them on radar and re-assess. The AWG-9 lost the target in the turn but displayed an estimated location that agreed with my mental plot, so I pointed my radar in that direction.

In just a few seconds the target re-appeared. "Jaws, single group, 115 at 22 miles, come left 090. They're at 18 thousand, let's go down."

Jake answered, "Boomer, second group in eight-mile trail."

We immediately recognized this tactic from our classes. While we were dealing with the wild card, one or two bogeys flew a tight delaying turn that put them about eight miles behind the lead. This would complicate our decision making. We couldn't dogfight the first bogeys or those in the second group would easily shoot us, but we couldn't ignore the lead bogeys either. Using Phoenix missiles we could each assign missiles to some targets, then attack the others with our other weapons, but Phoenix missiles were not an option in this scenario, so we had a real challenge. As briefed, Jake now focused his radar on the second group.

We were now inside of twenty miles to the lead group. Jaws descended to sixteen feet and leveled off. I switched again to the manual radar mode and got an accurate look at the bogey formation. Both the fighters and the bogeys accelerated so we were now approaching each other at one mile every four seconds. On the radio I said, "Jaws, lead group is lined-out right, eighteen miles, eighteen thousand."

Jake said, "Boomer, trailers at twenty-five miles." It sounds like a sizeable distance, but things would happen so fast in the next minute that I was feeling the tension. It was not uncomfortable, just exciting. We were completely prepared for this.

I switched back to track-while-scan and adjusted the scale of my display. The radar took a few sweeps to process information, about six seconds that seemed like minutes, and now we were thirteen miles from the lead group. On the ICS I said, "Jaws, look at the TID."

We had worked out a plan based on the theory that a picture is worth a thousand words. For most of the intercept to this point Jaws had been looking outside the aircraft. When we had fifteen miles to the merge I set up a picture on the display that he could see—the tactical information display—and told him to look. When I did that, he said, "Boomer is at left eight low," using the common clock code.

Jaws looked at his display to get the tactical picture, and I looked outside to locate our wingman. He said, "Got it," and I said, "Visual," so we both accomplished what we intended.

Turning back to the radar, I designated the lead target symbol with the hand controller and pushed the single target track button. Above the scope two small green lights indicated a radar lock, which would allow us to shoot a missile. Over the radio I said, "Jaws locked lead, ten miles, lined-out right."

"Boomer, trailers at sixteen miles, fifteen thousand, line-abreast." So the second group sped up a little and they were a little below us.

Jaws turned our fighter to the right to put the targets on the nose. He looked through the head-up display (HUD) on his windscreen, and a green diamond showed the target location based on our radar lock. Jaws had good vision and called, "Speck in the diamond." This let everyone know he could see something where the bogeys were supposed to be, which was good.

I divided my attention between ensuring the radar lock stayed good, checking Boomer's position, checking fuel, and actually making notes for the debrief. If the radar hiccuped I could manually get another lock, but that didn't happen this run.

"Fox One, lead A-4, eighteen thousand feet." Jaws squeezed the trigger on his stick to simulate launching an AIM-7 Sparrow radar-guided missile. A tone indicated the shot registered on the TACTS Range. He identified the target as an A-4 to show he was not just taking a wild shot.

For the next thirty seconds, things happened fast and there was a lot of information to process. Boomer made a radio call that he saw both bogeys in the lead group. Jake made a radio call about the trail group and took a radar lock. I updated Jaws on Boomer's position (left nine o'clock low, one mile). The bogey we shot was deemed dead by the TACTS controller. Jaws selected a Sidewinder heat-seeking missile, got a tone, and called a shot on the second bogey in the lead group. The controller relayed that that shot was a kill as well, so the lead group was gone. Jaws gave Boomer the lead to get us to the trailers, only eight miles away now. I went to the radar and got a lock on the second bogey of the trail group.

"Fox One, northern F-5, fifteen thousand feet." Boomer had identified and shot one of the trailing bogeys. On his call the entire formation was considered hostile so Jaws also launched a missile.

"Fox One, southern bogey that group."

The TACTS controller announced both bogeys killed, and then said, "Knock it off, knock it off."

"Jaws knock it off."

"Boomer knock it off, state 10.8."

Damn, that was cool! I thought.

Over the ICS Jaws said, "Nice work, Bio!"

We flew back to Telegraph Pass and set up for the next run. On the second run we did not have a wild card. Instead, that aircraft flew with the other bogeys so we had a 2v5. We also did not get kills on every shot before the merge, so we had some great engaged time.

We then flew a third engagement, a short setup of about twenty miles.

On one of these runs we bugged out at low altitude. In looking around, I saw mountains ahead of us. Jaws was comfortable with where the jet was going, so he looked back over his shoulder and saw me looking forward. When he looked back I actually said, "Watch the mountains!"

He came back, "Watch the bogeys!"

And so we added another rule to our contracts. On a bugout, when we left an engagement as quickly as possible, he could trust me to check behind us for bogeys, and I could trust him to watch terrain. Afterward, I never checked on Jaws because I didn't look forward on bugouts anymore. Since we never hit anything I believe he kept his part of the contract.

We landed at Yuma to refuel, grab lunch, and debrief, then went out for two more 2vUNK flights that day. All three flights lasted 1.0 (one hour), and reinforced what I had learned with John Boy just one year before—that most 1.0s are great flights.

And that was just one day out of five weeks! Now I knew why guys were so enthusiastic about going through Topgun.

⚜

The multi-aircraft events reinforced what we learned during the first few days of Topgun class, indeed from early days in Pensacola. The F-14 was superior in most respects to both the A-4 and F-5, as it was with the MiG-17 and MiG-21, but experience teaches smart pilots to never underestimate an enemy, regardless of his machine, and Topgun instructors proved this regularly. Yes, Topgun pilots had an unusually high level of experience, but surely there were also talented and committed enemy fighter pilots willing to defend their airspace. So we trained diligently.

One of the F-14's advantages was its powerful and sophisticated AWG-9 radar. It was the best among the world's fighters when it was introduced, and far better than the radar in the MiG-17 or MiG-21. The Tomcat's radar operated best over the smooth ocean. Over rough terrain it required a skilled RIO to sort out false returns from real bogeys, but still bettered other fighter radars for years.

Our trump card would have been the AIM-54 Phoenix missile, which we could launch at a target one hundred miles away, and which then used its own small radar to accomplish final tracking to a kill. Even better, we could launch up to six Phoenixes at different targets, although we rarely expected to carry more than two, as they weighed one thousand pounds each. Only F-14s carried the Phoenix missile, and no other missile in the world approached its performance. Unfortunately, we planned to "save" Phoenix missiles for use against Soviet bombers should they attack an aircraft carrier (and during the Cold War we always kept this possibility in mind), so we did not plan to shoot Phoenix missiles at enemy fighters.

This left us with the radar-guided AIM-7 Sparrow (Fox One) and heat-seeking AIM-9 Sidewinder (Fox Two), as well as our gun. So though we were a large sophisticated fighter with capabilities that could intimidate most enemy aircraft of the time, we carried missiles only a little better than our adversaries. But this was what I expected if it came to real combat during one of my deployments. So we trained hard. The Navy's MiG-ace pilot from Vietnam, Randy "Duke" Cunningham, often said, "The more you sweat in peace, the less you bleed in war."

I sweated in peace a lot during the Topgun class.

Meanwhile, Jaws proved that sometimes a little diplomacy could reduce the sweat.

Early in Topgun (during the week of 1v1s) we returned from a flight and I reported a problem with the radar in Renegade 204—it would not operate in the long-range modes. Even though we didn't use the radar much in a 1v1, I checked it out thoroughly while we were flying. My write-up provided detailed information, since I prided myself on being a good troubleshooting RIO and I had been the radar technicians' branch officer for more than a year. The following day we flew 204 again and I experienced the same problem, so I patiently wrote it up again and added "REPEAT" at the end. That should fix it, I thought. The next day we flew 204 for a third time and had exactly the same problem. I quickly passed through the "furious" stage, as I had given these guys a detailed description of the problem and as far as I could tell, they hadn't touched the radar. Exactly the same problem on three flights in a row! And I had been their branch officer!

When we got out of the jet, I ripped through the maintenance control area and headed back to the radar techs' shop like a Sidewinder after a MiG. It was late in the afternoon and the radar techs had been working all day in the hot sun. They were tired, while I had just finished a 1v1 hop and had a lot of energy. Fortunately I don't remember exactly what I said to them, but I expressed my irritation and disappointment. They made a few remarks, but didn't really say much, just kind of looked at the exploding RIO show.

When I was done, I felt better. I hung up my flight gear, got back together with Jaws, and we drove down to Topgun to debrief.

We went back to VF-24 when that debrief was over. I didn't know it but the Maintenance Officer (MO) then pulled Jaws aside with, "We need to talk." The MO was a lieutenant commander, one of the more senior RIOs in the squadron, and the radar techs told him about my visit. The MO explained to Jaws that since returning from deployment a few months before, VF-24 had received several Tomcats that needed a lot of work, and they were keeping the whole maintenance department busy. He had personally assigned 204 to us because it had a persistent radar problem, and he knew we could get by with it in our 1v1s. If we could just work with him, he would do his best to support us.

Jaws told him we were almost through with 1v1s and we would need good radar for the next four weeks. Jaws also said we would advise the MO of our scheduled takeoff times each day, instead of the general windows Topgun provided in their long-range plan. This would help the MO support our high-profile Topgun flights as well as the flying requirements for the rest of VF-24.

Jaws told me about all of this the next morning. It sounded reasonable.

The MO and the radar techs came through for us. We flew 204 the very next week for 2v2s and 2vUNK, and the radar was great. In fact, we had great radars for the remainder of the class.

Maybe my technique wasn't the best, but I contented myself thinking that I was the catalyst for process improvement. But the episode also made me slow down and think before talking to the sailors in the future.

In Week Four of the class, we went to China Lake for two days to fly on the Echo Range. A Topgun class would normally go during Week Three, but the range was not available because of testing requirements for a priority program. We faced the simulated surface-to-air missile threats that defined the Echo Range but also had to deal with Topgun bogeys. I knew that I would be the flight lead half the time, and I was ready.

We had a class at Miramar Tuesday morning, then took off at 11:00 AM for the flight up. We made a couple of runs through the range on our arrival flight.

For me this visit was completely different from my first short-notice hop the previous year. No confusion, no smeared palette of brown and blue. I felt completely in tune with the aircraft and our mission. Jaws jinked us through the range, while Boomer and Jake did the same two miles away. I easily kept track of them, as well as the radar warning gear, our location, fuel, and everything else I was expected to do. Topgun had us deal with the threat radars and surface-to-air missiles first, simulating one layer of an enemy's defenses, and then we moved into a second layer, bogey airspace.

Jake and I were now casually competing to be the best on the radar, so we aimed our radars up-range, where the bogeys were waiting, at every opportunity. Because of the violent maneuvering we were in manual mode, but a call like "Boomer, hits 350 at 30" helped build our SA. (In that case, it meant Jake had tentative targets 350 degrees at 30 miles.)

It was frustrating to "fight" against simulated missiles based on radio calls from ground controllers, and it felt good when the radar warning tones died down and we could fight real bogeys. We worked the radars, found the bogeys, took missile shots before the merge if we could, then either neutralized or engaged any remaining. While we were engaged, the instructors called, "Good break, continue" after virtually every shot they took (which wasn't many), so we could stay alive and fight our way back through the Echo Range at the end of the run. You can't get enough good training.

When we landed at China Lake that first day it was the same routine as at Yuma. We grabbed a quick lunch and debriefed the flight. Our jets were refueled. But as we started to brief for the afternoon flight, Spartan said we had been kicked off the Echo Range by a higher priority test project. He gave us the option to take the afternoon off, but Jaws, Boomer, Jake, and I all wanted to fly.

Spartan had coordinated with China Lake range control for an area where we could work. It was small, but included a well-defined valley with craggy mountains three thousand to six thousand feet high marking its edges. Because of the airspace rules, we had to stay below eighteen thousand feet.

Intercepts would be twenty to twenty-two miles at most. And in this area there were no surface-to-air radars.

Afternoon off? I don't think so.

We arrived on station at the western side of the valley a little before 3:00 PM. A layer of high clouds tempered the afternoon sun. Instead of our usual twenty-two-thousand-foot altitude, we started around fifteen thousand feet. There was no radar control so the Topgun instructors filled in with basic calls. I think they expected the lack of good radar control, the short set ups, and the mountainous terrain to cause us problems. They were wrong.

We called on-station and ready.

From the brief, we knew Spartan was in one jet, but we didn't know who else would be there, or how many.

"Recorders on, fight's on. Bogeys estimated 105 at 20 miles, altitude low." That was Sunshine's voice, using intuition to simulate calls from a radar controller. Sunshine was a RIO, so at least one jet was a two-seat F-5F.

Jake got the first contact and said over the radio, "Boomer, group 090 at 19 miles, two degrees low. Fighters steady 060." Working in search mode our calls were a little different than the lethally efficient rhythm we had developed on longer runs. But at this point it was a welcome change. Our technical skills, thought processes, communication, habit patterns, and crew coordination were all at their peak. We could handle the scenario variation.

After just a few seconds I replied, "Jaws same" over the radio, and proceeded to give Jaws a formation description over the ICS. I saw two bogeys on radar. I looked for more and didn't see any. A clean 2v2 would be nice at this stage of Topgun.

With first contact Boomer and Jake had the lead on this run. Jake and I remained in manual mode longer than normal, then took our radar locks. As we neared the merge, fighter radio calls included tally-hos to indicate we saw the bogeys, missile shots, formation descriptions, and quick game plans.

"Boomer's blowing through the lead."

"Jaws tally dash two."

In an unusual development caused by the last-minute changes to this entire flight, we shared a radio frequency with the bogeys, who usually had their own freq. So, even though I was talking and listening on an ICS and two UHF radios, I was keying on the voices of the Topgun instructors. They tried to make their calls short, but we could identify them.

We heard, "Tally one." OK, that's Spartan, but we already knew he would be here. And we had heard Sunshine.

"Wingman's high." That sounds like K. D.

And that was it. We heard no additional voices. Pretty soon it was easy to tell that Spartan and Sunshine were in an F-5F, while K. D. was in an F-5E. We had a 2v2.

"Knock it off, bogeys headed east."

"Roger, knock it off, fighters headed west."

Run after run they tried various means of challenging us, such as starting at extreme ends of the airspace, using wide formations, or starting low and then high. It didn't matter—Jake and I both had good radars and used them well; Jaws and Boomer had good eyeballs and used them well and then followed that up with some great flying.

Pretty soon we could tell that the bogeys were getting irritated at being detected and shot every run, no matter what they did. We could hear it in their voices. Well, that's how it's supposed to work when you put a couple of $30 million Tomcats against a couple of $5 million Tigers.

Besides, I thought, you guys trained us.

All four Tomcat crewmen enjoyed the rare experience of actually irritating Topgun instructors.

Since we were so close to China Lake, we were able to fight until our fuel was fairly low, so the flight lasted a long time, an amazing 1.7 hours. It was one of the more memorable flights of my career, with tight-turning F-5s wrestling us in the afternoon sun, the mountains on the edge of the Sierra Nevadas forming the boundaries of our arena, and purple late afternoon clouds as our audience.

The debrief was fairly short, and then we headed to the small Officers Club at China Lake to discuss the fine points before going into town for dinner.

Wednesday brought another bright, clear day and we flew Echo Range missions morning and afternoon, then bingoed back to Miramar. We were almost through with Week Four.

By now we knew the principles that Topgun recommended. They were not simple learning exercises or things they used to trip us up in debriefs, but exactly how they recommended we operate in combat. The principles were validated in flight and constantly scrutinized. (A scene in the movie shows Maverick breaking a "rule" and succeeding, and then being hammered in a debrief. This is an example of Hollywood drama, because it was not the way Topgun operated.)

One of the principles was that if you leave an engagement, you should not go back in. There were examples from combat (and other Topgun classes) of fighters becoming engaged and bugging out, and then re-engaging with bad results, such as being shot down.

On a 4vUNK hop in Week Five, flying over the Pacific, we were in a large furball. There must have been nine or ten aircraft within about five miles, a sphere of airspace in which they could influence each other. Some bogeys had already been killed. After Jaws and I took several shots we decided we should leave, so we coordinated with Boomer and called, "Jaws bugging north."

The answer was, "Boomer bugging west." Good.

Jaws pushed the nose forward to descend and went to Zone 5 burner. My job was now defensive lookout, so I focused 90 percent of my attention behind us, watching the swirling black dots recede as we rapidly accelerated through Mach 1. I told Jaws it seemed like a clean bug, and when I looked forward I saw the amazing spectacle of a shock wave sliding backwards on the Plexiglas canopy. It looked like a plate of glass that conformed to the shape of the canopy and moved aft as our speed increased. We hit Mach 1.3 (more than eight hundred knots) easily and were still accelerating. When I said it was a good bug Jaws pulled the throttles back from Zone 5 and the shock wave rapidly slid forward and disappeared as we slowed below Mach 1.

"Feel like poking our nose back in?" he asked.

"Sure!"

Jaws executed a max-performance left turn while I slewed the radar to its limits and set it for manual operation at short range. In the turn I saw black dots on my green scope. The small ones were A-4s or F-5s; the larger ones were F-14s still engaged. On the ICS I told Jaws I had contacts at nine miles and said, "Steady 190."

Squeezing the trigger on my hand controller, I took a lock. The symbology on Jaws's head-up display changed and the diamond showed the radar target. Although I tried to be selective, he said, "That's an F-14," so I went back to search mode, looked for a smaller blip, and took another lock.

The second lock led Jaws to make a radio call of, "Belly Fox One, A-4 chasing the F-14 at thirteen thousand feet." The A-4 immediately performed a roll to acknowledge that he was dead. We had shot at his belly, so he had no way to see the shot and no chance to defeat it.

Over the ICS Jaws said, "Let's not press our luck." We rolled into another max-performance turn, once again away from the furball.

Over the radio I said, "Jaws bugging north." We joined up with Boomer and returned to Miramar.

Since we were not on the TACTS Range, the debrief would rely on reconstructing the intercepts and engagements from memory and notes, and our cockpit tape recorders. After landing we taxied our jet through Miramar's hot refueling pits, where a sailor attached a thick hose and refueled the plane. Refueling took ten to fifteen minutes (it only seemed like longer), and while waiting one of us would play our mini tape recorder over the ICS. We listened, made notes, and refreshed our recollection of the flight. We rarely stopped on a specific point on the tape since we agreed to play all runs through before focusing on any incidents.

I'm sure most fighters listened to their tapes in the pits. If not, they should have. It clarified recollections and filled in gaps in my notes, helping me to come up with a fairly complete and accurate picture of the flight. After my lesson in the 1v1 debrief I wanted to be ready at any time to debrief a portion of the flight or explain what our jet was doing and why, and the mini tape recorder helped me prepare.

Our return to take a missile shot was mentioned in the debrief, thanks to a bogey who had been killed and saw the whole thing as he cruised above the action. Since we had made it work, the instructor lead stated the obvious (Don't do this) but didn't make a big deal about it.

Topgun was almost over.

On Wednesday of Week Five we fought Spartan for our 1v1 graduation hop. We all looked forward to this mission after the complex events we had been flying. It was a hard fight and a great final 1v1. It wasn't really a pass-fail flight to determine who would graduate, but they called it a Grad 1v1, which had a catchy ring to it.

On Thursday we flew the coordinated strike, essentially a "Class v UNK" on the Echo Range. Jaws planned and led the event, so our plane was the "command element" for the strike. Lead responsibilities added another layer of complexity, but Jaws had a great plan and the mission went well.

Thursday night we had a big class party, which Jake and I arranged, since many class members were from out of town. The class put on a small skit and the instructors presented a hilariously scathing overview of Class 05-82. It was a chance to finally relax.

Topgun graduation started at 8:00 AM Friday. After our party on Thursday, that start time goes in the Other column. The whole class gathered in Classroom 1, Navy students again wearing khaki uniforms while the Marines wore flight suits. By now we were all pretty good friends, we had just spent five weeks giving our best.

A few minutes before 8:00 AM one of the instructors started the music, and Ratchet strode to the front of the room as the second hand reached twelve. He had to feel good, his men having just completed another five-week invest-ment training sixteen fighter pilots and RIOs. The rest of the instructors followed him into the room and stood along the back wall.

Ratchet made some brief remarks, then signaled the start of a ten-minute slide show accompanied by music. The slides included photos of each class aircrew, along with shots of our jets and the Topgun jets, plus a photo of the president and other patriotic shots. Instead of rock, the music was majestic and martial, very inspiring under the circumstances.

After the slide show, Ratchet continued his remarks and congratulated us as a group. He then called attention to the photos of previous classes that adorned the walls. He picked up the new framed photo of our class from the podium and handed it to one of the instructors, telling him to put it "in the appropriate place." The instructor took the photo and deposited it in a trashcan held up by another instructor.

For us students it was a great gag.

Ratchet then called each of us to the podium and with a handshake gave us a brown envelope containing a gradua-tion certificate and a Topgun patch. The patch was a powerful symbol that we would cherish. It was unlike any other squadron patch. We would purchase additional patches and put them on our flight jackets and flight suits, but the first one was a gift.

When we had all received our envelopes, the instructors and the class members fell into an informal arrangement like two sports teams shaking hands at the end of a game. The two groups passed along each other rather tightly, and I think I shook hands with all of the instructors. Some of them said, "Nice job, Bio," and, "Bio, you and Jaws did really well." Several instructors said, "Hey, if you ever think about coming back, let us know." It all sounded to me like typical compliments given to guys who had spent five weeks trying hard and enjoying the effort.

I had seen the Topgun instructors around the base, in flight briefs, at the hold short, at the O-Club. But now after spending five weeks working closely with them, I felt that their reputation was well deserved, earned through individual effort all the time.

And then Topgun was over.

Jaws and I went back to VF-24 where we spent the rest of Friday starting to catch up on our ground jobs. Friday night the VF-24 officers had a party to celebrate several promotions. Two big parties in two nights. I was glad I was in shape for this kind of stress.

Saturday night was another party. OK, still no problem.

We got back to our squadron in time for more great flying as VF-24 cranked up the training program for the new officers who were trickling into the squadron, just as I had eighteen months before.

In the months and years following our Topgun class, two young men who were fellow students were killed in flying mishaps.

Lieutenant Doug Blum of VF-51 died just six months after Topgun when his F-14 crashed in the Mediterranean Sea one night. He was flying from the carrier USS *Carl Vinson* (CVN-70) during an eight-month around-the-world deployment. Doug was a competitive pilot and was well known around Miramar, even though he was a young officer. He and his RIO likely died instantly.

Navy Captain Manley "Sonny" Carter died nine years later when the commuter plane in which he was a passenger crashed near Brunswick, Georgia. When I read about it in the paper, I was amazed that Senator John Tower of Texas and professional golfer Davis Love Jr. were also on the flight. Everyone perished. Sonny was quite an accomplished gentleman, having been a professional soccer player in Atlanta in his early twenties while attending medical school. After graduating med school he became a Navy flight surgeon and a carrier-qualified Navy pilot. He flew a Marine Corps Phantom in Topgun, became a NASA astronaut, and went into space on a Shuttle mission.

Navy mishap and fatality rates had been decreasing for years, like those of the other services, but we all occasionally lost friends or acquaintances. Sometimes the incident provided a learning point, sometimes it was ironic, and sometimes just tragic, but regardless of the details it was punctuation to their life and service to their country. And whether or not it was "worth it"— paying for this fantastic opportunity with one's life—at least we could say they achieved a dream and had partaken in the extraordinary experience of flying jet fighters. That's a good place to leave it. Knock it off.

EIGHT

Gunboat Diplomacy in a Jet Fighter

Shortly after I returned to VF-24 I had an inkling, which developed into a full thought, and turned into my next dream.

Having achieved the dream of becoming an F-14 RIO (once becoming a pilot was no longer an option), I had to think of something to do when I completed my current assignment with VF-24. This is a routine administrative task for all Navy officers, recorded on an officer preference card. It's only a request, as the Navy will send you where they need you. My first thought was that I would like to be assigned to an "exchange tour" as a back seater in new Tornado fighters with Britain's Royal Air Force. This had seemed both exotic and sensible for an F-14 RIO.

But in the weeks after Topgun I started thinking about becoming a Topgun instructor. I don't know when it started, but I know exactly when it became my new goal: at a Thanksgiving party that Okie and his wife, Rita, had at their home. Okie, Rita, and their two kids had already hosted several squadron parties and made us feel welcome.

An hour into the party I started talking to Streak, who came to VF-24 after completing his tour as a Topgun instructor. One of the most talented pilots at Miramar—I saw somewhere that he had the base record for air-to-air gunnery, shooting bullets at a target being towed by another aircraft—Streak nonetheless was approachable and friendly. His easygoing, unflappable demeanor on the ground masked his intelligence, but in an airplane he was focused and competitive, usually winning. I told him what I was thinking and asked how I would go about becoming a Topgun instructor when I left VF-24.

Streak asked me one question: "What did they say to you at graduation?"

I thought back to the ceremony. "They said Jaws and I did a nice job, and if I wanted to come back I should let them know." Though I heard the words when I graduated, I hadn't given them much consideration. But I remembered them.

"You should go talk to them," Streak said.

And that was it.

Nothing changed for the rest of the party. I didn't tell anyone, "I'm going to be a Topgun instructor." I don't recall thinking about it for the rest of the long Thanksgiving weekend or during the workdays that followed. I don't remember if I went over to Topgun the Monday after

Thanksgiving or the next week. This tells me that, amazingly enough, I did not fret or agonize about my potential future as a Topgun instructor.

But one afternoon I phoned ahead, put on my khaki uniform, drove down to Hangar 1 and spoke casually to Ratchet, still Topgun's commanding officer. He asked when I was scheduled to leave VF-24 (eighteen months hence), what my job was (assistant personnel officer), and a few other fairly superficial questions. After our brief but cordial discussion he called Wahoo and said we were coming to talk to him.

Wahoo was a RIO who had been at Topgun more than a year, and based on my departure date fromVF-24, I could be his replacement.

Wahoo and Ratchet both talked to me as an equal, and again the conversation was fairly superficial. They asked me if I minded working hard (easy answer, No), would I mind traveling some (another easy one, No), and other perfunctory questions. After a few minutes we all said things like, "Well, I guess that's it." Ratchet told me two specific requirements: change my preference card, and have my CO write a letter recommending me as a Topgun instructor. Then I left.

As I walked down the familiar hall I thought, "If these guys didn't try to eliminate me, I guess they are confident I can do this." I also figured I wouldn't have a problem getting a letter from Commander Bertsch (who had succeeded Commander Switzer as CO of VF-24) because I worked hard and felt I had a good reputation in the squadron.

While in my mind I had started on the path to becoming a Topgun instructor, I tried to maintain perspective. I had generally been open with my friends about discussing my plans, but I realized there were still many steps to take from fleet RIO to Topgun instructor, so I kept this one to myself. I told Commander Bertsch and Streak, but didn't tell any of my contemporaries for a while.

Eventually I mentioned to Jaws that I had visited Topgun to talk about becoming an instructor and had gotten a good reception. He told me he was doing the same thing! I thought it was great and wasn't surprised.

But it was more than a year in the future, and we didn't talk about it much until the time got closer. Instead we focused like the rest of the squadron on another cycle of training, in preparation for the next seven-and-a-half month deployment, which was scheduled to start in six months.

Around this time I was designated a mission commander, which meant that I could be scheduled as the senior person in a group of VF-24 jets, and thus responsible for the conduct of the flight. This didn't feel like a burden but rather a credential that I sought, as did my contemporaries. Regardless of who briefed or led the flight, when I was mission commander I had a good deal of accountability. In training flights it was primarily for safety, but later it could be for combat mission effectiveness. I had been steadily trained, fed more difficult challenges, and found new goals, and I felt comfortable with the new title. Eventually most pilots and RIOs were designated mission commanders, but not until the senior officers of the squadron were convinced they deserved it. So there was suspense and competition based on when we received the designation compared to our peers.

Another big change was that I had enough experience to fly with new pilots who joined the squadron—first Beetle, followed by Petro, then Coyote. After more than three years of flying with instructors, experienced pilots, or contemporaries, this was an indicator of the increasing responsibility the Navy demands. These pilots had qualified as fleet F-14 pilots, but that just got them in the door of a fleet squadron. Now I was responsible to help them become more capable pilots, to "give back" the training that John Boy, Skipper Switzer, Streak, Jaws, and other experienced pilots had passed on to me. Some of my passdown items were vital to using our jet as a lethal fighter or operating off a carrier in the middle of the ocean. Other items involved finesse and technique, but these were not trivial, they were important to blending new pilots into our squadron as we again prepared to deploy and keep America safe.

⚜

For this deployment, the air wing shifted from *Constellation* to a different aircraft carrier, USS *Ranger* (CV-61). *Ranger* left San Diego for deployment on a Friday morning in July 1983. As usual, the squadrons had made arrangements with hotels in Hawaii for parties about a week later, and several wives had airline tickets for short Waikiki vacations with their husbands. After all, that's what carriers did when they left San Diego. Except this time we had to cancel everything when the battle group headed south and spent a month off Central America, "demonstrating U.S. interest" in the region. We were on the cover of *Newsweek* with the caption: "Gunboat Diplomacy; Reagan Gets Tougher with Nicaragua."

The dramatic change in plans was kept secret from most of us until the very morning we left. But in reality, aside from our expectations of visiting Hawaii in a week it didn't really matter where we went, we were on deployment for the next 225 days.

After spending a month off Central America we headed west and visited Hawaii and then the Philippines, conducting routine flight operations all the while.

The deployment seemed to be getting back on track. But while we were patrolling the Indian Ocean, the Marine Corps barracks in Beirut were bombed, killing 241 American servicemen. As a result, the carrier USS *John F. Kennedy* (CV-67) was held in the Mediterranean to provide options for American commanders. This event thousands of miles away affected us on *Ranger* because Kennedy was our scheduled relief in the Indian Ocean. We had planned to turn over patrolling responsibilities to Kennedy and spend three weeks in Australia during December, but instead we spent the next four months at sea.

Four months in a row . . .

It was not pleasant, but we survived.

We then visited the Philippines and Hawaii, and returned to San Diego. As deployments went, it was not good for recruiting. But it was a demonstration of how the Navy and each person on its ships was affected by real-world events, first the detour to Central America and then the change in carrier schedules caused by the Beirut bombing. The news was more than headlines to us. And the flying was the same as ever, with challenging missions, amazing scenery, many calm hours, some exciting moments, great performances by pilots and RIOs, and a few "I can't believe I/you/we did that" episodes.

I quietly looked forward to Topgun. I had changed my preference card immediately after talking to Ratchet, so the

Navy assignment office knew I wanted to become a Topgun instructor instead of going to England. During the deployment Skipper Bertsch wrote a letter recommending me. He handed me the envelope to mail. On the way to the ship's post office I held it up to a light but couldn't read it.

Jaws got his orders first, as expected, so in the middle of the *Ranger* deployment Jaws left the ship to start his tour as a Topgun instructor. Unlike the movie, fighter pilots who go to Topgun from a carrier in the Indian Ocean do so on a cargo plane such as a C-2, not their F-14. The versatile C-2 has two propeller engines for responsiveness and fuel economy, and the boxy fuselage provides the flexibility to carry cargo such as mail or replacement jet engines, or two dozen passengers. Not nearly as sexy as a Tomcat, but in the Indian Ocean the C-2 and its cohort the US-3 were the only one-way trips off the carrier, so those who flew in them did so with a smile.

By the time we returned from the deployment in February, I had received my orders to leave VF-24 and report to Topgun in March. I eagerly started the paperwork to switch squadrons. Once again, I was excited to be going to Topgun.

Intel Brief: Topgun's Origin and Mission

The Navy Fighter Weapons School, official name for the unit known as Topgun, was one of the responses to the poor performance of Navy fighters and their missiles in the first few years of the air war over North Vietnam.

When the Navy compared their Vietnam combat performance to previous experience, one measure was kill ratio, the number of enemy aircraft destroyed for each American fighter lost. (Kill ratio only considers losses from airplanes fighting airplanes.) In World War II, the U.S. Navy's kill ratio over enemy aircraft was 14:1, meaning we destroyed fourteen enemy planes for each Navy aircraft we lost. In the Korean War, American jets had a 12:1 kill ratio over enemy fighters. While some inaccuracy is expected in these numbers—people were shooting at each other, after all, and aircraft could be lost for other reasons—they provide a rough indicator of effectiveness.

During the first few years of air combat in Vietnam, the Navy's kill ratio was around 2:5:1, quite a bit lower than in the previous wars. This was more surprising when one considers that the United States employed sophisticated, high-performance, missile-armed fighters opposed by what was thought of as the relatively primitive air force of North Vietnam. There were many complicating factors, but that kill ratio indicated profound problems, so Navy leaders ordered a study, led by Captain Frank Ault; the results were known as the Ault Report.

One of its major conclusions was that air-to-air missiles needed to be more reliable. Fighter pilots many times aimed at the enemy and squeezed the trigger only to find the missile did nothing, or flew off on its own. This was partially due to the pounding these weapons took from frequent aircraft carrier takeoffs and landings. Industry and government responded with solid-state electronics and other advances that greatly improved reliability.

A second conclusion was that pilots had not been well trained in close-in maneuvering, which could be attributed to the attitude that missiles would eliminate the need for dogfighting. But when missiles failed or an enemy fighter managed to get into a position of advantage, dogfighting proved a valuable skill.

One way to address this training problem was to establish a core of specialists to train fighter crews in air combat maneuvering. To provide a greater benefit, these instructors should fly aircraft that were different from the Navy's fighters and replicated the capabilities of likely enemy fighters.

The Navy's response to the Ault Report led to the establishment of Topgun at NAS Miramar, initially as a department in an existing squadron (the F-4 Phantom training squadron), which evolved into a stand-alone aircraft squadron. The Navy (and Air

Force) also established other adversary squadrons at fighter bases to prepare crews to face enemy fighters.

As for Vietnam aerial combat, Topgun training and other measures resulted in the Navy's kill ratio improving to 13:1. That's a good return on investment.

NINE

Murder Board

Like all orders, mine to be a Topgun instructor were sent to both VF-24 and Topgun, so they were common knowledge in both squadrons. Since it looked like I would soon make the switch, I started going to Topgun staff meetings and social events in April. When another Topgun class started in mid-May I was one of the guys in the back row. Sitting in on the lectures was an effective way Topgun maintained the currency of instructors, as well as integration among the staff.

Each time I went to Hangar 1, I took off my red VF-24 nametag and put the gold Topgun nametag on my khaki uniform. The other instructors treated me like I was one of them, or about to be.

The only problem was my written orders were modified to delay my arrival, and phone calls between the CO of

VF-24 and the Navy personnel office added further delays. I was still assigned to VF-24 and new commanding officer Dan Shewell was playing hardball, keeping me and a few others on hand until our numerical replacements walked into VF-24's ready room in Hangar 4. VF-24 still relied on me to be the RIO Training Officer, so I continued to manage part of the training program, prepare comprehensive reports, and do all the other tasks in this job I had sought. It was ironic, now that I wanted to leave. Fortunately, Streak was the VF-24 operations officer, my immediate boss and the person responsible for squadron scheduling, so he had the schedules officer accommodate as many Topgun events as possible. I'm sure he remembered how dynamic his early weeks were as a Topgun instructor.

In late May Topgun evaluated their lecture schedule and came up with one that would be a good fit for their incoming RIO, me. It was a lecture in the Fleet Air Superiority Training (**FAST**) program. In addition to the five-week flying class I had attended, later made famous in the movie, Topgun applied their expertise to preparing F-14 and E-2 squadrons to defend carrier battle groups against a large-scale raid by Soviet bombers and jammers. This was a plausible threat during the Cold War, and defeating it was one of the primary design considerations for the F-14, its AWG-9 radar, and the AIM-54 Phoenix missile. Unlike the Topgun class that trained a small percentage of selected aviators, FAST was a one-week program that provided high-quality lectures to entire squadrons, plus challenging simulators to about half of their crews.

My lecture would be Maritime Air Threat, an overview of the threat posed to American aircraft carriers by Soviet bombers and anti ship cruise missiles. Maritime Air Threat was given by former F-14 pilot Steve "Legs" Schallhorn, a likable guy finishing his tour as a Topgun instructor and headed for a major career change, leaving for medical school to become a Navy Doctor.

Maritime Air Threat was next scheduled to be given on Monday, July 23, and Legs had to start medical training on the East Coast the week before, so it was up to me to take over the lecture and deliver it that day. Seven weeks may seem like plenty of time, but taking over a Topgun lecture, even for FAST, is quite an endeavor.

I knew Legs from when I went through the class, and I had seen Maritime Air Threat when VF-24 went through FAST. Soon I would be expected to give this lecture in front of dozens of Navy aviators. Some would be appreciative, some bored. Some would sincerely ask difficult questions, while a few would try to show off their specialized knowledge of a small point at my expense. It all came with the gold nametag.

As Legs and I sat at one of the long tables in an otherwise empty Classroom 2 at 7:15 AM on a Tuesday morning, I could hardly fathom these future audiences. We got to work immediately.

Legs first ran through all one hundred slides. The lecture started with a short recap of Soviet history and aircraft development, then moved to the main portion consisting of facts about the current bombers (the Bear, Badger, and Backfire) and the anti-ship cruise missiles they carried. The closing portion set the stage for the rest of the FAST program. In fact, Legs's lecture had references to other FAST lectures throughout, demonstrating close coordination within the program.

After the overview, Legs introduced me to how things worked "behind the curtain." He described how Topgun instructors got our detailed intelligence from highly classified publications that were not widely available, and supplemented them by talking to intelligence experts in Washington. He told me how professional artists with security clearances made our 35mm slides. He revealed how to prepare for an hour-and-a-half Topgun-quality lecture: You don't just memorize it, you have to know it.

Then Legs started to teach me the mechanics of giving a Topgun lecture. Instructors did not wear wristwatches during lectures, an acknowledgement that some guys in the audience would be distracted comparing their watch to the instructor's. Instructors always lectured in the khaki uniform, but in the "working" style with no ribbons, so the audience wouldn't be distracted wondering about the stories behind the awards. In my case this was not a problem because I wore only a single ribbon, the Sea Service Deployment Ribbon. Indicating nothing more than I had completed a deployment, it is the most basic award available to a fighter RIO. There were dozens of other guidelines.

I had heard these in the "Teaching and Learning" lecture during Topgun class a year and a half before, but now I had to apply them. Legs continued with practical aspects of lecture delivery: never put your hands in your pockets, stand beside the podium so you're not tempted to lean on it, always hold the pointer with two hands for precision, and many more.

These revealed the essence of the Navy Fighter Weapons School. Your medals or your cool watch did not matter, what was important was what you were teaching and whether or not you could convey the information to the class (and then go out and fly what you taught). The rules were clearly stated and firmly enforced, as were the high standards for flight discipline.

Legs's comments helped prepare me for the ultimate test, a "murder board" review by all other Topgun instructors that determined whether a speaker was cleared to go before a class. In it the instructors would ask hard questions to test my knowledge and dumb questions to see if I handled them politely. They would watch my delivery intently and check my facts. The murder board was the most difficult audience an instructor would face, and if you got a thumbs-up you were ready to go out on your own. If the instructor got a thumbs-down he would correct his problems, practice more, and try again.

After two hours with Legs it was time to return to VF-24. I walked down the stairs in Hangar 1 with the MiG-kill silhouettes and a familiar feeling of, "Other people have done this, and so can I."

On that day and during the weeks and months ahead I thought about the men who had started Topgun, tenacious and proud Navy pilots and RIOs with breathtaking combat experience over Vietnam. The first instructors were members of a world-leading Navy that was not doing so well in its air war over Vietnam, but who were determined to do better. And better they did, in dramatic fashion. I also thought of those who faithfully passed the torch before I put on a gold nametag. They agreed that even flying legends must write neatly on the board and follow the other presentation rules. They supported the stressful murder board process. The men (and later, the women) who passed the torch enforced these and the other demanding standards that helped

Topgun achieve and retain the respect it had in the fighter community.

I drove back to VF-24 in time for an afternoon post-maintenance check flight. Because they required thorough system checks after an aircraft had undergone significant repairs, these check flights were only assigned to more experienced pilots and RIOs. They were usually incident-free but occasionally revealed a problem that was not quite fixed, at which time the crew might have to rely on their judgment and experience to get the jet home.

Among the hundreds of items to complete was a high-speed run, for which the checklist instructions to the pilot were: "Jam throttles—max afterburner." The crew was to check various high-speed functions such as automatic wing-sweep while accelerating. On that day we went Mach 1.7, more than 1,200 mph. In the thin, clear air at thirty-five feet, far above the ocean and away from clouds, there was little visceral sense of speed, only the rush of wind over the canopy frame (largely muffled by our helmets) provided a sensory cue to match the numbers on our instruments indicating we were covering a statute mile every three seconds. No drama, 1.7 times the speed of sound. It was great to still be flying Tomcats!

The next day VF-24 deployed to the small Navy airfield at El Centro, California, for a weeklong air-to-air gunnery detachment. Going to El Centro, one hundred miles east of Miramar, allowed us to focus on this specific phase of training with minimal distractions. The training cycle for new aircrews was repeating again.

For me this detachment was different. I had eight flights in six days, but I had one eye on my upcoming challenge, and took a set of classified notes for the Maritime Air Threat lecture so I could work on memorizing the information associated with one hundred slides. I figured I needed to memorize the facts first, and then work on my delivery. The VF-24 Intelligence Officer locked my notes in El Centro's classified storage safe, and I studied when I could. Even with the brisk pace of flying and the studying in between, this would be the least stressful week of my summer.

Soon I had only a month until my murder board. I worked at VF-24 in the morning and at Topgun in the afternoon and evening. The combination of flights, lecture prep, ground job, squadron meetings, and social events continued to give me a full schedule. I had thirty-five F-14 flights at VF-24 in June and July, so I was not short-changing my old squadron to accommodate my future.

And on cool San Diego nights, as I walked to my Trans Am sitting alone in the Topgun parking lot, I went over in my mind the opening lines of my lecture, a phrase that I had trouble remembering, or a set of facts that had to be delivered carefully to make a point. I worked on the day's roughest spot until it became smooth. Another one would surely replace it.

Suddenly it was early July, only weeks to go until my murder board, and I felt the pressure. My workdays ran from about 7:00 AM to 9:00 PM or later, plus half days on weekends. I ate a lot of triangle sandwiches for dinner, delicious meals sold in triangular plastic packages in the snack trailer near Hangar 1.

I had gathered the hundreds of facts within Maritime Air Threat, searched for relevant new information to add interest for those who had seen the lecture before, and included references and teaching points from other lectures. I wrote it all down in a script coordinated with each slide. I memorized all of the information and then worked on a compelling delivery, doing my best to keep an audience's attention for ninety minutes.

Exactly two weeks before the murder board I had my first pre murder board. We called them "pre-boards." Legs and two other instructors sat in Classroom 2 at 1:00 PM on a Friday afternoon while I delivered the lecture, the first time I gave the whole lecture in front of an audience. This group saw the result of my hours of study, research, repetition, and standing in front of an empty classroom late at night talking to chairs. Realizing I only had two weeks to go, they started talking about a fall back plan. Legs would be on the East Coast when the lecture was scheduled, so they discussed flying a two-seat F-5F over to bring him back to Miramar for one last appearance.

Hearing a backup plan being formulated did not give me comfort.

In that first pre-board I got through all of the slides but I had problems. My evaluators thought I treated the pre-board as a practice session, when they wanted me to treat it as a lecture to a class. I could fix that. They pointed out the times when I stumbled over transitions and forgot significant points. Those errors could also be fixed with more practice. But some of my other problems would require a significant effort and long hours because I needed to change my whole approach. I can summarize my faults by describing the actions I would have to take to fix them:

- Tell the audience what they need to know, not everything I know.

- Listen carefully when a question is asked.
- Know when to stop talking.

I needed to tighten up my entire delivery. To hear such criticism after a month of hard work was neither discouraging nor depressing. The instructors' comments were constructive and objective, and they were holding me to the standards they themselves met. Occasionally they mentioned a problem that another instructor had experienced and had overcome, to let me know I was not the first person to be in this situation.

They talked about flying Legs back, but they didn't give up on me.

The two weeks between my first pre board and my actual murder board were a blur of long days. But I received good criticism so my practice sessions were worthwhile. I got some final advice from Legs as he left Miramar for medical school, and then I had two more pre boards.

My real murder board started at 1:30 PM on a Friday afternoon, in Classroom 2. I had come a long way in the last two weeks, largely through the insightful comments of the instructors who sat in on my pre boards.

Before the murder board started I had written very carefully on the white board:

Maritime Air Threat

LT David "Bio" Baranek

The assembling audience included instructors who had been there since I was a student nearly two years before—Spartan, Secks, Harpo—and others who were almost legends to me because I first met them while I was in the audience. But there was another portion of the audience even more familiar to me: Boa (who I got to know during a one-day class on the

F-5), Flex (a RIO I knew from around the base who had been at Topgun only a few months longer than me), and Jaws, who made it to Topgun about six months before I arrived. Roughly eighteen instructors sat in for my murder board.

I started with the historical perspective and moved on to descriptions of the bombers, very conscious of following the delivery rules. Things went well, and after forty-five minutes it was time for a break. No major mistakes so far; the time was flying by. I was nervous. I had a head full of knowledge and had practiced so many times that I was confident I could at least get through the lecture, but I wasn't yet comfortable in front of an audience of experts like this one.

During the break a few instructors came up to give me encouragement, but most acted like normal students and left the room to get a snack, make a phone call, or just walk around.

We started the second half and again things were going smoothly as I described the impressive cruise missiles that Soviet bombers could launch against American carriers. One of the instructors sitting in the front row asked, "Bio, why does this slide showing the AS-4 missile look different from the slides for the bombers?"

"Oh, that's because Steve (one of our artists) is in the process of making new slides in this style and the bomber slides are still at the photo lab."

About half of the heads went down as my evaluators made a note. I didn't recognize any problem, and continued. They would tell me about it soon enough.

The rest of the lecture went fine. I finished the second half and we took another short break, then came back in for the critiques.

Every instructor had at least a half-page of observations, some had more. They went around the room while I stood at the podium and made notes. The first instructor went through all of his comments, and once in a while when he said something several others would cross a comment off their lists. For example, my slides had one or two typos and almost everyone noticed them, so a lot of guys after the first crossed these comments off their lists. No one wanted to repeat a previous comment.

My biggest blunder was my response to the question about the difference in slides. I answered as if I were talking to another Topgun instructor, when I should have responded as I would to a FAST class, acknowledging the difference without mentioning Steve the artist or the photo lab. Not fatal, but something to work harder on.

Most comments involved classified information about bomber tactics, cruise missile capabilities, or additional suggestions for integrating with other lectures. All were valuable improvements to the lecture.

And then Secks, the Training Officer, gave the verdict: I was good to give the lecture to the FAST class on Monday, but he wanted me to practice it again on Saturday and Sunday. I think he said, "Nice job," too.

They wouldn't have to bring Legs back to give "my" lecture.

We finished about 5:00 PM, which was quick for a murder board, especially a first lecture, and everyone went to the O-Club. It was a typical Friday afternoon crowd of a few hundred people. It seemed like most of Miramar's pilots and RIOs were there, 90 percent in bags. There were a few dozen women, but it was still early. I was a little dazed after almost four hours in the spotlight, but it was a normal Friday for everyone else and I didn't attract any special attention. I was still between squadrons and split my conversation between VF-24 and Topgun groups.

Several Topgun instructors commented that this might be the first time a Topgun lecture would be given by an instructor who had not checked in to the squadron yet, even though it was "only" a FAST lecture.

I spent most of Saturday and Sunday as I had for the past few weeks, at Hangar 1 practicing Maritime Air Threat. Now that I had met the essential requirement and was going for refinement, practice was more enjoyable and less stressful.

Monday morning I had a 6:30 AM brief at VF-24 for a 2v2 flight. That was a nice way to start the week. How far I had come from my first flights in Pensacola, which were so stressful they wiped me out for the rest of the day, to now when I hardly broke a sweat in an hour-long flight with three or four intercepts followed by ACM. After the debrief I changed into my khaki uniform (with gold nametag) to make the noon start for my first lecture.

I walked into the large auditorium used for classified lectures and gave Maritime Air Threat to pilots and NFOs from two F-14 squadrons and an E-2 squadron. The audience totaled about eighty. Although not a Topgun room it was a familiar auditorium, I saw some familiar faces in the audience.

The lecture went smoothly.

That was it, my first Topgun lecture, anti climactic in itself. I felt quite comfortable, even in front of the crowd. The weeks of hard effort and long hours, the extensive knowledge

I gained, and the teaching skills I developed would pay off for the next few years. I would eventually lecture to almost every fleet F-14 pilot and RIO and almost every fleet E-2 pilot and NFO. The up-front investment soon became insignificant compared to the payoff.

That first lecture wasn't perfect, but my critique sheets revealed no serious flaws. Critiques were a staple of every Topgun instructor for every lecture, and we reviewed each one conscientiously. The six other FAST instructors also looked at my critique sheets and saw their murder board efforts and their confidence in me rewarded.

With another hurdle cleared I put more emphasis on my VF-24 duties during the rest of the week. But I continued to spend some time with Topgun and the ongoing FAST class.

The weekend after I gave the lecture I attended my first Topgun instructors' reunion, held at a hotel in San Diego. Some present were true legends in the Navy fighter community, names and faces that I knew from the aviation interests of my youth, who welcomed me into their fraternity. My murder board and initial lecture behind me, having a beer with these legends and being part of a group whose reputation I respected made it a great evening for me. I didn't make a point of saying I had not yet officially joined the squadron.

Monday morning I was back at work at VF-24. I had yet another 2v2 on Tuesday, and Wednesday morning Drifty and I flew a low-level training route. I was scheduled to fly a 2v2 on Thursday but it was canceled.

And then without advance notice several new pilots and RIOs walked into VF-24, much like I had done thirty-nine months before, and I suddenly had Skipper Shewell's blessing to leave. Squadrons normally met pilots or RIOs at the end of their last flight with buckets of water or the base fire trucks, a bottle of champagne, and other festivities. But for me, plans changed so quickly that my last-flight celebration slipped away, as my last flight in VF-24 had been that low-level with Drifty. There would be other "last flights" in my future.

I checked in to Topgun the next day, Friday, August 3. This simplified my life, plus it allowed VF-24's next RIO Training Officer to finally take the job he had been waiting for. I spent my first week as a Topgun instructor on leave, catching up on a long list of personal things I had put off during the previous few months, and sleeping in. When I got off leave I had my first full workday at Topgun. I was the squadron duty officer.

On my second day I took my first F-5 flight. The squadron was between classes, several new instructors had reported over the summer, and some of the old guys had moved on to their next jobs, so we needed to do a lot of "instructor-under-training" (IUT) flights. My first hop was a 1v1. I flew with an experienced instructor in the two-seat F-5F against a new instructor pilot in a single-seat F-5E. Flight time was 0.8 hours and it was a good introduction to the jet.

The very next weekend I left for a trip to give FAST training to squadrons at NAS Oceana in Virginia Beach, Virginia. As a new guy I rode a commercial airliner over on Sunday, with two pilots and our intelligence officer, Russ Novak.

Every Navy squadron had at least one intelligence officer whose duties included keeping themselves and aircrews up-to-date on enemy capabilities, as well as more mundane tasks such as handling the squadron's classified material. After he was commissioned, Russ had completed a six-month intelligence officer course and other training, and then spent three years with VF-2, a fleet F-14 squadron like VF-24. VF-2, however, had specially configured Tomcats that could perform reconnaissance as well as the fighter mission (roughly half of the F-14 squadrons had the reconnaissance mission), and managing that program was one of Russ's primary concerns in the squadron, so he picked up the call sign Kodak.

How did he get to Topgun? The old-fashioned way—he earned it. Topgun's commanding officer after Ratchet was Boomer Wilson, who had been Kodak's CO in VF-2. Kodak had worked hard and done well, and when Boomer needed an Intel Officer he could count on, he selected Kodak. Kodak gave a FAST lecture and a Topgun class lecture so he definitely proved his worth and provided a great deal of additional support whenever he could. Although not a flier, he fit in well. We became pals and ended up making that Sunday flight to Virginia several times a year.

The four of us on the United Airlines flight would be joined by reinforcements making their way east from Miramar. Since there was no Topgun class we could take some fighters on the trip, so several instructors left on Friday and Saturday and took cross-country flights, eventually arriving at Oceana Sunday afternoon. They brought two A-4s, two F-5Es, and one F-5F, arriving in time to park their jets, change out of their flight suits, and get to the airport to meet our flight. They drove to the airport in a gray Navy van and picked up two rental cars to add flexibility for the week. Ten instructors left Norfolk International Airport headed for dinner at The Raven, a small restaurant and bar one block from the surf in Virginia Beach.

Every time I went to Oceana on a FAST trip, we had dinner at The Raven the Sunday night of our arrival. Several instructors had done their fleet tours in Oceana and had friends in the area who joined us for dinner, making it a bigger crowd.

Sunday turned out to be a long day, and at 8:00 AM Monday morning I was standing in front of an audience of about eighty F-12 and E-2 pilots and NFOs. I was tired and it was only the second time I gave the lecture, and it was my worst performance. Several critiques commented on a few misstatements and long pauses in my delivery, but most were surprisingly forgiving. My fellow instructors didn't make a big deal about it, but they didn't have to. We all read the critiques and I knew they saw the comments on my lecture. I learned a lesson about being ready and it stayed with me the rest of my tour.

With my lecture complete at 9:30 AM, my duties for the rest of the week in Oceana fell into two categories:

- I handled my share of the simulator sessions. Fleet pilots and RIOs sitting in a realistic F-14 cockpit defended their simulated carrier from attacks by dozens of simulated bombers that were attempting to reach cruise missile launch range. In addition to the sheer number of targets, radar jammers added to the challenge by introducing false targets or blanking out the Tomcat's radar. The fighter crew could overcome the jamming, but they had to work at it.
- I flew in the two-seat F-5F providing adversary support to Oceana squadrons.

That week I flew 2v2s on three mornings and spent every afternoon in the simulator. Through this intense exposure I got a sense of my job. I was new and had a lot to learn, and my fellow instructors led (or nudged) me forward each step.

Running the simulators came fairly easily for me. After just a few sessions observing, I took my turn supervising fleet pilots and RIOs as they faced the enemy in linoleum-tiled rooms in a cinderblock building in Virginia Beach. For thirty minutes they played their part in a doomsday scenario, while I provided necessary communications over the intercom, watched the computer-generated "God's-eye view" of the action, and constantly checked various read-outs to evaluate their performance. Then another Topgun instructor ran the next crew while I spent about twenty minutes in a small room debriefing my crew, reinforcing what they did right or explaining what they did wrong. I was not far removed from my "students." Just weeks before, I too had been charged with this mission. Now I tried to ensure they had a real understanding of my debrief points. I suspect all teachers seek this.

All of the RIOs who were FAST instructors took turns at the simulators, and it required knowledge of everything in the FAST course, such as bomber tactics and details of how the F-14's missiles operated in the jamming environment. I quickly felt comfortable with the complex scenarios and enjoyed my role. I had experienced instructors like Denk and Flex to lean on, which added to my confidence. (We had an identical simulator setup when we gave the FAST course to squadrons based at Miramar.)

We ran FAST and flew ACM in Oceana Monday through Friday and Saturday morning flew to Key West, Florida, for a two-week detachment focused on instructor training. I had fourteen ACM flights in nine days at Key West, all hard-core dogfights. Ten of them were 1v1s lasting less than one hour, which means we kept the engines at high power and burned our fuel quickly.

The focus was on the performance of the new instructor pilots, which made my life easier at the time but meant I missed some in-depth understanding that comes with preparation, stress, execution, debriefing, and coaching. The pilots' instructor-under-training (IUT) flying syllabus was similar to the murder board process that shaped Topgun lectures. (During my tour as an instructor, Topgun formalized an IUT flying syllabus for new RIOs, something I didn't get.)

No one treated me like a freshman, but I felt like one. At least I was on the varsity team, and in the months ahead I would come to feel like I really belonged there. Freshman, varsity, IUT—those were details. I was a Topgun instructor.

We got back from Key West and worked for three days before going to Tailhook. There I caught up with some old squadron mates from VF-24, including Cab, one of the RIOs who had been in VF-24 less than a year. After a few minutes of conversation, Cab said, "Bio, how did you get to be so good?"

I immediately recalled when I had asked Window the same question two years earlier. I was modest, telling Cab I had been doing this a few years more than he had, and had gotten some great training. As it turned out, Cab earned a great reputation and later became a Topgun instructor, too. Maybe "How did you get to be so good?" were the magic words.

TEN

Our Toughest Fights

It's my turn. "I'm Dave Baranek, call sign Bio. I made two deployments with VF-24 and have 1,200 Tomcat hours." That was all I could say at this point. Left unsaid: I'm new here, so I won't be giving any lectures to your class. But I know what a Tomcat can do, so I will be flying against you, evaluating you, and debriefing you. I may be new, but I came to play.

"I'm Mike Galpin, call sign Flex. I made two deployments with the world famous Bounty Hunters of Fighter Squadron Two, and have 1,200 F-14 hours. . . ."

"My name is Ricky Hammonds, call sign Organ. I have 1,200 F-14 hours. . . ."

We continued through the roster as each instructor introduced himself and described his role.

It was the day after we got back from Tailhook. A group of us had returned from Vegas Sunday morning and went to the San Diego Chargers NFL game Sunday afternoon with our girlfriends and wives. And at 7:00 AM Monday another Topgun class started.

So I was standing for the first time in the back of Classroom 1 with all the other instructors as Skipper "Joe Dog" Daughtry went through the intro routine, including the jokes Topgun skippers passed down to each other. The class only heard the intro speech once and enjoyed it, as I did when I went through. Those few who came back as instructors heard it five or six times a year. It was a small price to pay. The instructors were an easy audience in public, but did not give the Skipper any slack when we talked about professional performance. He was the Skipper with the rank of commander, but he wore the gold nametag.

In my first few weeks on the staff I learned that lieutenants ran Topgun.

In a normal Navy squadron the CO and XO, both commanders, ran things aided by a handful of lieutenant commanders. But the lieutenants steered Topgun to a large degree, along with our Marine Corps and Air Force counterparts, who were captains. Topgun usually had twelve to fourteen lieutenants assigned, plus four lieutenant commanders and a commander. The senior officers gave us top cover from higher-ups, who had probably forgotten what it was like when they were lieutenants and could handle almost anything that came up.

During this class I sat at the back table for many lectures, filling in knowledge gaps and refreshing certain important lectures. The happy haze of self-congratulation and sense of accomplishment—"I'm wearing a Topgun nametag"—did not last long as I watched the more experienced instructors lecturing, and recalled the effort I put into the relatively simple Maritime Air Threat lecture. The lectures seemed like a lot of material now that I was responsible for knowing them, and I tried to absorb as much as I could.

I didn't fly much in the first week of a class, as all flights were 1v1 and Topgun wanted to use its most maneuverable aircraft to provide the greatest challenge for students. Among the three types available (A-4, F-5E, and F-5F) the two-seat F-5F was the least maneuverable, being a little larger and heavier than the others. But the F-5F was still adequate for 1v1s, so we RIOs bagged some hops in Week One.

We rarely used the names given to these aircraft, usually referring to them by their designations. The F-5E and F-5F carried the official name of "Tiger II" and the A-4's official name was "Skyhawk," widely used during its years of service with the Navy. When I was at Topgun it was usually called just the A-4, or even the "Dog." I never asked about the origin of that name, reasoning it was based on the fact that the jets were fairly old but likable. Just a guess. Sometimes we'd have instructor events where the A-4s would fight the F-5s, and the whiteboard always said "Dogs vs Tigers."

On Thursday morning the second week of class I had a 9:30 AM brief for a day of 2v2 flights on the TACTS Range near Yuma. I sat in on the lecture that started at 7:30 AM in Classroom 1, after which we went next door to Classroom 2 for the flight brief. Like all instructors except those giving a lecture, I wore my flight suit all day.

Jambo briefed this flight. Also known as Lieutenant Jim Ray, Jambo had been an F-14 pilot in the VF-213 Black Lions before becoming a Topgun instructor. This was a typical class brief (similar to when I had been a student) and illustrated why precision and reliability were important at Topgun. He was briefing half of the class fighters—two sections, four jets, eight students—and he had to give them the information they would need for the entire day: times on the TACTS Range, simulated missions as American fighters in combat, training objectives as Topgun students, and more. Each of the main topics involved additional details such as a short overview of tactics the fighters should use, their simulated weapons loadout, and the type of bogeys that intelligence projected they would encounter. That day it was the MiG-21 with advanced heat-seeking missiles.

In addition to the tactical material he covered, Jambo assigned radio frequencies, told the students where to meet for debrief at Yuma, and reminded them not to violate the U.S.–Mexico border. Jambo was the mission commander, so if there was a mishap his briefing would be reviewed to ensure he provided adequate and correct information, even that he established the appropriate mindset for the event. That was just another small burden the mission commander always carried.

He then covered essentials designed to improve flight safety. He picked one student at random to go to the white-board and draw a diagram depicting effectiveness ranges for a missile, called the weapon's envelope. The students memorized an envelope for each weapon they carried and for threat weapons, a total of about eight detailed diagrams. Each day they were quizzed on one of them. Most students drew the envelope correctly, but the few that needed help were gently chastised.

Jambo next reviewed the training rules that added a margin of safety to all practice dogfights. For example:

- Aircraft are not allowed to fly within five hundred feet of each other during the fight. This is known as the five hundred-foot bubble.
- No aircraft is allowed to simulate a gun shot when approaching another aircraft head-on. (The resulting flight path angles would present a danger of collision.)
- Maneuvering was limited below ten thousand feet above the ground. This is the soft deck.
- No maneuvering at all below five thousand feet above the ground, the hard deck.

We had sixteen restrictions on dogfighting that wouldn't apply in combat, but reduced accidents in training. The parameters could all be determined from another aircraft in the fight, and breaking a training rule was cause for an immediate knock-it-off call that ended the engagement. If the violation were serious, the instructor might end the flight and order the fighters to return to base immediately. This was rare, but it happened. Since we were required to review the rules before every dogfight flight, many squadrons (including Topgun) had a summarized version printed on their kneeboard cards.

Finally, Jambo's brief ended like all ACM briefs, with one person from each type of aircraft in the flight reciting the procedures to follow if an aircraft got into a spin.

As with the weapon envelope, he selected a student to recite the procedures for the F-14 and we heard, "Stick forward, neutral lateral, harness locked. Rudder opposite turn needle/yaw. If no recovery. . . ." The F-14's eight steps and additional comments took about twenty-five seconds to recite, and were followed by another six steps for getting out of an inverted spin. It was rare that a student could not recite the procedures verbatim; if that happened he was ridiculed by all since this was basic knowledge for every military flier. This shortcoming would be passed to other instructors so he could be tested in the next day's brief.

Jambo then picked an instructor to recite the A-4 procedures and another instructor for F-5 procedures, which I still remember: "Neutralize controls, power back, lock harness. Stick—full forward. Aileron—full into direction of spin. Rudder—full opposite spin. Flaps—set to maneuver." And then the procedures for an inverted spin: "Flaps—up; visually check up. Stick—aft as required. Ailerons and rudder—neutral."

The chosen person always recited his procedures as quickly as possible, and it was interesting to watch their hands move as they mimicked operating the required controls.

With spin procedures completed, Jambo dismissed the brief.

The other half of the class was to fly in the training areas over the Pacific that day, and they were being briefed in Classroom 1, a mirror to our activity in Classroom 2. But since he followed the class lecture in Classroom 1, that briefer had to rush into the room the moment the lecture ended and had only a few minutes to get his whiteboard set up. Sharing rooms like that showed how Topgun operated on a shoestring, with barely adequate facilities. But the government-issue wood paneling and window air conditioners made the rooms more comfortable than those of most Navy squadrons, so we thought we were doing OK.

After the mass brief, instructors split up and headed for the training office, the ops office, or some other place where we could discuss our plans away from the students. Topgun presented students with a variety of enemy tactics that had been identified by U.S. intelligence agencies, and we tracked the scenarios that each student saw. We would show them bogeys that approached from different parts of the range, followed each other by six to eight miles, or flew a high-low altitude split. The bogey lead spelled it all out for his bogeys, the other instructors. Each of the bogey presentations should elicit a different game plan by the fighters and required different skills of the pilots and RIOs. I think students would agree Topgun kept the class fighters challenged for all five weeks.

With one and a half months of experience and thirty flights, I was comfortable with the basics of the F-5, and I was about to see how a day with the class went. I was flying with Mike Blue, call sign Vida (after the Oakland Athletics' famous pitcher of the 1970s, Vida Blue). Vida the fighter pilot was an intense and colorful East Coast Tomcat pilot who had been at Topgun a year longer than me. He would keep us out of trouble while I got up to speed, and challenge the fighters to boot.

After the bogey brief the instructors went to the locker room to get into our gear. We put on our G suits and survival vests, then grabbed our helmets and helmet bags. We talked a little about cars, movies, and ground jobs but most of the chatter was about relevant topics: the students, rendez-vous points, or whether the "Gila Monster" burrito was the best item on the lunch menu at the Yuma flight line café. (Unanimous—Yes.)

There were similarities and differences in suiting up to fly the F-5 compared to the F-14. Our flight suits, G suits, and boots were the same, but at Topgun we had lighter helmets. The F-5 program was managed by the Air Force so the survival equipment vest was lighter, on the theory that if you ejected from an F-5 there was a good chance of your being over land and recovered quickly instead of over water as in a Navy aircraft. A major difference was that in the F-14 we strapped in to a seat that had an integrated parachute, but in the F-5 we carried our 'chutes out with us and then attached them to the seat. Packed tightly in nylon pouches with straps and lanyards, they weighed about thirty pounds and looked like large backpacks. Extra weight, but we all thought they were cool. The walk from the hangar to the jets wasn't that long.

Once we got to the jet, the feeling was very different from manning-up a Tomcat. Vida and I preflighted our F-5 in much less time than we had spent preflighting the F-14s we flew in the fleet. The F-5 is small, its cockpit is not as high off the ground as the F-14's, and after engine start we left our canopies open since the F-5 does not have air-conditioning when it's on the ground (the Tomcat did). Systems checks went much faster than in a Tomcat, and the F-5's simplicity made it unlikely that there would be a problem after start.

All of these factors allowed us to walk to the jet and start up only a few minutes before takeoff, compared to thirty minutes or more that was typical of an F-14 start.

Of course, there were downsides to this simplicity, one of the biggest being that we had no radar, not even short-range radar like most fighters since the Korean War. Air forces that used the F-5 as a combat aircraft equipped them with radars, but when the Navy procured these aircraft they removed the radars for simplicity and economy, so we relied on our ground controller when we operated over the TACTS Range. When operating without a controller, such as over the ocean, we listened to the fighter radio frequency and used their calls to find them. They knew we were listening, and it was important to our evaluation of their performance.

Since we were a two-seater, Jambo assigned Vida and me as bogey lead for this flight. Jambo took the lead for the other section of bogeys going to TACTS, an F-5E and an A-4 to challenge Topgun 3 and 4.

Our wingman was Hollywood, flying an F-5E. He manned-up and started one jet away from us on the Topgun line. When Hollywood was ready to taxi he gave us a thumbs-up. Watching helmet movements we could essentially make eye contact even with our visors down. As soon as his thumb came up I was on the radio, "Miramar Ground, Topgun Forty-seven. Two F-5s, taxi with Charlie." The word Charlie indicated I had listened to the airfield information broadcast, the third update of this day denoted by the letter C.

Ground control replied, "Topgun Forty-seven, taxi twenty-four right."

Next I switched the radio to Topgun Base and told the duty officer we were leaving the Topgun flight line: "Base, Forty-seven and Forty-five leaving the line."

Base: "Have a good one."

Headed for the hold short area, Vida and I kept track of the class Tomcats as they started and taxied. Besides lacking radar, another indicator of the simplicity of these jets was they only had one radio. After years of flying in Tomcats with two radios it took a little getting used to, but at least the radio was in the backseat, since I didn't have a radar.

As Topgun One and Two called Miramar Ground for taxi, I called the tower for takeoff for my flight. We bogeys had to fly about forty miles farther to our station at the eastern side of the range, so launching a few minutes ahead of the fighters made the timing all work out.

"Topgun Forty-seven flight, cleared for takeoff twenty-four right. Contact San Diego Departure 269.1."

"Topgun Forty-seven flight cleared on the right, switching."

Hollywood, Vida, and I lowered our canopies at the same time. I rechecked that my ejection seat was armed and my caution lights were out. Vida and I both looked over our left shoulder and saw Hollywood raise his head after completing his checks. He gave our jet a quick look and then gave us a thumbs-up.

We were cleared to take off so Vida pressed the brake pedals, advanced the throttles, and nodded his head forward. Thrust of 6,500 pounds strained against the brakes. If we were using afterburner our F-5 would produce 9,300 pounds of thrust, but military power was adequate and would save a little fuel that we could expend on education for Topgun One and Two. An F-14 by comparison produced 35,000 pounds of thrust in afterburner.

Vida raised his head, he and Hollywood released their brakes, and our small fighters rolled down twenty-four-right. A few seconds later we were airborne, the pilots tightened the formation, raised the landing gear, raised the flaps, and turned right.

Since we were headed to Yuma, once we climbed a few hundred feet above the ground we made a smooth right turn from the runway heading of 240 degrees all the way to our departure heading of 360 degrees, due north. I called departure control: "Departure, Topgun Forty-seven flight airborne."

"Topgun Forty-seven, Departure. Radar contact, cleared to one-six thousand."

I repeated the altitude as required, "Topgun Forty-seven, one-six thousand." It was mid-morning so air traffic was relatively light and we got clearance to climb to sixteen thousand feet, allowing us to bypass the series of altitude changes specified for this departure route. Between navigation and other RIO duties I looked outside. I always liked to observe this part of San Diego, where rock outcroppings and giant boulders deflected roads and neighborhoods, while the suburbs reached north and east into the high desert. We navigated along the standard departure route, but after we climbed a few thousand feet the departure controller cleared us direct to our next waypoint, further simplifying our lives for the next few minutes.

The flying to come would include hard-as-possible maneuvering, so I wiggled in my seat to get comfortable and tighten my straps. Early in my Topgun days I noticed that the F-5 moved when I wiggled in my seat. The whole jet moved. The sixty-thousand-pound F-14 didn't even notice my presence, but in the F-5 I could watch the wingtips move as I settled in. This was a "personal size" fighter.

On one wingtip we carried a simulator for a Sidewinder missile. The simulator consisted of a heat-tracking seeker head like a regular missile but mounted to an empty missile-sized tube that fit the missile rail. The Navy and Air Force bought thousands of simulators in addition to the actual missiles, allowing pilots to gain realistic experience and immediate feedback as to whether the missile was tracking a target. The AA-2 Atoll used by most MiGs was similar enough to the Sidewinder that the bogeys carried the same simulator as the fighters.

On our other wingtip we carried the TACTS pod that would tie us in to the system. By design it was the same size as a Sidewinder missile so any aircraft able to carry a Side-winder (a good portion of the U.S. inventory) could carry a TACTS pod. The pods carried by every aircraft were iden-tical, but the TACTS technicians identified aircraft type for a realistic display.

On the departure and flight over, air traffic control-lers advised me to change frequencies as we passed into a new controller's area, and since we were in close formation I used hand signals to tell Hollywood the new frequency. After ensuring he was looking at me, I tapped the side of my helmet to indicate "radio," then used standard finger signals to indicate the new frequency. I indicated numerals 1 through 5 with fingers held vertically, and turned my hand ninety degrees for numerals 6 through 9. Showing a "6," for example, looked like I was pointing at something. Zero was a closed fist. This ingenious method allowed fliers to signal any number using one hand, important for pilots who had to keep a hand on the stick. Aviators had passed along frequen-cies this way since their earliest training.

We flew to Yuma at twenty-three thousand feet. To reduce the workload on our wingman Vida gave him a signal to fly a loose formation. Since he could not see hand signals when he was farther away, Hollywood simply said

"Two" after each of my transmissions to let me know he was with us on the radio.

For the flight so far I had stayed out of the way of the full-size control stick in the backseat, but then Vida said, "OK, Bio, you've got it." He was going to let me fly the jet during this relatively tame portion of the flight. Should there be a problem, he was shadowing the stick in the front cockpit and would immediately have control.

I grasped the control stick with my right hand, my left instinctively resting on the dual throttles on the left console. Our jet started a slow descent, so I pulled the nose up a little and we climbed through our assigned altitude. I pushed forward and we descended. I made us porpoise a few times, climbing and diving a hundred feet or so and trying hard not to stray any farther from our assigned altitude, which would lead to an inquiry from our air traffic controller.

Vida said, "Easy with it!" I had a little experience already so I was working the trim control, a "fine-tuning" thumb-operated button on the top of the stick, to get back to our altitude and configure the jet so it would stay there.

New to the piloting side of things, it took all of my concentration to keep us on assigned heading and altitude. But each flight I would get a better sense of control forces, and pilots would give me more tips. Flying the jet myself would help me in lecturing the class, briefing, and debriefing. Later I would fly with new pilots on their instructor-under-training flights, and personal experience helped me to be more effective.

But I only had the stick during non-demanding segments of the flight. It was a new thrill, and the fact that pilots were amused by my stumbling progress didn't bother me. When we got close to Yuma, I told Vida he had to get back to work because I just wasn't able to fly the jet and make my radio calls. With practice I would get better.

With Vida back on the stick and throttles, I checked us in to Yuma range control. We quickly switched to the TACTS bogey control frequency. Hollywood said, "Two's up," and we checked the signals from our pods to the control trailer.

Navigating visually using terrain features visible from twenty-three thousand feet, Vida took our formation to the starting point for the first run, well north of the "normal" bogey station so we could approach the fighters from a different bearing. And since we were already at a cruising altitude for the flight over, we climbed above thirty thousand feet to make the students look a little higher. Variations like this were good training. Our starting location and altitude were not a big problem for F-14 RIOs using their systems properly; it forced them to think a little more than if they faced bogeys on the most common set up on the TACTS Range, bearing 115 and flying at twenty-three thousand feet.

As always when we flew on the TACTS Range, we had the benefit of a bogey controller, a Topgun instructor sitting in the TACTS trailer at Miramar. He had omniscience regarding events on the range, but to provide a realistic simulation he provided less-detailed information at the start of a run, commensurate with the capabilities of an air defense search radar. Later in the intercept he might give us more detailed calls, depending on the radar capability of the bogeys we simulated.

Vida established us in a steady left-hand turn at three hundred knots. Hollywood was in loose formation on our right side, about a mile away and slightly behind us. It was a little after 11:00 AM on a beautiful September day.

The bogey controller interrupted our serenity with, "Fighters are checking in now." He was sitting at a console next to the fighter controller and could hear fighter communications over loudspeakers in the room. Vida steadied up heading east, flying away from the fighters to get a little more distance before the run started.

Our controller then said, "Recorders on, fight's on, fight's on." Everything changed.

Vida called, "In place left," advanced the throttles to military power and started a hard turn to head toward the fighters. I punched my micro-cassette recorder on. Hollywood performed an in-place turn and ended up on our left side, still slightly behind us.

"Bogeys steady 270. Fighters bearing 280 at thirty-three miles." This was our controller setting us up so the fighters were 10 degrees right of our nose, but at thirty-three miles we couldn't see them and their bearing would change a lot in the next few minutes. Our controller's calls were similar to what we figured an enemy controller would provide to aircraft trying to intercept American fighters. Except he didn't have an accent.

The two student-manned Tomcats executed a variety of turns based on their controller's calls and their own radar picture, while we flew due west as if we were flying to defend our airspace, unaware of the Americans' actual location. Then, at about twenty-two miles, we made a hard right turn and put them on our nose, under direction from our "enemy controller." Since this was a 2v2, our goal was to work on fighter technique in a multi-aircraft intercept and then have them maneuver in a multi-aircraft engagement. So we stayed together in a combat formation, wider than you would see at an airshow, but close enough to help each other deal with the Tomcats.

By now we were doing more than 400 knots and the fighters were at about 450, so every four seconds we were a mile closer. I was used to the relentless countdown of mileage, but contemplating the fact that we were closing a mile every four seconds always amazed me.

We were in a gradual dive and the fighters were climbing, but they were still below us. Looking down over the rough terrain desert we could see the F-14s as specks moving against the background when they were about eight miles ahead of us, typical for this altitude and environment. If we had been level or below them, we would have seen them sooner.

Seconds after we saw them we heard the "beeps" of missile shots as the Tomcat pilots positively identified us as F-5s and launched Sparrow missiles. Based on the scenario and learning objectives for this flight, we didn't launch missiles during the intercept.

Seconds after the beeps, our controller said, "Vida, you're dead," based on TACTS system indications. We expected that would happen. On this first engagement we planned to give the fighters credit for one of their shots before the merge, even though TACTS evaluated both missiles as kill shots. The system did not consider the various component failures that could result in a "miss," but only whether the missile was launched in parameters. Navy aircrews knew that missiles of the day didn't have 100 percent success and trained for this reality.

Vida and I performed a quick wingover roll to acknowledge we were dead and climbed overhead to watch Hollywood engage the F-14s in a 2v1. Both bogey aircraft switched to the fighter freq for this engagement so we could call shots on them and hear any shots they took, as well as for safety.

It turned out to be a good fight—for Topgun. The fighters did what a lot of fighters did, flew roughly the same attack when faced with a single bogey. Easy debrief point. One fighter should have kept pressure on the F-5 while the other got separation. The engaged fighter might kill the enemy aircraft quickly, but even if he didn't, the enemy would have to remain in a small piece of the sky defending himself. The second Tomcat should have taken eight to ten seconds to get away from the turning fight and then made a max-performance return to launch either a Sparrow or Sidewinder missile.

But on that morning it took Topgun one and two longer than it should have taken to kill Topgun Forty-five. While Vida and I watched from about twenty-eight thousand feet, almost two miles above the fight, Hollywood worked out with the Tomcats. In and out of afterburner (mostly in), set the flaps to maneuver, 3g, 5g, 6.5g, -2g, flaps up. One Tomcat over his right shoulder, the other one ahead and to the left, check fuel—no problem, step on the left rudder to increase left roll rate, steady up and pull back on the stick, "Snapshot, F-14 nose low, continue."

The fight continued.

"Fox Two, belly shot, F-5 left turn!" A missile shot from Topgun Two, finally.

"F-5's dead, knock it off." This was Hollywood.

"Topgun One knock it off, state 10.3"

"Topgun Two knock it off, 10.0."

The bogeys switched back to the bogey control frequency and Vida said, "Visual, left eight high, I've got 4.2."

Hollywood looked high on his left side and said, "Visual, 3.6," and flew to get into formation. There were only two jets on this frequency so we dispensed with call signs. It was cool to be on the inside of something I had wanted for so long.

Our small F-5s didn't burn gas like the big fighters, and Yuma was only thirty miles from where the final fight would end. An F-14 with four thousand pounds would be thinking about heading home in order to land with some safety reserves, but we planned to get another thirty-five-mile intercept and engagement, plus a short setup.

On the next two runs we gave our students real 2v2 engagements at the end of their intercepts, so I got my share of high g's and hard maneuvering. Plus, from "fight's on" to "knock it off" I captured as much information as possible about the action so I could contribute to the debrief. In time I would be the mission commander, briefing the event, leading it airborne, and then running the debrief.

I continued to use a combination of symbols, numbers, and abbreviations to record the action, as I had done in Tomcats, and as Topgun taught in the Teaching and Learning lecture. The top of my card recorded the intercept:

*160 / 80—The sun was on a bearing of 160 degrees and 80 degrees elevation, something we always recorded since it might affect keeping sight during a fight

BH 270, 300↑, 31K↓—Bogey heading 270 degrees, speed 300 knots increasing, altitude 31,000 feet but descending.

280 / 33—Bearing 280 degrees, range 33 nautical miles.

283 / 27—Bearing 283 degrees, range 27 nautical miles.

283 / 22 RT—At 22 miles separation, we made a right turn to come nose-on to the fighters. They were still bearing 283 degrees from us.

Throughout the intercept, I noted significant events such as turns, deceptive tactics, or missile launches by either side. Once we gained sight of the fighters, I switched to arrow diagrams, which we sometimes called spaghetti. (Furball, spaghetti—same idea.) The most effective way to use diagrams was to draw the fight in segments, because continuous lines showing several aircraft would quickly become confusing. Sometimes I just drew snapshots of everyone's relative position, to at least capture "markers" for my recollection, since a dogfight might last two minutes or more, with constant three-dimensional maneuvering and many significant moments such as missile shots.

At knock-it-off for the third engagement, Hollywood joined up and we headed for Yuma. One thing I noticed about all Topgun instructors was how quickly we got joined up and ready for the next stage of the flight. It was a quick trip from the middle of the R-2301 range to the airfield at Yuma. The students were a few miles behind us.

We grabbed lunch and headed for the trailers while a crew of Topgun enlisted people refueled the jets and completed the turnaround inspection to prepare them for the next event.

Vida led the debrief. He used the whiteboards, the 1:72-scale models on sticks, and the big-screen TACTS replay to reconstruct every intercept and engagement in detail. He highlighted points from lectures. Referring to the Tomcats performing similar turns, he said, "Just after the merge of that first engagement you maneuvered in-phase. Remember what we put out in the 'Combat Section Tactics' lecture about getting out of phase."

He had dozens more observations, and praised the students when appropriate. "When Topgun One got separation and came back in for the AIM-7 shot, he did a nice job following Jaws's recommendations from the 'Radar Missiles' lecture."

We wrapped up the debrief with Goods and Others, the list of positive and negative performance items that ended every Topgun debrief.

Two hours after landing at Yuma we were on the range again. Taking off and landing at Yuma, we got three full-on 2v2 intercepts and engagements on this flight. But with extensive use of afterburners our flight time was only 0.8 hours. I guess our F-5s could burn gas like the big fighters after all. We landed at Yuma again to debrief. With no more range time available, we made the thirty-minute flight back to Miramar in mid-afternoon.

During my first class as an instructor I flew twenty-nine hops. The average flight length was 0.8 hours, due primarily to a lot of dogfighting—high-g, max-burner, multi-aircraft aerial wrestling matches. At the time I rarely thought about how far I had come in five years, from wobbly first flights in the tubby T-2 to three Topgun class flights a day in the sleek F-5. Between responsibilities to the class, instructor banter, inhaling lunch, and taking the occasional photo, I didn't have much time for philosophizing.

ELEVEN

Preparing for Combat

Topgun was a complex machine with many moving parts, the most significant of which was the five-week class. The class had to be coordinated with the eight squadrons that sent aviators, because they had to schedule the crews as well as their aircraft and a maintenance team, especially squadrons from bases other than Miramar. The other large training program, Fleet Air Superiority Training, required scheduling all the officers from three squadrons for a full week, and required the most capable simulators at Miramar or Oceana. Other moving parts included the murder board schedule, instructor training, aircraft maintenance requirements, and more. Coordinating all of these parts required that we hold meetings of all staff officers, known as "staffexes" (staff exercises).

When we finally had a staffex during Week Two of the Topgun class in September, it had been a while, and a lot of business had piled up. Oceana, Key West, Tailhook, and the start of class had kept the schedule full. Staffexes got the entire staff together to address long-range issues and the administrative and discretionary items that oiled the gears of the Navy Fighter Weapons School machine. For example, Kodak was making arrangements for an intelligence update trip to Washington and needed to know who required face-to-face meetings with CIA experts. Spartan was planning a day of lectures to Marine Corps fighter squadrons at their air station in El Toro, seventy miles north of Miramar, and needed to get instructor commitments to lecture. Tex needed to update the "Wish List."

The Wish List. This was new to me, so I listened intently for a few minutes.

An unwritten rule said Topgun instructors had to be graduates of the five-week class. So in a closed meeting at the end of each class, the instructors evaluated the students and selected those they would like to see return and become instructors. Their names were placed on the Wish List.

Former instructors in many Navy and Marine Corps fighter squadrons kept tabs on the prospects. Some on the list had no interest in returning as instructors, and for others the timing just would not work. The whole thing was coordinated with the Navy Bureau of Personnel. It was a coarse system but it worked.

When I learned this process I felt I was really in the club. Several events suddenly fell into place. The handshakes at my own graduation when instructors said, "If you ever think about coming back, let us know." Streak's advice at Okie's Thanksgiving party to visit Topgun. How my preference card and the letter from Skipper Bertsch seemed to make things happen. I had been on the Wish List, and all they needed was for me to indicate my interest.

Of course, I was in a room full of guys who had been on the list, and at the end of every class new names were added, while some old names were removed. It was fascinating to see the process work and think how it affected my life, but it was just another item on the agenda for that staffex. We updated the list and moved on. (The method of choosing Topgun instructors eventually changed, so the Wish List no longer exists.)

When the agenda items were complete, Tex asked for items from the floor. Several instructors said the squadron duty officer needed to keep better track of class fighters as they checked in on the Topgun Base frequency. One instructor complained about the combination locks used on the gates to the flight line. Other instructors raised items that were mundane but affected how we operated every day. I was in the dangerous stage of being new but having been around long enough to feel comfortable, and I made a suggestion regarding the class, something so trivial I can't remember it.

My comment seemed to catch Tex off guard. He looked at me and said, "OK Bio, that's a good idea. Check on it and get back to me by next week." He added, "Sunshine, make sure you get that on the list, 'action for Bio.'"

This was new, I was assigned to follow-up on what I suggested.

Guys in VF-24 had a lot of *ideas*, and many of them went no further than, "Yeah, somebody should check on that." But no one did. Here, however, each of us was both empowered and accountable, which turned out to be a good combination. I took care of my action item and took a moment to think before making suggestions at future staffexes.

With the squadron back at Miramar we returned to a normal schedule of having a staffex about every two weeks.

In October several of us made the trip to Washington arranged by Kodak and talked to intelligence specialists about highly classified information. Although we could not reveal most of the details to our lecture audiences, the discussions helped us add perspective and emphasize certain facts in our lectures and training.

In November I drove to Marine Corps Air Station El Toro, one hour up the highway from Miramar, to give Maritime Air Threat to a crowd of Hornet pilots who would soon be deployed on a carrier, the trip arranged by Spartan. Later in November we ran a weeklong Fleet Air Superiority Training course for three Miramar squadrons. The FAST team was small and I came up to speed quickly. I felt comfortable in front of the FAST audience giving my lecture, and running the simulators was even better. Radar jammers were designed to obscure and confuse fighter radars, and techniques for beating them were mysterious to most fighter guys, but I felt confident when I taught them, having studied the manuals and watched runs from the console outside the simulator. I developed my own baseline procedures to guide students and wondered how we would do if a U.S. carrier were attacked in the real world. If things didn't go well, would people look at the Topgun FAST syllabus for inadequacies? Would they find that I had done my best?

My seat at the simulator control console was a great perch. I watched enemy tactics unfold on the overview display and saw how fighter crews performed in a critical thirty minutes defending their ship, then I debriefed them. Six to eight times a year FAST simulators took up half of my days for a week and provided an immediate sense of accomplishment.

I identified some essentials that I could teach consistently. For example, I told the pilot and RIO to actually write down the initial compass direction bearing to a jammer so they could accurately track how it changed during the first two minutes. Most guys tried to simply remember it, but did not remember well. I tried to build on things the students knew and presented my essentials to all the pilots and RIOs I trained. This helped me maintain enthusiasm for running FAST simulators for the next two and a half years. In addition, I learned in great detail about the complex capabilities of the Phoenix missile against radar jamming targets, as well as the other missiles and the F-14 radar. A good teaching technique is fine, but there is no substitute for knowing more than the students know.

After two months as a Topgun instructor, it was time to step up to the next level of responsibility. In mid-October the Training department evaluated the lecture plan in consideration of instructors who were leaving and determined that I should give "F-14 Combat Intercepts."

This was a tactics lecture in the five-week Topgun class. This was the big-time.

Some lectures presented information that was essential to Topgun, but wasn't "tactical." This group included Teaching and Learning, Briefing and Debriefing, and Course Rules (which explained Miramar flying procedures to students). The instructors adhered to Topgun's high presentation standards, but generally presented unassailable facts.

Tactics lectures described how Topgun thought Navy fighters should operate in actual combat. They included Combat Section Tactics (how two fighters operate together in combat), Division Tactics, lectures on how to employ each missile, and others. They were the reference material for flight briefs and debriefs, and had to be integrated with each other. In addition, a tactics lecture could easily become derailed by a student's question if the instructor wasn't prepared.

Every instructor gave at least one tactics lecture. Most gave one tactics lecture and one of the informative lectures, and a few gave two tactics lectures. FAST lectures were blended into this scheme, too. My Maritime Air Threat was an informational lecture, but the FAST course did include several tactics lectures.

F-14 Combat Intercepts was always given by a RIO, and I was pleased to be selected.

The outgoing instructor for F-14 Combat Intercepts used a "chalk talk" method that increased audience participation. He set the stage with a scenario and then asked students for their actions and concerns as the intercept counted down to merge plot, structuring their inputs into key areas. But to me the technique seemed to perpetuate old tactics and experience from training. It was called F-14 Combat Intercepts to emphasize the differences between our artificial training environment and the way we would go to war. The RAG taught us basic intercept techniques, and then we operated in relatively undisciplined and non-demanding environments during most of our flying in the fleet. It was the best we could do, but it wasn't always the challenging training needed.

Every instructor who took over a lecture sought to upgrade it, and it was time to upgrade F-14 Combat Intercepts.

I didn't think of all this the day the training department told me in mid-October that I was going to take over the lecture. I just wanted a tactics lecture. My murder board was set for December. I figured two months would be enough.

To start preparing I watched the lecture during the class and on videotape. I made notes and started to frame my lecture. I had 1,200 Tomcat hours, hundreds of successful intercepts and engagements, and had been selected to return as a Topgun instructor. I was a good RIO and figured I could give an informative lecture.

As I sat at a desk in the small, crowded Topgun library, surrounded by classified reports and books on fighter combat, Jambo came by and asked what I was going to say about radar sorting, evaluating the radar picture so that both fighters have the same understanding of the bogeys. I explained how I would handle this subject based on what I had learned almost four years before in the RAG and through my experience since. Jambo asked more questions and made some suggestions. My RAG experience was a starting point, but not the Topgun-level answer.

Then Hollywood asked about the range guidelines I was going to suggest for various activities, such as when to stop looking at the bogey formation and take a radar lock, and when to break the radar lock and try to gather more information in the search mode of the radar.

Jaws asked what I was going to say about communications between the pilot and RIO, and over the radio between the fighters and their controller. Jaws knew that something as simple as effective communication could make a big difference in whether the fighters succeeded or failed.

I discussed their concerns, thought, and wrote. Other instructors came by with areas of concern, and I thought and wrote more. It was soon obvious that on my own I could not take the lecture where it needed to go. Several instructors suggested I talk to Boa about how Air Force F-15s were running intercepts. It turned out the Air Force had more standardized procedures than I had ever heard of. The concepts were familiar, but the Air Force presented them and practiced them rigidly, so I incorporated the material. My fellow instructors demanded it, and I saw it as an opportunity to advance the Tomcat community.

A new instructor showed up, a Marine Corps F/A-18 Hornet pilot called Player, who was up to speed on the latest radar intercept concepts. The Hornet was a new single-seat fighter and its instructors borrowed heavily from procedures used by the Air Force's single-seat F-15, so Player joined the ranks of instructors helping to shape the new F-14 Combat Intercepts lecture.

My murder board was scheduled for the first Monday in December. By mid-November several instructors saw me still writing a script in the library and asked about my progress. "Bio, shouldn't you be doing pre boards by now? This is a tactics lecture."

They weren't nagging me. They thought I was behind schedule. As before, I began to spend more time in the library, staying there until 9:00 PM (after starting my days before 7:00 AM), and I worked weekends.

I worked through the Thanksgiving holiday and had my first pre-board the Monday after, one week before the scheduled murder board. I barely knew the material, much less had the ability to present it at the Topgun level. Questions from the small audience brought me to a stumbling halt.

I had a second pre-board on Tuesday and it went about the same.

On Wednesday, Sunshine asked if I wanted to delay a month. Shine, as he was frequently called, was a focused Marine Corps F-4 RIO who had been at Topgun longer than most other instructors. He managed the murder board process, and the audiences from my pre-boards had told him I wasn't ready. I agreed that a one-month delay was a good idea, so the murder board was re scheduled for January 4. This was a small disappointment as well as a relief. I was not alone, though, as several other murder boards had been delayed in my short time at Topgun. Instructors told me about others who spent too much time writing and not enough time practicing and how they ultimately delivered great lectures.

It may not be right the first time, but it will be right eventually. I continued my work and had two more pre boards, including one at seven thirty on a Saturday morning.

Of course I was still doing my ground job and flying with the class. I had ten flights in the first half of December and then that class ended. The FAST team went to Oceana the week before Christmas, we had dinner at The Raven, and I gave Maritime Air Threat and ran simulators. The rest of the time was similar to my trip to El Centro the summer before, when I got my classified notes out of a vault and worked on my new lecture. I actually had a pre-board in Oceana with several FAST instructors.

Suddenly it was December 27 and I was back at Miramar with only eight days until my tactics murder board. "How did I get here?"

Shine was concerned about my progress, and possibly about my commitment. He was taking a week of leave over New Year's, and I was his biggest concern before he left. Shine asked when he could see my new lecture.

I told him I could do a pre-board on Thursday, but he was "busy all day." He was also busy Friday, and he was leaving Saturday morning. I had plans to attend a party with my old VF-24 friends Friday evening, but Shine said that was the only time he was available.

Friday evening. "OK, what time?" I said.

"How about 10:30 PM?"

"No problem."

I reviewed my notes and practiced Thursday and Friday, then went to the VF-24 party. It started at 8:30 PM. Unlike the old days, I stayed one hour then went to Topgun for the pre board with Shine. It was cold and damp when I unlocked the gate to the Miramar flight line a little after 10:00 PM. Sunshine showed up just before 10:30, completely unaffected by the unusual situation of practicing a lecture at this date and hour. It didn't really bother me either. I guess "goes with the gold nametag" went a long way.

Sunshine seemed to have guarded confidence when we finished the pre board at 1:00 AM that I would be ready to lecture the next class. But he delayed my murder board one more week, to January 11.

Delayed again. Any sense of relief was gone, replaced by a sense of focus. What was I missing? Some of it turned out to be familiar advice from my first murder board: Tell the audience what they need to know, listen carefully to questions, know when to stop talking. But for this tactics lecture I had to learn another rule in the final weeks before my murder board: Know the answer to every question before it is asked.

This is not an impossible requirement. Think of martial arts and using an opponent's strength or weight against them, or of TV lawyers admonished to never ask a question to which they don't know the answer.

The final two weeks of preparation turned out to be some of the most valuable time I spent at Topgun. It forced me to better understand all aspects of Topgun's teachings, so it functioned as my instructor-under-training syllabus.

A few days before my murder board I had a pre board Monday afternoon at five. I knew the material well and was working on delivery and question handling. Hollywood, Vida, and a couple of other instructors sat for the pre board. A new Topgun class had started that morning, so it was a long day, but we were used to them. I talked for fifty-five minutes and took a break. When the second half of the lecture started, my audience members sat down with sodas and bags of chips in front of them. A few minutes after I started talking, they noisily opened their snacks and really enjoyed eating.

In between slides I said to Hollywood, "I know, you guys are trying to distract me."

"Bio, what are you talking about? We're just having a snack."

This was a reminder of something I'd heard before. I needed to treat every audience like a class full of students, not a practice session. I got back on my game plan and the rest of the pre board went well.

For the rest of the week I focused on practicing diagrams on the board, perfecting references to other lectures, and a few other refinements. I even practiced when to stop talking.

The murder board for F-14 Combat Intercepts started early on January 11. At 6:28 AM I started the Talking Heads song "Life During Wartime" on the cassette player in Classroom 2, in front of seventeen instructors who wanted me to succeed but wanted more that I uphold Topgun standards. At 6:30 AM I started the lecture. I began with a very brief scenario about being on deployment and suddenly becoming involved in combat operations. It was simplistic but plausible, given the nature of Navy deployments.

I stood beside the podium and launched into the material, facing a room full of instructors. I viewed them not as other instructors, but as an audience. They were alert and engaged even at that early hour. Murder boards were not a chore for the staff but an occasion to verify that another instructor lived up to the reputation and assist them with making the grade. I didn't need to look at my slides, and pushed the advance button with confidence, only glancing at the screen over my shoulder to see that I was in synch with my slides. I always was. I used the pointer precisely, swept my gaze around the room, and drew tidy diagrams on the whiteboard to illustrate a few points and answer questions. I spoke clearly.

Even though I had given my Maritime Air Threat lecture to real audiences eight or ten times, I was nervous for this lecture. As soon as it started, I was also impatient to know if I would pass or fail and to hear the comments, but that was two challenging hours away.

After the opening scenario I spent a few minutes summarizing fighter intercepts over Vietnam. I addressed ways that crews could prepare themselves and their weapons system before the intercept started, and then moved to the core of the lecture, a hypothetical 2vUNK combat intercept that I described from a range of thirty-three miles to merge plot. I dissected and categorized it:

- What to do with the radar—primarily RIO actions—to maximize the lethality of two powerful fighters.
- What to do with the aircraft—primarily pilot controlled, such as airspeed and formation—to take full advantage of the lead-wingman tactical formation and emphasize that this wasn't just a RIO lecture.
- Communications, both over the radio and on the ICS, which I knew from experience to be critical to success.
- Other considerations such as weapons employment and visual lookout. These points added tactical details and integrated other class lectures.

The lecture included a great deal of information that was new to Topgun. I didn't invent the material, but I blended it into a coherent lecture that fleet RIOs and pilots could understand and apply. They would be held accountable for the material, tested in a training area above the Pacific, over the desert, and the Echo Range at China Lake. They might be tested in the real world.

After fifty minutes I took a break, starting my tape again to finish "Life During Wartime." The murder board was going fine, but not perfect. As usual, a few instructors came up to encourage me or give me a little coaching, but most just took a break. Five minutes later they returned to their seats and I picked up my intercept with twenty miles to the merge.

The second half of the murder board continued to go well, and about eight twenty I said, "If there are no more questions, please take five minutes for critiques," the standard closing for a Topgun class lecture. I started my tape again, picking up Blue Öyster Cult's "Godzilla," classic hard rock. My murder board was over.

After just a few seconds of music, Sunshine signaled me to stop the tape, then asked everyone to take a short break and return for the debrief portion of the murder board.

During this break Sunshine conferred with Secks, who as Topgun's training officer was responsible for the five-week class and its content. When we reconvened, Shine started the debrief with his typical understatement and polite manner: "Nice job, Bio. I know you put a lot of hard work into this, and it shows. You get a thumbs-up to give the lecture to the class on Monday. You need to work on a few things, I am sure they will all come out in the comments, but you're taking this lecture where we want it to go."

It was a relief. After all of the preparation, the late nights and weekends in the Topgun Library, the solitary practice sessions and grinding pre-boards—yes, it was good to hear the words, "You get a thumbs-up."

On to the critiques.

First comment: "What the hell was that music?" Several heads went down as others marked this off their notes. Apparently "Life During Wartime" wasn't very popular, and my tape didn't sound good on the simple tape player and cheap speakers we had in the classrooms. Most other instructors played ZZ Top, Van Halen, Foreigner, Phil Collins, The Who, or some other popular act. I could fix this.

Other comments were more substantial. Several instructors corrected flaws in my references to their lectures, others suggested additions and deletions, and some corrected details in my statements and slides. Pre-boards had caught most of these mistakes but missed a few.

Many instructors wanted me to review key points for their own benefit, because after I gave the lecture to the class it would be Topgun's official recommendation on how an F-14 crew should run a 2vUNK intercept. We would hold students accountable to these standards.

A big part of the lecture was increased precision in all aspects of flying, including radio terminology. (All U.S. forces were working on this.) One of the basic ways it affected us was the use of the term "bogey." We decided to conform to emerging practice and use "bogey" to refer to an *unknown* radar contact, while an identified *enemy* aircraft was to be called a "**bandit**." This change had been under consideration at Topgun and we decided to implement it.

With the majority of the lecture imprinted in my mind, the changes made during the murder board debrief were easy to incorporate.

Then Jambo made a comment that would be difficult to implement. "Bio, you need something to get you fired up before this lecture. Maybe take a shot of whiskey or something." He got smiles and head nods in agreement. I took this in a constructive manner and figured that my dull delivery was partly a result of the stress of the murder board. I knew I could put more energy into the class lecture.

It took more than two hours to get to the final instructor in the back row. It was 10:30 AM and there was a class going on, so everyone got back to work. We didn't adjourn to the O-Club or even go to lunch, everyone was busy. I went to the locker room to change out of my khakis and into my flight suit. I'm sure I exuded "relief." From now on I would have a lecture to add after my name when I introduced myself to new classes.

At 1:30 PM that afternoon I was in a brief for a 1v1 against the class. I flew with the new Topgun CO, Commander Tom Otterbein, call sign Otter. Our flight was unremarkable, just another over the Pacific 0.9 in an airspace designated Warning Area 291, or W-291. I was still thinking about whether I should actually drink a shot of whiskey before I gave my lecture on Monday.

Otter had flown F-4s and F-14s. A calm and skillful fighter pilot with a dry sense of humor, he had the respect of the entire staff. Through good timing, Otter was able to accomplish something important shortly after he became CO.

At some time in the hazy past (that means, before I got there) Topgun instructors had obtained blue flight suits that were distinctive from the standard issue olive green worn by their fleet brethren. They put a couple of light blue stripes on these bags to make them even more spiff, and wore them with pride. When they talked about the long hours and working weekends associated with Topgun, they said, "It comes with the blue suit." Eventually those blue flight suits wore out and were not replaced. Otter became aware of a plan to provide one blue flight suit to every Navy pilot and NFO, regardless of what he flew, as a morale builder. But somehow Otter obtained a blue flight suit for each Topgun instructor a full year before they were issued to Navy fliers in general.

One day he walked into a staffex with a big box and gave a short and humorous speech, then opened the box. For eighteen fighter pilots and RIOs it was like Christmas morning. Otter said it was some kind of test batch, but we didn't care about the details. Blue bags were back, baby! We all found one in our size or close enough, then quickly made plans to have them embroidered with the light blue stripes like our forebears. I couldn't believe I was there at the right time for the return of the blue flight suit. For the next few weeks it seemed like we said, "It comes with the blue suit" several times a day, then it receded to a more natural frequency of a few times a week.

I gave F-14 Combat Intercepts to the class the Monday after the murder board and it went well. The murder board process worked again. I was confident about delivering the material and also that I was getting through to the class. I adhered to Topgun's lecture standards almost subconsciously, and technique details such as controlling the pointer with two hands felt natural. I enjoyed answering questions. Guys eating snacks were a non-issue. And in contrast to my days as a junior officer in VF-24, I realized that I could now lecture for two hours without notes to a demanding audience and not even break a sweat. I considered Jambo's recommended shot of whiskey to get pumped-up but decided against it. It was, after all, 7:30 AM.

As I looked around the class, it was hard to imagine that the students might see me the way I had viewed the instructors lecturing me a little more than two years earlier. But when I looked at their critiques after the class, in addition to a few helpful suggestions I found compliments such as those I had written when I was in their place. On a personal level it was rewarding to read them. On a professional level, I felt like I was now earning my place on the team.

Around this time I also started briefing class flights. Briefing and leading a Topgun flight with two student fighters and several instructor bandits was more demanding than the flights I had briefed at VF-24, but with some experience and constructive comments I came up to standard.

I was building flight experience in the F-5, and I became qualified to fly with pilots under instruction. New pilots took their first F-5 flight in the two-seat F-model, with a *pilot* in the backseat. Their second flight was usually in the two-seater as well, but with a qualified RIO in back. Once I became qualified, these were flights on which even my little experience to date actually flying the jet helped.

One of my favorite maneuvers in the F-5 was a "rudder reversal," an effective way to get separation from a tight dogfight and then point at the fighters so we could launch a missile. (Missiles have a *minimum* range based on their guidance systems and small wings.) F-14s did not frequently perform rudder reversals because of the risk of losing an engine due to the turbulent airflow involved, but it was a comfortable maneuver in the F-5 and pilots used it when appropriate.

Tex taught me how to fly a rudder reversal by performing several and talking me through his actions. Then it was my turn.

We started at fifteen thousand feet and at least 250 knots airspeed. I made sure we were in full afterburner, then pulled the nose up to a climb angle of seventy degrees. Our speed decreased as we climbed. At 200 knots I came out of afterburner. At 150 knots I used the small handle next to the throttles to set the flaps to the "maneuver" position, which was halfway deployed. Critical steps happened at 100 knots, when I smoothly and quickly pressed the left rudder pedal all the way to the floor, which started the aircraft nose coming to the left. The trick was to also quickly and smoothly move the stick forward and right the proper amount to make the plane pivot around its middle. We went from seventy degrees nose up to ninety degrees nose down in about two seconds. Then I neutralized the stick and rudder, raised the flaps, and started to track the imaginary fighter as we rapidly accelerated in the dive. Remember, I only did this when we were not actually fighting another aircraft.

The first time I tried it, I pressed the left rudder pedal to the floor and the nose started to come left, but I didn't move the stick correctly and the jet flopped over on its back. It was interesting to feel the aerodynamic forces push the plane in a way that I did not intend, but that I had caused through my control movements. I'm not sure if it was the small size of the jet or the fact that I was doing the flying— probably both—but I felt very much "in touch" with the air flowing over my wings. As soon as we started to tumble I checked our altimeter, but we had plenty of altitude and being out of control in an F-5 was no cause for alarm. Tex said, "Neutralize," and as soon as I neutralized the controls (centered the stick and rudders) the nose fell toward the ocean twenty thousand feet below and we gained airspeed.

Before the next attempt Tex told me to press the rudder pedal a little slower and move the stick more to the right as I moved it forward. My next rudder reversal worked, and the one after that was even better. It felt great to make this eight-ton flying machine pirouette at my command.

A few months later I launched from Miramar with a pilot on his second F-5 flight, one of my early hops with a new pilot. He flew with another squadron that, like Topgun, used A-4s and F-5s on adversary missions, and our squadrons worked together frequently. He had been to the required one-day class, gotten instruction from pilots, and taken his first F-5F flight with a pilot in the backseat. It was a beautiful morning with a rich blue sky and a few puffy clouds as we flew out to a training area. We had briefed specific objectives for the flight and started with some basic aerobatics above San Clemente Island. We then moved on to rudder reversals.

Flying fifteen thousand feet above the northern part of the island, near the Navy's practice landing field, we were doing more than 250 knots when the pilot pushed the throttles forward to afterburner and pulled the nose up smoothly to the prescribed 70-degree climb. As we climbed and decelerated, he told me he was coming out of burner, moving the flaps to maneuver, and preparing to press the rudder. I told him we were too fast for the rudder, but he said, "I think it's 120 knots . . . here goes." I pulled my feet out of the way when he pressed the left rudder, and watched my control stick move in response to his inputs, quickly forward and to the right. The nose of the jet started to track left in response to his rudder inputs, but then we flopped over on our back.

I checked the altimeter and saw we were at twenty-one thousand feet, so we had time to recover. But then I thought, "I'm the more experienced member of this crew. I wasn't certain of the parameters for the maneuver, and now we are out of control." This was different from when a pilot was showing me the maneuvers.

We were inverted and spinning, and I said over the ICS, "Twenty-one thousand feet, eighty knots." There was no cause for alarm. We could fall for thousands of feet before alarm became appropriate.

We were not under unusual physical stress, as g forces were low and the spin was quite smooth once established. I used my right arm to push against the canopy rail and turned my head hard to look up and over my right shoulder to see San Clemente Island spinning below me. The edges were blurred but the center, directly below our aircraft, was easy to pick out. I saw with some relief that it was vacant. This is where our jet would impact if we didn't fix this spin.

Having been out of control in the F-5 several times, I knew recovery was straightforward so I enjoyed the view for a few seconds, waiting to see what the new pilot would do. Maybe it was only one second, but it seemed longer. Then I said, "Flaps up," and turned to look at the wing leading edges to see the maneuvering flaps retract. He pulled the stick aft as I said, "Stick aft," the next step in the "Inverted

Spin" emergency procedure we all memorized. Our spinning stopped as the aircraft nose pointed toward the ground.

Instead of falling, we were flying again.

The pilot said he wanted to try again to see if he could get it right, and I said, "Sure, but I think you're supposed to program the rudder in at 100 knots instead of 120." We discussed this point as we accelerated to starting conditions. He thought he had simply not put in enough forward stick. So when we tried again, he stepped on the rudder at 120 knots and put in a lot of forward stick, and we flipped over and spun a few more turns. He recovered the aircraft quickly.

The pilot was "certain" he had been told to feed in the rudder at 120 knots, and was just doing something else wrong. Amazingly, I could not convince him that the critical parameter was 100 knots. Part of the problem was that I wasn't certain of the number myself. I couldn't even talk him into trying to step on the rudder at 100 knots, and we spun four more times that day. The final few were brief, for as soon as the jet flopped on its back he'd neutralize and pull back on the stick and we'd be flying again. It all happened with an incredible lack of drama or stress.

When we landed, the pilot dropped his flight gear off at his squadron before we debriefed, and I saw Rat as I walked through Topgun Maintenance Control. I said, "Rat, I hate to admit this, but I just got out of a Fam 2 flight and we couldn't get the rudder reversal to work. Do you feed in the rudder at 100 knots or 120?"

"Oh, 100 knots. If you do it at 120 you'll spin every time."

Yes, of course.

I had prepared for, practiced, and succeeded in teaching students how Topgun wanted them to fly in combat. I had briefed, led, and debriefed Topgun class flights. And now I knew that I had to be just as well-prepared when I strapped on an F-5F for a simple practice flight in the training area. It comes with the blue suit.

TWELVE

Hollywood Comes to Miramar

I walked out of the training office one afternoon headed for ops to check the next day's schedule, and found Sunshine in the hall really dressing down a new instructor about his flying. Another pilot, who had been an instructor for a while, had joined them. My walk between the offices was too short to satisfy my curiosity, so I changed direction and walked to the other end of the hall for a drink of water. Although I passed the fantastic plaques and photos, all of my attention was focused on just one sense, hearing.

Shine had been around Topgun a long time and was one of the keepers of the flame, a firm adherent to the squadron's highest standards. He personified integrity and profession-alism, and confidently mentored new instructors whether pilots or RIOs. I couldn't tell whose side the experienced pilot was on, he didn't say much. I missed some of the conversation from the far end of the hall, but on the way back I heard Shine progress from the new guy's flying performance to his attitude. Passing them when I walked into Ops I wondered if we were going to lose a pilot.

I was being overly dramatic. Of course the new pilot didn't give up, he was a fighter pilot. I guess Shine gave him the wakeup call he needed, and he soon proved himself in the air, in flight briefs and debriefs, and murder boards.

I realized that people who saw some of my pre-boards might have wondered if Topgun was about to lose a new RIO, but I didn't give up, either. Sunshine wasn't nagging this new guy, just like he wasn't nagging me. Topgun had standards and it took intensity and commitment to maintain them, as much from the old guys as the new.

You could say tigers raise tigers.

Like the little drama in the hall, my activities for the first half of 1985 were typical for a Topgun instructor. I gave my F-14 Combat Intercepts lecture an average of once a month. Half of these were to Topgun classes, the rest were to groups such as squadrons that requested the lecture for training and classes for senior officers coming through Topgun for updates. I gave Maritime Air Threat an average of twice a month.

One day Jaws and I flew an F-5F to the naval air station at Lemoore, California, three hundred miles north of Miramar, to give lectures to new Hornet squadrons that were focusing on air-to-air training. I carried our pressed khaki uniforms in the rear cockpit and tried not to wrinkle them during the forty-minute flight, which wasn't easy with all of the trays of

Once I joined Topgun as an instructor, this was the photo of me for the board showing all instructors. The light blue t-shirt was standard. Most of us had moustaches, but they weren't required.

DAVE BARANEK

All Topgun instructors had a callsign slide prepared by the artists who supported the squadron, which we used near the start of our lectures. This was a pretty generous interpretation.

⌃ F-5s in loose formation cruise in the early morning toward the ranges at China Lake, California, for another day of work.

⌃ Air Force Captain Mike "Boa" Straight and Marine Corps Captain Terry "Circus" McGuire, both Topgun instructors, use the nose of an F-5 Tiger II to make notes after a flight.

Photo © George Hall

⌃ Hollywood (left) and me on the stairs in the Topgun hangar discussing a flight. The silhouettes behind us represent enemy MiGs shot down by Topgun graduates. They had just been repainted and the names and dates not yet added.

≈ Lineup of Nissan Z cars and Corvettes in Topgun parking spaces at Miramar. Several other instructors had cool cars, but most drove "normal" vehicles.

≈ Commuters. Three F-5s fly 16,000 feet above San Diego, returning to Miramar after a mission off the coast. In a few moments we would begin our descent into Miramar.

⌃ F-5 climbing out from the Naval Air Facility at El Centro, California.

⌃ A few months after becoming an instructor, I started briefing students for flights in the Topgun class. It was demanding, because you had to cover everything from flying safety to tactics.

⩓ Self-photo in the rear cockpit of a Topgun F-5F with an F-5E joining in formation.

⩓ A Topgun F-5 in formation with a black F-4 Phantom from the Navy test and evaluation squadron, VX-4. These aircraft were adversaries during a series of test flights at NAS Fallon, Nevada, against the Navy's front-line fighters, the F-14 and F/A-18.

⏫ Right after climbing out of an F-5. It was interesting how quickly you got used to wearing all of the gear: g-suit, harness, survival equipment.

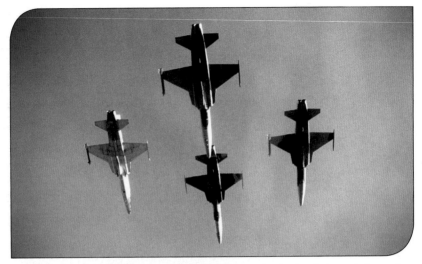

⌃ Four F-5s in a diamond formation. We got in this formation for the photograph, it wasn't something we used against the class.

⌃ Former Soviet MiG-25 Foxbat pilot Viktor Belenko shakes hands with Topgun instructors Rat, Circus, and me after his familiarization flight in a two-seat F-5F Tiger II. Belenko frequently spoke to Topgun classes about his past.

⩗ A group of instructors leaves the NAS Key West flight line in style at the start of the training detachment. With no students around, we relaxed a little.

⩗ Heading out to film scenes for the movie "Top Gun," three black Topgun F-5s join on Clay Lacy's Learjet over the Pacific. The Learjet carried director Tony Scott, cameras, and technicians.

⌃ F-5s cruise above the Pacific, heading toward a rendezvous with the Learjet and F-14s to film scenes for the movie. Look closely and you can see some of the black paint has peeled off.

⌃ An F-14 Tomcat fighter flies behind the Learjet carrying cameras during filming for "Top Gun," right after the director called "Cut!" over the radio. Glare on my canopy makes it hard to see the Learjet.

⌃ With "Rat" Willard, the Topgun squadron's primary coordinator for the movie, after completion of another filming sortie. The black helmets and flight suits were loaned to all instructors flying the F-5s while filming.

⌃ At the cast and crew party on completion of filming in the San Diego area, actor Anthony Edwards (who played the character Goose) with my wife Laura and me. I tried to "dress Hollywood," while the actors "dressed Miramar."

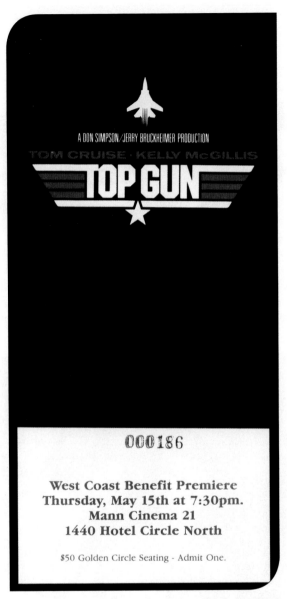

A DON SIMPSON/JERRY BRUCKHEIMER PRODUCTION

TOM CRUISE · KELLY McGILLIS

TOP GUN

000186

**West Coast Benefit Premiere
Thursday, May 15th at 7:30pm.
Mann Cinema 21
1440 Hotel Circle North**

$50 Golden Circle Seating - Admit One.

⌃ A ticket to the premiere in San Diego, officially the "West Coast Benefit Premiere," as the first showing was in Washington – a nod to the Navy's official cooperation.

✿ At the cast and crew party on completion of filming in the San Diego area, my wife Laura plants one on actor Tom Cruise (who played the character Maverick).

✿ Topgun instructors and wives / dates / friends with a limousine on the way to the San Diego premiere. The group filled six limos. This is Bio, Laura, Kodak, MaryAnne, Mary, Jaws, and Nancy Forth.

⌃ Topgun instructors in blue flight suits outside the Miramar Officers' Club as we start an evening of club-hopping as a farewell to the skipper, Commander Dan "Dirty" Shewell. We rented limos to take us around.

⌃ My wife Laura with Kenny Loggins after Dirty's change of command ceremony. Loggins wrote the movie theme song "Danger Zone," which became a hit, and was invited to the ceremony.

⌃ Just for fun: after a day of hard dogfights at Yuma, a student pulls his F-14 up next to my Topgun F-5 and lights the afterburners. Seeing things like this made me long to return to the mighty Tomcat.

⌃ Jaws, me, Nick, and Rat on the Topgun flight line after my last flight in the squadron. My pilot for the flight, Zone, took the photo. I was the only one drinking champagne, the others had to get back to work.

Cover: VF-24 F-14 zooms vertically into the sky above the
Indian Ocean. This aircraft is carrying an AIM-7 Sparrow missile
and external fuel tanks.

35mm slides that also shared my cockpit. The return flight was easier since I just stashed the uniforms out of the way without worrying about wrinkles.

I briefed and led two or three flights in each Topgun class and flew an average of eighteen flights per month. Like all instructors I still worked a fair number of Saturdays, spent two days a month as SDO, attended one murder board a month, and also went to a squadron party roughly every month. It comes with the blue suit.

As a group, we were regulars at the Miramar O-Club. If there was a class going on we would spend time with the students, but we usually merged into a crowd of blue flight suits intently discussing some new development in aviation or the Navy fighter community, or some squadron issue that grabbed our attention. Of course, we told a lot of stories from our days of flying fleet aircraft, mixed in with new stories of our lives as bandits and instructors. Wednesday was the big day at the Miramar club and that was our main day to wear blue bags, although they showed up on other days, too.

I was happily immersed in "Navy fighters," working hard and loving it. I felt I had accomplished something by getting to Topgun. I enjoyed the flying and was making progress improving my flight briefs and flight lead skills.

I didn't need more amusement, and yet more amusement came along.

In the spring of 1985, movie producers Jerry Bruckheimer and Don Simpson saw an article in *California* magazine describing actual Tomcat crews going through Topgun. Written by Ehud Yonay, the article was illustrated with dynamic, professional-quality photos taken by former Topgun instructor Chuck "Heater" Heatley. We all saw the magazine when it came out and thought it was neat, and that was it. Bruckheimer and Simpson, however, were inspired. Working with Paramount Pictures, they contacted Navy officials at the Pentagon and pitched their idea, and the Navy gave the project an official green light.

One day several limousines brought the producers, a cinematographer, and other Hollywood people to Miramar to meet with Rear Admiral Tom Cassidy, the two-star in charge of Navy fighter and E-2 operations on the West Coast. Once he was personally satisfied, Admiral Cassidy called Topgun and found that Otter and Rat (Topgun CO and XO) were just getting out of a couple of jets after a day at Yuma. He told them to come over immediately, and they walked in wearing their bags, which the Hollywood group loved. After the admiral described the idea, Otter looked at Rat and said, "You've got it, XO." Rat would be Topgun's point man for the project, and they came back to Topgun carrying an early version of the script.

Otter told us about the movie at a staffex a few days later. He briefly outlined the story of a fictional F-14 pilot and RIO going through the Topgun class. The talented pilot has a conflict with almost everyone except the female intelligence analyst with whom he has a relationship, and there was a lot of other Hollywood drama thrown in to make it interesting. A young actor named Tom Cruise would be the star. Most of us had barely heard of him.

My first thought was, "Hey, they picked the Navy and the F-14, instead of the Air Force (which also has a Fighter Weapons School) and the F-15 Eagle fighter." Then I thought the movie wouldn't actually happen, or if it did it wouldn't have much effect on me.

By the time Otter briefed the staff, Rat had spent some time with the script. He said it had major flaws, but when he mentioned this to higher-ups in Washington they told him this movie was going to be made, so he'd better help fix the script if he didn't want Topgun to be embarrassed.

Many of us brought bag lunches and ate them in the Topgun ready room (if we weren't off flying all day), and Rat read excerpts during lunch to show us what we were facing. To develop the story, a writer and several others had spent time at Miramar listening to unclassified lectures, briefs, and debriefs, and had been fascinated by the terminology we used. They wanted to capture it to give the movie more authenticity. Unfortunately, they had several misunderstandings during their visit, which were carried over to the original script. Terms were misstated and misused. For example, we used a term "P_S" for an aircraft's ability to maneuver. It meant "specific excess energy" and we said it "p-sub-s." This was used in the early script as "pieces of s." Another one was their use of the term "went ballistic;" the writer was captivated with that one and just didn't use it right. These small errors caused great amusement in the ready room. (Some of the terms didn't make it to the final script.)

It turned out that Paramount and the Navy were lucky that the project was assigned to Rat, because besides being a great fighter pilot and instructor, Rat was meticulous and tactful. I sometimes called him "Diplo-rat" because he would take a subtle approach to a difficult situation when others might have been more blunt and offensive.

Despite these rough spots, the writers' time at Miramar contributed to making the script as good as it was. They heard the eclectic language of aviators and solicited more.

Sobs (pronounced "sobes," rhymes with "robes"), a great RIO and great storyteller, used to say, "Do some pilot shit!" when things weren't going well. That made the movie. They also used my exchange with Jaws from a low-level bugout, "Watch the mountains!"

Working mostly on his own time—evenings and weekends—Rat was able to fix the small mistakes fairly easily. Other repairs took more thought, but he tackled them, too. In one of the key points of the movie's plot, for example, the writers knew that one of the main characters would have to die to provide a dramatic hook, and it wouldn't be star Tom Cruise. So the choice was his RIO, Goose, played by Anthony Edwards, and they asked Rat to come up with a plausible scenario where a RIO would be killed and the pilot survive.

As a Tomcat pilot before his Topgun tour, Rat was familiar with a weakness of the F-14's powerful engines—the danger of engine stall and resultant loss of thrust when airflow was interrupted. This could happen during certain dynamic maneuvers or by flying through the turbulent jet-wash that trailed other aircraft. If one engine stalled, the other engine at full power could quickly drive the aircraft into a flat spin, and because of inherent inertial factors recovery was dicey. This was something all Tomcat fliers were aware of. People had been killed in flat spins, some of them our squadron mates. But the basis for the RIO's demise was a real incident from Tomcat testing, during which the test F-14 got into an unrecoverable spin, and the crew ejected but did not jettison the canopy first. In the burbling airflow associated with the falling spinning jet, the canopy floated above the cockpit long enough for the RIO to hit it when his seat rocketed out of the plane, and he fractured a leg. It could easily have been worse. This was Tomcat community lore and served as the basis for Goose's death.

The official technical adviser for the movie was a former Topgun instructor, Pete "Viper" Pettigrew, who had Vietnam combat experience and was one of the few Navy pilots to shoot down a MiG-21. He worked with the Paramount crew extensively to make the movie happen and was rewarded by having his call sign used for Topgun's commanding officer in the movie. He also had a small on-screen role as Perry Siedenthal, the "older gentleman" who Charlie joins in the O-Club scene.

Sometime in spring 1985, Tom Cruise came to the Miramar O-Club to see what it was like on a typical Wednesday night. I usually went to the club Wednesday nights, but I was busy, and didn't think I was missing anything big anyway. For most of the instructors, it was, "Tom Cruise? I think he was in *Risky Business* and that high school football movie." (That was *All the Right Moves*.) Only a few instructors made it to the club that night, and Thursday morning they said he was young, skinny, and had long hair in a ponytail, which was from his work on the movie *Legend*. He attracted some attention, but no large crowds or screaming fans.

Many of us met him and other young movie stars on a Tuesday afternoon. There was no class going on, so most of us would leave the squadron about 5:00 PM. The event was arranged hastily. The day before, we were told some of the actors would be at the Rusty Pelican at 4:30, and they wanted some instructors to stop by and to talk with them. The Rusty Pelican was a new seafood restaurant a few miles from the north gate of Miramar. Great bar, great food, nice design, a cool and popular place in suburban San Diego, and we were all familiar with it. The bar was quiet when a dozen guys in uniforms showed up and gathered with a few who were clearly not military. I met Tom Cruise, Anthony Edwards, and a few others. Our group had the bar to ourselves.

At the time Tom was almost twenty-three, four years younger then me, and I was the youngest instructor in the squadron. He was polite and deferential while remaining enthusiastic. Tony Edwards was the same age as Tom, and we knew him from *Revenge of the Nerds* and *Gotcha*. They were just a couple of years younger than most Topgun students, not a big difference.

The group was relaxed and dynamic, all interested in the same thing: talking about flying jet fighters. I leaned against the bar with a couple of other instructors and Tom asked me, "What's the most fun part of flying? What's the scariest part?" I told him about high-g dogfights, about flying at low altitude and high speed, about the almost unlimited power and maneuverability. I used my hands to illustrate the relative position of aircraft when it was important. I told him about my ejection and a few other actors moved in to listen, but I gave the short version because other guys had their stories. Anyway, it wasn't about me, it was about the military flying life. Each of us used slightly different words to express similar sensations or to highlight different subtleties.

The actors were sponges. I figured they did this for every role, and today it was our turn to leave our imprint. Being fighter pilots and RIOs we told a lot of stories about ourselves, so it was a match made in heaven.

We were there an hour before a twenty-something girl came over and asked, "Are you Tom Cruise?!" We realized our quiet hour in a nice bar with Tom Cruise was over. The bar area was filling up with the after-work crowd and we had accomplished our mission, so people started to drift away. I stayed another ten minutes and then left.

The movie crew started filming scenes a few weeks later, near the end of June, and continued through July. Rat kept us advised of progress and we started to see articles in the San Diego paper. Filming started in the town of Oceanside, shooting scenes in a beachside house "where Charlie lived." They filmed scenes in an order dictated by various production concerns such as the availability of locations or people, not in the order they would appear in the movie.

Even though I had met the actors, the project still seemed a way off. But it was homing in on Miramar. Filming progressed from Oceanside to a Navy base in San Diego that had more photogenic buildings than Miramar, then onto the aircraft carrier USS *Ranger* while it was pierside at the base on North Island. Paramount then had two days of shooting at an old bar in eastern San Diego.

The bar, the Roxy, was located on El Cajon Boulevard near 55th Street in what could be called a well-worn part of San Diego. Paramount was rejected by the management of the real Miramar O-Club, who didn't want to close their doors for two days, so they rented the Roxy instead. Word was passed around Miramar that they wanted real pilots and RIOs as extras in the scenes, but you had to be available for two days. That way Paramount could use film shot on either day, because the same people would be in the scenes. I don't think any Topgun instructors went, leaving this glamorous duty to RAG instructors and others, many of whom can be seen in the film.

In another fateful encounter, the location director for the film wandered into a small barbeque restaurant and bar in downtown San Diego one afternoon for a beer. Even though the place had nothing to do with the real Topgun, he liked the atmosphere and found the owners amenable to the disruption of shooting a movie. Thus the Kansas City Barbeque became the "sleazy bar" where Maverick, Charlie (Kelly McGillis), Goose, and his wife (Meg Ryan) drank beer and sang "Great Balls of Fire" at the piano.

We got more reports in early August about the actors and filming when production moved to the aircraft carrier USS *Enterprise* (CVN-65), about one hundred miles off the coast conducting standard training ops in preparation for deployment. The Paramount group flew out by helicopter and spent four days filming basic carrier ops, such as the burner cat shots used so effectively in the opening credits. Others shots involved the actors around the aircraft, such as the scene at the end of the movie where Iceman and Maverick invite each other to be their wingman. (Iceman says, "You can be my wingman any time.") None of the filming involved the actors actually flying in aircraft. According to second-hand reports, most of the ship's crew was fascinated by the movie-making, although it had to be distracting while the ship and air wing tried to prepare for their real-world deployment.

The movie people stayed busy, next filming the helo rescue scenes, where an orange-and-white Coast Guard helicopter hovered above Maverick in his raft as he held the lifeless body of Goose. We heard stories about how cold the water got after multiple takes and how the whole scene happened right next to a seawall. In the film it looks like they are in the open ocean, but illusion is Hollywood's specialty.

While Paramount filmed everywhere else, we completed a five-week Topgun class. (That was the reason none of us could get away to spend two days at the Roxy.) We also held another one-week senior-officer refresher course, had several staffexes, squadron parties, and the annual Topgun reunion. We heard about the movie and talked about it a little, but it still did not affect most of us, except Rat in his work on the script and other behind-the-scenes coordination.

About mid-August, filming came to Miramar. On weekends, when it was relatively deserted, the crew filmed scenes around the base. The scene where Viper (Topgun CO in the movie) welcomed the new students was filmed in VF-24's ready room in Hangar 4. The real Topgun classrooms were rejected as "not photogenic," and VF-24 had just renovated their ready room. The film crew dressed it up with flags and photos and asked several VF-24 junior officers to write realistic things on the whiteboard seen in the background. They wrote names and other information as they would for a flight brief. One guy told me that since we had both been in VF-24, they included Jaws and Bio.

To provide a tangible goal for students in the movie, and another plot element, the writers developed the idea of a "Topgun Trophy," awarded to the best crew in each class. There was no trophy in reality, but they made a convincing model anyway. Someone brought the trophy to Hangar 1 and showed it around Topgun, and we saw that the brass plates for "previous winners" had the names and call signs of the current Topgun instructors.

We heard after the fact about filming of the scene where Maverick and Goose make a low fly by of the Miramar tower. (This is where the harried air boss says, "That's a negative, Ghostrider, the pattern is full.") Someone coordinated special permission for the low-altitude flying to keep everyone out of trouble with the Federal Aviation Administration. In fact, many scenes in the movie show maneuvers definitely prohibited for normal flying and dangerous without planning and skillful aircrew, but Rat and the others involved prepared carefully and captured some very dramatic flying without endangering people or equipment. Even though we all flew jets for a living, the few who saw the Tomcat's passes by the tower said they were very low and impressive—high praise among a group of fighter guys.

In contrast to much of the shooting around Miramar, the crew made a small announcement before the volleyball scenes were filmed, requesting wives and girlfriends to come by to watch as Paramount wanted a female audience for the game. It may be hard to believe, but the turnout was a small and orderly group, just right for their needs, as most of the actors simply weren't well known then. We instructors were debriefed after the filming and heard that director Tony Scott had incredible energy all day and cussed a lot, and the actors were not very good volleyball players. The action consisted not of volleyball games but of multiple takes of very short segments.

We were all learning about Hollywood reality.

At some point in here we heard that several of the young actors went on F-14 flights, and of course the next phrase in these stories was " . . . and got sick." I don't remember who got sick and who didn't, but they had my sincere sympathy.

A backseat flight in an F-14 was a great experience, but for most people there was a price to pay and being a star didn't change that. I think the actors enjoyed the flights nonetheless. I'm sure the Navy parachute riggers and plane captains who helped Tom Cruise, Tony Edwards, and others get into their G suits and strap in to F-14s enjoyed their encounters with celebrities.

The filming finally affected Topgun instructors when Paramount moved our lockers out of our locker room. Our actual lockers. We thought this was interesting, since they were unremarkable. One day after we finished flying, they took our lockers out and put in replacements that held all of our flight gear and other stuff, with our names on the front. A few days later our original lockers returned, and again the change caused nary a ripple in our daily operations. Sure enough, when we watched the movie the next year, there were our actual lockers. The "students" were using them, while at the real Topgun there was no student locker room, but that was more Hollywood "reality." I'm not sure where they filmed those scenes, but I know those were real Topgun lockers.

In a more typical encounter, I met Michael Ironside (Jester) when several of the actors were looking around Topgun to get a sense of the place. I recognized him from various movies and TV shows, such as *Scanners* and the alien invasion series *V*. I also spent half an hour one day showing several actors how to climb up an F-14 like a pro. RIOs started by reaching up with our left hand to grab the handhold, and put our left foot on the bottom rung. Pilots started with the opposite hand and foot because they went forward at the top of the climb, instead of aft like RIOs. Even though I was flying F-5s now, I had climbed the F-14 ladder probably one thousand times and it still felt natural.

The week of August 12 we filmed most of the flying scenes involving the MiG-28. This really brought Hollywood to Topgun, and we experienced the pursuit of perfection and accuracy, in Hollywood terms, that drove everyone associated with *Top Gun*. At this point we became a part of this project. I saw that everyone was committed to making the best movie they possibly could, and that they were good at their jobs.

Producers Jerry Bruckheimer and Don Simpson assembled, enabled, and managed the team to transform their vision into celluloid. Writers Jim Cash and Jack Epps Jr. wrote a script designed to entertain and capture audiences. Gifted director Tony Scott translated that story from fantastic vision to camera-capable scenes. The actors, technicians, and dozens of others did their parts. And, of course, Viper, Rat, and other Navy personnel provided the reality check that made the result respectable.

Early in the project there had been a discussion about aircraft options to support the story and show both enemy fighters and Topgun adversaries. The pointy F-5 looked more sinister, and so it was cast as the MiG-28. There is no MiG-28 in reality; they made up this type to avoid any direct comparisons with real aircraft or air forces. That left the camouflaged A-4s to portray the aircraft flown by Topgun instructors during the class. Paramount decided to paint the F-5s black to remove any doubt about which were the bad guys, so over a weekend three single-seat F-5Es and one two-seat F-5F were painted a flat black, a paint that was apparently easy to apply and remove. These fighters became props in a movie but would remain in the hands of Topgun instructors.

Director Scott wanted dramatic lighting, so he shot as much as possible in the morning or afternoon, avoiding midday. Long before the flight briefs he studied the script and personally drew storyboards, small sequential sketches of the action, which he then refined with Rat. The storyboards looked like hand-drawn comic books, featuring line drawings of airplanes, clouds, even close-ups of actors' faces showing emotions. They were impressive for their clarity and accuracy.

The group had filmed other flying scenes before my involvement, so when I walked into the brief at 4:00 PM on Monday, they had found their rhythm and had become a smoothly functioning team.

Key players in filming the aerial scenes were Tomcat pilots Bozo and Loner, junior officers with VF-111 and VF-51, fleet pilots handpicked for their skill, consistency, and maturity. Besides being good, they were in the right place at the right time. I knew one of the RIOs, Tracy Skeels, whose call sign was T. C. for Too Cool. Several other pilots and RIOs also flew in support of the film, including a young lieutenant, Scott Altman, who later became a space shuttle astronaut.

Typical for a flight brief, we nodded and said hi but didn't make a point of formally introducing ourselves to everyone in the room. A few actors watched the brief quietly to get a sense of how fighter guys operated in our natural habitat.

All of the flying scenes that week were filmed over the Pacific from the specially equipped Learjet flown by Clay Lacy, and he was at all briefs. Fighter pilot, racing pilot, and successful businessman, Clay brought experience and innovation to the project as well as his fantastic jet with the high-quality cameras and special viewing windows. He had specific permission to fly his civilian jet from Miramar, an exclusively military airfield.

I was to fly with Rat, who briefed the flight. He started by covering the standard administrative items such as takeoff times, the operating area, and radio frequencies, all normal information required for a group of planes to operate together. He then briefed the mission—filming for the movie—using the storyboards, diagrams on the whiteboards, and of course the aircraft models on sticks. We would have two F-14s and four F-5s available, but the first scene would involve only the two-seat F-5F flying in formation alongside the Learjet. On a call from the Lear, both Rat and I would look up, acting as startled as we could. Although there would be nothing above us, Rat explained how this shot would be used for the scene where Maverick's Tomcat is inverted above the MiG-28. The F-14 would be added later in one of the few special effects in the film. The rest of the flight was to consist of the F-5s maneuvering below and behind the F-14, while it flew below and behind the camera-equipped Learjet.

These scenes seemed straightforward and not too risky during the brief, but Rat displayed the same conscientious attention to detail as if he were briefing a 4vUNK. When we finished the brief, the F-14 crews went to their squadrons in Hangar 3 to man-up, while Clay Lacy, Tony Scott, and other aerial camera people headed to the Lear.

We MiG-28 crews had to change into our costumes— black flight suits, helmets, and gloves to reiterate that we were bad guys. The first sign of danger occurred when I walked into the hot wardrobe trailer to get my black flight suit. The trailer smelled like a locker room that had been left for a week to rot. No, it was worse than that. I don't know the history of those flight suits, they seemed brand new when I caught my breath and pulled one outside into some fresh air, but someone should have told the wardrobe people they were washable.

Next I had to get one of the black helmets, which were beautifully painted and coated with a shiny layer of polyurethane. The front of each helmet bore a red star in a yellow circle, the insignia of no air force that we knew of, but suggestive of a "Communist" force. It wasn't my lucky day in the wardrobe department, because I could not find a helmet that fit. The best one I could get was a few sizes too small, but I figured I could make it work for this flight.

I had been on unusual flights before so I knew the dangers of distraction. The same elements that conspire to ruin an aviator's day remain present no matter what the mission. So walking up to a black F-5F with a big red star on the tail provoked a smile, and then became another opportunity to focus on the essentials. I had seen the aircraft on our line since they were painted but hadn't bothered to take a closer look, so, as I noticed during my preflight, the paint wasn't glossy, but flat, and in some spots it was already starting to peel. Still, black looked good on the sleek F-5. We climbed in and started up.

The Learjet and F-5s made radio calls once they were taxiing, so the Tomcats took off. The Lear took off next, and as soon as we had the required separation Miramar Tower cleared the F-5s for takeoff.

We launched at 5:00 PM, making coordinated section takeoffs from the dual runways. The summer sun was still bright but low enough to provide side lighting and avoid heavy shadows. As we headed toward our operating area we switched radios again, and soon all seven aircraft were on the same frequency, along with a ground-based Navy radar controller watching his scope to warn us in case another aircraft flew into the area. The Tomcats ran a radar intercept on us, then gained sight and remained out of the way a few thousand feet above and behind us. Rat made a radio call to detach the three F-5Es, and they joined the Tomcats.

My small helmet squeezed my head more painfully than I expected, so I slipped it off for a few seconds before the cameras started rolling. This is dangerous while flying, but the relief was priceless. Besides being too small in size, the helmet's wiring was faulty, so while Rat came in loud and clear on the ICS, all radio transmissions were weak and hard to hear, even with volume turned to maximum. Because of the controlled nature of this flight I decided these conditions did not create undue risk.

A small voice said, "We are steady 210 (degrees), 250 knots." This was Clay in the Learjet. Rat could have flown formation alongside without this information, but the numbers made it easier and safer. Rat flew us into forma-tion on the Lear's right side, and I saw the glass window that made up a large panel on this side of the fuselage. One high-quality camera sat behind the glass, others were mounted on the top and belly of the Lear.

"A little forward. That's good. When I count to three, both of you look up as quickly as you can. Remember, you're startled. One, two, three!"

I looked up. It was hard to act startled in all my flight gear and oxygen mask.

No feedback, just a small voice, "OK let's do it again. Remember, you are startled that there is an F-14 above you. One, two, three!"

They didn't teach us this in Pensacola.

I couldn't tell who was talking, probably Tony Scott, the director. With my helmet problems it was difficult to hear. We did it three times. I wasn't sure if we didn't get it right until the end or they just wanted multiple takes. Then we set up for the maneuvering shots.

Rat directed a turn to keep us all inside the working area. Since we operated here frequently, staying in the area was second nature. As the RIO in the F-5F I normally would have handled most of the flight lead navigation and communications, but Rat had it for this unusual mission. The Lear started a left turn and stabilized on a heading of 30 degrees. The Tomcats and F-5s were still above and behind, so Rat called the F-5s down along with one F-14 and we set up for shots of an F-14 being pursued by multiple MiG-28s. The second Tomcat stayed out of the way as a spare, so that we could continue to have a productive flight even if the primary F-14 had to leave early for some reason. I removed my helmet again for a few seconds of relief.

The Learjet stabilized at eighteen-thousand feet and three hundred knots, the Tomcat about two hundred feet below and behind, and the black F-5s strung out diagonally below and behind the gray fighter. The F-14 pilot manually swept his wings back, which would make it look like he was flying faster. It definitely made the aircraft look sleeker, and the reduced maneuverability was unimportant for this mission.

"Action!"

On the director's call, the F-14 started to bank left and right, always staying within about twenty degrees of the Lear's tail. Each of the F-5s had an assigned altitude band, and we banked within that band. The lower aircraft could keep sight of those above and ahead of them, but it was safer for all if we stayed in our assigned bands.

Rat and I were at the top of the F-5 stack, and we tried to follow the F-14's motions, as if we were pursuing it, while the belly camera in the Lear recorded everything. These scenes would be used to show the MiG-28s threatening Maverick, Cougar, Iceman, or whoever was in trouble. A real dogfight was an exceptionally dynamic contest that filled a spherical part of the sky three to five miles in diameter, and would be very difficult to photograph. We were going to film the components and convey the sense of the action through skillful editing and fill-in shots.

After about a minute we heard, "Cut! That's good, fellas. Let's get a little tighter on the formation so we can see who is at the end of the line down there."

"Organ, can you bring it in a little?"

"No problem."

"Rat, state 4.0." With that call the three F-5E pilots checked in with their fuel states and the F-14s followed. Everyone had plenty of fuel. My helmet hurt, so whenever there seemed to be an opportunity I slid it off my head for a few seconds.

Rat called for a left turn to stay in the area. The Lear made a gentle left turn, tailed by six fighters. When he had completed the turn, Clay Lacy called, "Steady, 210." Rat said, "OK, whenever you're ready."

"Action!"

We performed our maneuvers again. After each time we would get a few comments and plan a few adjustments for the next time. We went through this routine until the F-5s reached Bingo fuel, then we went home in three groups: black jets, gray jets, and high-end executive biz-jet (a group of one).

That night Rat drove to the hotel where Tony Scott and other members of the film crew were staying and watched the dailies with them. This was the raw film from the day's shooting, quickly processed and viewed unedited. Those present learned a few important lessons for shooting on later flights.

Rat was excited at the squadron on Tuesday, reporting that the shots of the F-14 flying alongside the Learjet were very good; they made the Tomcat look impressive. But some of the lessons would require fixes. For example, when they filmed the F-5s maneuvering below and behind the F-14 the cameramen used a common Hollywood technique to speed up the action, reasoning that we were flying slower than normal dogfight airspeeds for safety, so the film should be sped up. Unfortunately the result looked silly, so future scenes would be filmed at normal film speed. In addition, the first flight Monday morning had filmed head-on passes of the F-14s and the MiG-28s using the five-hundred-foot separation specified by training rules. (I wasn't on that flight.) When they looked at film from the cameras mounted on the F-14s, the dramatic shots that were to show Maverick's point of view, the passing F-5s were small dots in the corner of the screen. That wouldn't work at all, but we had time to recover.

Fortunately someone also learned that you could wash flight suits, so future trips to the wardrobe trailer were no longer to be feared.

Tuesday morning Rat went to visit Admiral Cassidy at his headquarters building across the street from Hangar 1. They had discussed previously how we would conduct the movie flights and had decided to be conservative, which was to be expected. Flying was risky enough—no one wanted to lose a plane or injure people to film a movie. But now Rat knew the conservative approach would not accomplish the goal, so he and the admiral discussed alternatives. They reasoned that the rule requiring five hundred feet of separation was designed for pilots in the heat and uncertainty of air combat training, but the controlled situation of filming the movie should allow aircraft to safely pass with less separation. The admiral said that Rat had to personally lead flights with close passes, and if there were any type of mishap he would stop production of the movie. Rat thought these were reasonable conditions and came back to continue filming.

Tuesday afternoon I went out on my second movie flight, the mission to film head-on passes when Maverick encounters MiG-28s (described in the first chapter), scenes used at the beginning and end of the movie. The black flight suits were clean and I found a helmet that fit. I thought, "This is the way Hollywood is supposed to treat Topgun instructors."

On the flight out to the area I figured I would make myself distinguishable from the other RIOs in black flight suits so I could tell which scenes I was in, and I rolled up my sleeves halfway. Before we started filming, someone in the Lear came up on the radio and said, "In the two-seater, we need the RIO to roll your sleeves down." I'm sure many movie extras have gone through a similar experience. Now I can say, "Me, too."

Wednesday morning I made a third flight in support of the movie and found the detailed planning and careful briefing still in evidence even though we no longer considered the mission novel. My first two movie flights were 1.3 hours each; this one was a 1.4. That was longer than my average Topgun flight of 0.9, indicative of the relatively benign nature of these flights. A lot of bank and not much yank allowed the pilots to stay at intermediate throttle settings and burn less fuel, despite the adrenaline rush I experienced with the unusually close passes. I flew with Rat again on this third movie flight, and when we landed I got one of the plane captains to snap our photo, in black flight suits with black helmets in front of a black jet. Yeah, we're the bad guys.

Even though the Navy supported Paramount in making the movie, taxpayers did not pay for any of it. Rat was tasked with tracking the cost associated with the Navy's movie ops, and he did an admirable job of determining total operating cost for the aircraft, the largest item. He described the accounting to us over bag lunches in the ready room. He started with the cost of jet fuel, a number that every squadron tracked—about $1 per gallon at the time—and then took into account such costs as depreciation on $30 million F-14s based on their expected lifetime, consumables such as oil and nitrogen that were used to service the aircraft after each flight, and the salaries of pilots and RIOs involved. He came up with a figure of about $7,600 for each hour that the Tomcats flew in support of the movie. Cost for the F-5 was about $5,500 per hour, and the hourly rate for the older single-engine A-4 was about $3,500. He then had a separate log of ground personnel actions that directly supported the movie, such as moving aircraft for camera shots. Paramount willingly accepted the charges. A year after the filming was complete, a Navy auditor inspected Rat's records looking for errors or omissions and found none.

Although I enjoyed my flights, probably the best flying related to the movie took place over the desert near NAS Fallon in Nevada. Located sixty miles east of Reno, Fallon is where carrier air wings go for some of their most demanding training before overseas deployments. I'd been there several times, both with VF-24 and with Topgun. For Tony Scott, Fallon provided clear skies, remote airspace, and dramatic mountains that made for perfect background scenery as well as good locations for cameras. Topgun's real class flights were on ranges near Yuma and China Lake, but those were not available for dedicated filming, so the range near Fallon was an acceptable substitute.

I had most recently spent a week at Fallon in June, fighting F-14s and F/A-18s from the Navy's fighter weapons and tactics development squadron, VX-4. That was a great bit of flying and I would have enjoyed more, but the filming trip conflicted with a FAST detachment I had to take to Oceana in late August.

By this time most of the MiG-28 scenes were complete anyway, so their primary goal was to show Maverick and other students going through the class, fighting A-4s. They would shoot a few scenes with the MiG-28s, though.

The Paramount group rented a local motel, with Tony Scott in a suite that he pretty much converted to a briefing room. He placed a whiteboard on the wall and had the airplane models on sticks, but he was missing the surly squadron duty officer behind a desk. They held flight briefs in his suite, and despite the unofficial atmosphere, the professionalism remained. Paramount wanted the best shots it could get, Rat wanted to make Topgun and the Navy look as good as possible, and no one wanted to crash a jet or get killed.

At the start of the detachment the director personally scouted locations. He found a great spot where the camera crew could set up, with a view down a canyon so they could shoot the F-14s and A-4s at eye level instead of always looking up. The site worked well until the pilots realized there was a hill to deal with as they flew past the camera, and a mistake could be fatal. So Tony found a second site, almost as good for the camera and a lot better for the pilots. Early each morning the crew would truck the big cameras up to this cliff, along with radios, food, and a lot of water. Rat or another pilot stayed with the film crew all day to coordinate with the aircraft. They filmed in the morning and then waited for the afternoon light, keeping with the low sun angles for the look that Tony was after.

I think he got what he wanted.

When the filming was largely complete we had a cast and crew party at the O-Club at NAS North Island, which had been the location of the graduation scene in the movie, where students received orders to carriers. (The scene in which Viper says, "Maverick, you'll get your RIO when you get to the ship. And if you don't, give me a call. I'll fly with you.") The location scouts had decided it was more photo-genic than the Miramar O-Club, even though Miramar's club also had a great patio and nice pool.

We received a few days notice to show up for the Sunday evening event. I was pleasantly surprised to see most of the stars in attendance, and it turned out to be great fun. Almost all of the instructors made it, too. Even though Tom Cruise was a new star, we knew he was "somebody" by the coverage of his activities in the San Diego paper. Still, he was polite about meeting people and having his picture taken—of all the times to forget my camera! Fortunately, Kodak came through and got some great photos of instructors and stars.

Hollywood was leaving Miramar. It was time for us to get back to staffexes, FAST, and all of the other things that didn't make the script, as well as the Topgun class, the O-Club, and things that did make it.

In the interest of accuracy, I must add that they filmed the scene where the MiG-28 crew is surprised on another flight, too, with another RIO (Shine, Flex, or Sobs). It's almost impossible to say which version was used in the movie, but I think it was me. I wish they had let me keep my sleeves rolled up.

THIRTEEN

Make-Believe Turns Real

It's my turn again. "My name is Dave Baranek, call sign Bio. I've made two deployments with VF-24 and have 1,200 F-14 hours. I'll be giving the 'F-14 Combat Intercepts' lecture and briefing the flights against jammers later in the class."

"My name is Terry McGuire, call sign Circus. I have 1,000 hours in the world's finest fighter, the F-4 Phantom. . . ."

"I'm Jim Ray, call sign Jambo. I have 1,200 F-14 hours. . . ."

"My name is Pete Caulk, call sign Horse. . . ."

On it went through all the instructors.

Another Monday morning, this class started at 7:15 AM. At 7:45 we had a staffex in Classroom 2 while the Topgun class continued in Classroom 1. Paramount had been gone for weeks, and we hardly heard or talked about the movie anymore. I was scheduled for an afternoon brief for a 1v2 against a couple of RAG student pilots. Since the class would be in lectures all day we would fly against anyone at Miramar who wanted bandits. It sure beat sitting at my desk.

About 11:00 AM someone said, "Bio, Rat's looking for you."

Rat asked, "Can you go to Hollywood for a few days? Actually, unless you have a good reason, you're going. They want you up there tonight." Rat chuckled. He was a really nice guy, with a great way of asking people to do things, but he always thought out his approach beforehand and would convince you if you didn't agree.

I didn't have a good reason not to go; in fact, I wanted to make the trip. Rat said the writers had only scripted dialogue for about twelve minutes of flying scenes, but it looked like the movie would include almost twice that much, and they wanted help with all of the flying-related dialogue. Since communications was a big part of my F-14 Combat Inter-cepts lecture, he decided I was the best instructor to go. Admiral Cassidy's staff was getting my airline ticket, and I was to meet Smegs at Topgun at 3:00 PM. I drove home, packed a bag, then went back to the squadron.

Smegs was John Semcken. He had been a Tomcat pilot and went through the Topgun class but was getting out of the Navy. I had met him going through the RAG several years before. In a colossal case of good timing, he had been assigned to the Miramar public affairs office for his final year of government service, and so for several months he spent all of his time assisting with the production of the movie. Smegs worked at a level below Viper and Rat, in close contact with the production assistants, cameramen, and other crew who made the movie. He was a lieutenant about my age, and he put in many long days, often seven days a week, arranging, explaining, helping, listening, suggesting, coordinating, and otherwise supporting the project. Navy lieutenants were good at doing whatever needed to be done. We all knew Smegs even before the movie. At any one time there were fewer than two hundred lieutenants in Tomcat squadrons at Miramar, so it was possible to be familiar with pretty much every one of them. The movie people had complimented him on his enthusiastic hard work and effective assistance, which made all of us look good, so we were proud of him.

We arrived at San Diego's Lindbergh Field about twenty minutes before takeoff (this was in those days before tight security) and got on a commuter flight for the forty-minute trip to Burbank's Bob Hope Airport. Smegs and I didn't know each other well so on the flight up we filled in a lot of background. When we landed we may as well have made a deployment together, and this rapport turned out to be good for the work ahead.

We walked out of the airport, two guys in khakis carrying small bags. We were told to look for a white station wagon with Paramount on the side, and there it was. There was the only white wagon, we were the only two guys in khakis, so it was easy to make a positive ID and get going. An attractive young brunette was driving. It was a little after 5:00 PM and she had no trouble with the Los Angeles rush hour traffic.

When I think back on those years, I am sometimes amazed at all that happened on some days. The evening ahead would be one of them.

First stop was the other side of Bob Hope Airport. We went into a hangar that Paramount had leased to support production of the movie, in which they had built a convincing model of an F-14 cockpit. I met the talented special effects expert who built this beautiful full-size copy—based solely on some photocopies he had from the F-14 flight manual, unclassified volume. The front and sides had mounts for cameras and operators, and behind the mock-up was a screen onto which they could project sky and clouds as background. This would be the stage for the actors' flying scenes. It tilted and pitched, which would help provide a realistic look when the actors were sitting in the seats.

While Smegs talked to some of the other people, the effects guy and I climbed a ladder and looked in the cockpit. Wow, this guy is good. He told me how he found a round cathode-ray tube to substitute for the RIO's display in the F-14 and rigged it so he could display numbers and symbols. Then he asked me about labels for a few switches that he had not been able to decipher from the photocopies. I think he wanted to make me feel useful, but it also showed his attention to detail. These labels wouldn't be seen on camera, but we fixed them anyway. For a few of these puzzlers he had used nonsense labels, but for most of the unknowns he had spent time trying to figure out what would be in a Navy fighter. He took notes as I said, "That one should say Hydraulic Isolate; that's Missile Options; that's ACM Threshold; that's Azimuth Center." I had spent hundreds of hours looking at these switches while flying CAP missions over the Pacific, orbiting the carrier waiting to land, training in the simulator, studying the manual, or otherwise learning my trade.

He was proud of his work, and I was sincerely impressed, which made him even prouder. The entire crew at the hangar was committed to doing the best they could. It felt great to be able to help them just from my residual knowledge.

We only stayed at the hangar about thirty minutes, then got in our white wagon and drove to the main entrance for Paramount Studios, 5555 Melrose Avenue in Hollywood.

There was good security at their gate. The Paramount logo on the side of the car helped, but the guard checked the identity of our driver and verified that Smegs and I were on his visitor list. We entered the grounds of Paramount Studios. It looked just like the "movie studio" shown in countless films, with clean streets, no sidewalks, and large buildings packed closely together. I am sure Paramount uses their own property when they need to, so I had probably seen these buildings as props on the big screen.

Our driver took us to a large building a few blocks into the property. It was similar to an airplane hangar, and once inside we walked through a maze of offices and working spaces, with structural beams, plumbing, and other exposed utilities. It reminded me of our squadron spaces, a working area where function and serviceability took priority over aesthetics. Smegs and I threw our bags in a corner, not knowing where we would end up this evening.

Shortly after going inside we met up with Tony Scott. Smegs knew him from assisting with filming at Miramar, but I had met him only briefly. Now he expected to work with me for the next day so I registered with him. He was a very energetic Englishman, forty-one years old at the time, quick, and friendly. He restated our mission: to help develop dialogue for the flying scenes. We would work on radio communications and pilot–RIO comments within the cockpit, and would help the film editors with continuity. They had pieced together more than twenty minutes of short segments showing aircraft flying, but they weren't sure if it made sense.

A few minutes after we arrived, Tony got a phone call telling him of the death of famous civilian pilot Art Scholl. Scholl had been filming spins from his Pitts aerobatic biplane and was killed that afternoon when he crashed into the Pacific. Scholl had performed in air shows and aerobatic competitions since 1958 and worked with the entertainment industry for years. An expert at unusual flying, he was piloting an aircraft that was designed for dynamic rolls, loops, and spins. He had spent the day with a camera attached to his plane to record the view from an aircraft in a spin, for the "dual engine flameout" scene that results in the ejection and Goose's death. The person on the phone told Tony that Scholl made a brief radio transmission, "I've got a problem," before his crash. The call affected Tony personally and his demeanor became quiet and thoughtful. One of "his team" was gone.

I didn't know what to think. Being an aviation fan I had heard of Art Scholl (as I'd heard of Clay Lacy) and it was strange to think he had died filming a movie, this movie, that very afternoon. We all looked at each other, made some perfunctory comments, and sat in silence a few seconds. Tony said, "I've got to call his wife," and someone retrieved her home number. He knew she would be in shock, but he wanted to talk to her, and he did. A human whirlwind just moments before, he was thoughtful and consoling on the phone. He didn't hurry through the call, but there wasn't really very much he could say, especially so soon after the accident. The call helped us realize that Tony's expression of sympathy was all anyone at the studio could do at the time.

With this realization and with some determination we came back to the matter at hand. It had been busy and noisy when Smegs and I arrived, then became still and quiet for the few minutes around the phone calls, and then the pace and noise level gradually returned after a few more minutes. When the movie came out it was dedicated to the memory of Art Scholl.

The next event further helped restore normalcy by getting us out of the room for a while. When the actors had been taken for F-14 flights at Miramar, there was a movie camera mounted atop the instrument panel in front of them. It was planned to use this footage in the movie, and most of the actors had lines of dialogue for these sequences. We walked over to the theater to watch the footage.

It was a little before sunset when a dozen of us went from the production building to the theater, Smegs and I in our khakis, the others mostly in jeans and comfortable clothes. We talked quietly trying to get back to the task at hand and trying to get to know each other better so we could be more productive.

This was a full-size movie theater on Paramount's grounds, lavishly appointed, with large plush seats. Several actors were waiting—Tom Skerritt, Tony Edwards, a few others—but I stayed close with the production people and the groups didn't mix. Everything was set up and Tony called the shots, moving back to his high-energy, high-speed mode. We took our seats quickly, he said "Go," the lights dimmed, and the film rolled.

What we saw next was both hilarious and pitiful.

The screen was filled with the image of a young man from about the chest up, an actor, in the backseat of an F-14. He was wearing flight suit, helmet, mask—all the right gear—but he looked uncomfortable. For these clips the F-14 pilot had a switch to control the camera and coordinated with the actor when to turn it on. For the first few seconds of this segment the actor looked into the camera with resolve. Then the clouds and horizon in the background started to swing and swirl. You could tell by the moving straps and hoses that the Tomcat was maneuvering briskly, and the actor's head wavered and bobbed with the varying g load.

It was pitiful because after just a few seconds the man's gaze began to fade, then his face and his entire being began to wilt as he became sick from the maneuvering. The maneuvering and the wilting continued until the pilot turned off the camera.

It was humorous because he was in the theater laughing, and his buddies were laughing too. Apparently there was no permanent damage.

The clip lasted about thirty seconds and was followed by another, as they had all been spliced together for easier showing. The second clip started the same way, an actor looking forward with intensity. This time he tried to do what a pilot or RIO would do in a dogfight, look around to track bandits he was already fighting or scan the sky for new threats. But that lasted just one glance over his right shoulder because turning your head while the plane maneuvers is very disorienting if you aren't used to it. Small black F-5s swirled in the background, as this was a dogfight scene involving MiG-28s. In this clip the actor kept his head turned to the right, tried to look up, but then surrendered to the g's and let his head fall to his shoulder before the film stopped. Like the first, this clip was unusable.

The full-size theater could be called "practically deserted" with the audience of about twenty people, but it was filled with howls of laughter. The actors kidded each other with comments like, "That's some of your best work!" They also admitted, "I was so dizzy," and, "I got so sick."

Again, the next actor started with the determined look straight ahead but never progressed to looking around. His facial features softened and fell, to the delight of our small audience, and he finished with a pleading look at the camera. He seemed to physically shrink and several of us thought he actually turned green before the clip flickered out.

The film they shot could have been used for actors playing either pilots or RIOs, since 99 percent of the audience wouldn't be able to spot the differences between the F-14's front and rear cockpits. I can't even guess who we were watching, but they were all amusing.

The film ran a few minutes, then Tony said what everyone already knew, "We can't use any of this!" He cussed when he said it, but he wasn't really irritated; the cockpit mock-up at the hangar would work fine.

We walked back to the production building around 7:30 PM and returned to the upstairs editing area. Tony figured that everyone was hungry so he ordered a few pizzas. Smegs and I sat at an editing machine while Chris Lebezon, the assistant film editor, showed us what we would be working with. The motorized machine had a film reel on each side and a small screen in the middle. Simple controls allowed us to run the film forward or backward and vary the speed. On the right side of the front of the machine, a small plaque read:

Flashdance (1983)
Beverly Hills Cop (1984)

Chris explained that both of those movies had been hits and they were edited on this machine. He hoped it brought luck to this project. We watched a few of the flying scenes and took a break to grab some pizza, then continued working.

The assistant film editor's job at this time was to piece together short film segments, most only two or three seconds long, into logical aerial combat sequences. We started by looking at a sequence he had already assembled showing an F-14 engaged with a Topgun A-4, Maverick and Goose fighting Jester. We continued with the other flying sequences. Working with the director, Chris had organized the clips to support the plot. I wasn't familiar with most of the story points, so Chris explained the purpose of each sequence as he was showing it: Maverick and Goose facing challenges, Maverick revealing his skill as a fighter pilot, the pair making errors, and other key points. Tony was in the area and joined the discussion at times.

Although I had heard good things from Rat about the footage they were getting, this was the first time I had seen it myself and I was amazed at its quality and dramatic effectiveness. Even on the small screen of the editing machine, I thought the shots made the F-14 look spectacular—powerful, complex, and sleek—but also functional in its dirty gray paint. The footage came from different vantages, including cameras in the Learjet, ground-based cameras in Fallon, a camera in the cockpit of an F-5, and pod-mounted cameras attached to the outside of an F-14. As for the maneuvering shots, the Paramount crew had captured great images of a dynamic environment, and the aircraft were big enough to fill the screen.

Smegs and I spent about thirty minutes running through the flying scenes. We wanted to get a sense of it all before we started recommending changes. We both soon developed several suggestions and went through each sequence in detail. A few segments in the Maverick vs. Jester dogfight seemed out of place. Chris was pleasantly surprised at how quickly we came up with detailed recommendations, but with our experience at air combat this was second nature. He shuttled back and forth between clips and tagged them for rearranging. We moved on to the other flying scenes such as the 2v3 dogfight, other class flying scenes, and the MiG-28 encounters.

When we finished reviewing the flying sequences, Chris had to make the changes, so Tony talked to us about other things. For example, they weren't sure how to show progress through the movie, to let people know the class lasted longer than just a few days and was an intense period that required a significant commitment. I suggested they do a voice-over at the start of each flying scene to set the stage and provide perspective. Tony thought that was a good idea so Smegs and I came up with some simple descriptions of flights. Several of these were used in the voice-over, such as, "Gentlemen, this is hop nineteen, multiple aircraft, multiple bogeys. Your training is half over." We discussed a few other points, then Tony sent us back to our primary task for the trip, to develop dialogue for the flying scenes.

Smegs and I now sat on an overstuffed couch and watched the reedited film on a small screen while the film editor managed the machine. As we watched we easily fell into a pilot–RIO situation and almost instinctively spouted appropriate statements.

"Tally two A-4s, left ten o'clock level. Continue left turn."

"I'll target the left bogey."

"Roger, I'll target the right."

We had both done this hundreds of times, and the film was so good we could develop a dialogue on the spot, including intercom comments between the pilot and RIO as well as radio calls. We ran through all of the flying scenes and just said what we thought needed to be said. When we were finished, Tony was very happy. "That's what I want, boys! This is f***ing great!"

He asked us to do it again and add more comments. It was 9:30 PM or later but everyone was doing fine so we ran through it again. Tony told us to talk more. We told him one of our goals is to say as little as necessary and make each statement important, but he wanted a lot of raw material to work with, fighter talk, so Smegs and I went into gabby mode. We also came up with a few more rearrangements for the film clips.

While those changes were being made, Tony asked me what the RIO would say if he was in a dogfight, lost sight of the adversary, and then the next time he spotted the enemy plane it was in a firing position. I thought for a moment, then said, "The f-word."

"We can't say that," Tony replied, "because we'd get an R rating and we want PG."

"OK, he might just say, 'Shit!'"

"We can say that and stay PG."

By now I felt comfortable enough to mention to Tony three things that bugged me about the filming: the Tomcats were flying too close to their opponents (whether A-4s or MiG-28s); a wingman does not fly engagements in tight formation as shown; and we saw camera pods on one of the F-14s. Tony responded to each of these concerns.

He said the fighters and bandits had to fly close to make it look good on film. At realistic distances some or all of the aircraft would be specks. OK, that was true.

He said the wingman had to fly together so it was easy for an audience to interpret. OK, he's the professional.

Finally, he said the camera pods would only bother a few military pilots and others watching for details, and they would just have to accept it.

I didn't argue, I got back to work.

Smegs and I watched the flying scenes again. At this time they were purely flying scenes, without the shots of the actors in the cockpit mock-up. Those scenes would be filmed after our visit because we were developing the dialogue for them. We filled in more holes in our commentary, and by now we had developed a sense of what was coming next. Tony was happy with our progress so he sent someone to get a tape recorder.

The reel of flying scenes was rewound to the beginning while Smegs and I sat on the couch and the tape recorder was set up in front of us. Most people in the area were wrapping up their work, so a small crowd gathered in the room. When we were ready, an assistant turned on the tape recorder and Chris the film editor started the film. Smegs and I started talking, ICS, radio, and other comments, all one stream. It was easy for us, even with the extra chatter the director requested, and took about twenty quick minutes to run through all of the scenes. They didn't applaud when the last scene ended, but it was clear that the assembled crowd enjoyed the show.

About 11:00 PM Tony figured we were done for the day, even though he still seemed full of energy. He said he would buy us dinner and we accepted. We had accomplished a lot. Smegs and I grabbed our bags and headed downstairs with the rest of the crew, and by the time we walked outside Tony was rolling by on his powerful motorcycle. He waved and cruised past us, then took off. One of the Paramount people said he loved his bike and had just gotten permission to ride again after satisfying a contractual clause that prohibited it until the picture had reached a certain point of completion. Smegs and I got back into the white Paramount station wagon with the same driver who had picked us up at the airport.

We went to a nearby Mexican restaurant, the El Adobe Café, and sat at a large round table, five or six people in jeans and two in khakis. We ordered beers before dinner and Tony pulled out some cigars. I joined in. It wasn't something I did frequently, but I'd smoked a few in my day and this seemed like an appropriate occasion. Everyone at the table was happy with the movie's progress and the conversation was full of stories about flying, filming, and other adventures. We toasted Art Scholl.

Our Paramount driver dropped Smegs and me at the Beverly Hilton hotel about 12:30 AM. We checked in and went to our rooms.

I thought, "Wait a minute, I'm in Hollywood!" and went down to the bar for a beer. I wanted the evening to last a little longer. Three other people were keeping the bartender company but he broke away to bring me a beer. I saw a jukebox and thought I would try to kick-start the evening, so I played a couple of my favorite Van Halen songs, "Panama" and "Hot for Teacher." They did not sound good in a quiet bar at almost 1:00 AM, so I finished my beer and went to bed. It had been quite a day, even for a Topgun instructor.

We had arranged for a 10:00 AM pickup. Waking up that late was like a day off for me. The Paramount wagon rolled up to the hotel on time with a different driver. At the studio we went upstairs to the same working area, rejoined the same group, and quickly got back into rhythm.

Smegs and I watched the flying scenes again as a warm-up. We didn't even turn on the tape recorder, but it still sat on the table. While we were going through our dialogue, Tony decided to have a stenographer capture it and called to have one sent up immediately. Then he thought it might be valuable if one of the writers could sit in and listen to our comments, our inflection, and absorb as much of the intangibles as possible. He made more calls and found that one of the writers was available.

The room was filling up but we had worked with most of these people the previous night and we weren't nervous, anyway, just a couple of fighter guys talking fighter talk. The stenographer showed up and sat to the side of the couch, but in the "front row" of the crowd.

When the writer showed up, Tony introduced us, but I didn't write his name down or remember it. I'm sure he didn't remember mine either. We told him that fighter guys tried to say as little as necessary and make everything count. He said something similar to what Tony had told us, they had more than twenty minutes of flying scenes and dialogue would only make it more exciting and interesting, so the more raw material we could give them, the better.

With that, Chris started the reel and two of the gabbiest fighter guys ever seen started talking.

"Maverick, contact. Section, twenty degrees left at thirty miles, lined-out left."

"Cougar same."

"Maverick coming left. Altitude two-five thousand, speed 450."

"Cougar."

Tape recorder, stenographer, screenwriter—Tony wasn't taking any chances.

"Maverick, speck in the diamond. Tally two, targeting lead."

"Cougar has the trailer."

And so on.

Twenty minutes later, Smegs and I stopped talking. Someone turned off the recorder, the stenographer set her pencil down, and the writer took a deep breath. The crowd may have applauded this time, but they had made us feel comfortable and helpful, so applause was unnecessary. As people drifted back to their work I told the writer I was concerned that some of our comments were too technical, that a movie audience may not understand them. He said, "Don't worry, by the time I finish with them, you won't even recognize them."

My mind flashed forward to the movie's release. I envisioned overly cocky dialogue and my fellow instructors punching me in the arm. "Bio, what did you tell them up there?!"

Too late now.

We had accomplished our goals for the trip. And with bonuses such as seeing the cockpit mock-up, I enjoyed it more than most business trips. We had a small lunch and then Tony arranged for us to meet producers Don Simpson and Jerry Bruckheimer, the creative team that imagined this and many other megahits. Smegs and I spent a few minutes talking to them in an office, telling them sincerely that we thought the movie was coming along very well. And then it was time to go to the airport.

I got back to San Diego late Tuesday afternoon. I had one flight each day Wednesday and Thursday and three flights Friday.

Now I thought Hollywood was gone from Miramar and from my concerns, but not just yet. Rat asked each of the instructors who flew in the movie to write their name and call sign as they wanted it to be shown in the movie's credits. The credits. Damn, that would be cool.

Circus went with Terrence McGuire instead of just Terry, and Hollywood went with Gregory Dishart instead of Greg. I thought about my Mom's advice, but I was a lieutenant, dammit, so I wrote "LT Dave 'Bio' Baranek" instead of David.

A few weeks later someone said the credits were too long and Paramount could not include the instructors. I was disappointed but figured there wasn't much we could do about it. Besides, that week I had six flights, gave two lectures, and attended a murder board and a staffex.

Now Hollywood had definitely left Miramar.

FOURTEEN

Waiting for the Cork to Pop

When the movie people left Miramar, we immediately got back to our normal busy lives flying fighters and doing the other work of Topgun instructors. After all, each of us had sought this assignment, and from my own experience found it more fulfilling than imagined. We had been doing our regular jobs all along anyway.

It's an understatement to say we had no idea how big the movie was going to be.

In the month after I returned from Hollywood I had twenty-seven flights. The Topgun class finished on Friday, October 18, and on Sunday I flew to Oceana for FAST with Kodak, Sobs, Flex, Jaws, and the rest of the FAST team. Because I was on the East Coast I visited intelligence agencies for an update and returned to Miramar in time for a staffex, murder board, and the start of the next class on November 4. Even with all of the traveling and other activities, I kept up an average of eighteen flights a month throughout the year.

But the movie kept coming up.

A professional photographer friend sent me some slides of movie-related action created at special effects company USFX for scenes that could not be filmed otherwise, such as the complete destruction of MiG-28s and an F-14 from missile hits. The photos showed extremely detailed aircraft models up to six feet long. If you just focused on the model, it looked so real that everything else in the picture seemed out of place. After building these beautiful replicas, USFX filled them with flammables and charges and then suspended them from a crane outdoors so they had a real sky background. Using high-speed cameras they dropped each model and blew it up in the few seconds as it fell. For the movie, this footage was slowed down according to the scale of the models, resulting in jaw-dropping shots of exploding aircraft that looked real, even on the big screen.

I had seen "how they did it" shows on television so I had some concept of Hollywood special effects. But now the models were of airplanes that I flew, and the movie one that I had worked on, which added to my fascination with these photos. I showed the slides to other instructors, and several of us used the shots of the exploding black F-5/MiG-28 model in our class lectures.

By the end of the year yet another new Topgun commanding officer had been around for a few months. Topgun CO was a "bonus command" option for someone who had completed a successful tour as CO of a fleet squadron, so the Topgun front office was home to a parade of luminaries among Navy pilots. Their arrival and departure dates were frequently affected by larger issues such as availability of an air wing commander (CAG) position or command of a large replenishment ship, which was a stepping-stone to the prestigious job of commanding an aircraft carrier. With these considerations in play I was not surprised to have four COs during my two and a half years as an instructor.

Topgun One was now Dan Shewell, call sign Dirty (after the San Diego nightclub chain Dirty Dan's). He had also been CO at VF-24 near the end of my tour. Dirty was a colorful fighter pilot who started in single-seat F-8 Crusaders in the late 1960s and was a Topgun student in the third class to go through the school.

As Topgun One he commanded an organization that was growing in stature, not because of the movie but because of a change in our official responsibilities. We were now more formally involved in applying the expertise of Topgun instructors to Navy war planning and weapons system development. During those years thoughts of a major war were always on military minds, and it made sense to include Topgun with other Navy organizations that worked on issues much larger than 1v1 and 2vUNK. Dirty blazed many trails as Topgun joined these new projects and communities.

He enjoyed getting around San Diego, too, and one Monday he said, "Let's have the next MiG-killer Debrief at the Kansas City Barbeque, the place they used to film some scenes in the movie. I had dinner there over the weekend and it would be a great place for us."

The MiG-killer Debrief was one of several social events we put on for each class, and coordinating it was one of the small jobs I picked up when Tex left the squadron. I was in contact with about twenty men who had destroyed enemy MiGs in the skies over Vietnam and now lived in San Diego, pilots and RIOs whose names were among those stenciled in the stairwell in Topgun's hangar. Each class we would ask one of them to spend an evening talking informally with the students going through the class, telling the real story of their experience. Some recounted how their training helped prepare them, others told how it was deficient. They talked about radar and missile problems, and life-and-death combat. They explained how teamwork helped American fighters succeed against challenges such as hit-and-run tactics, and how in many cases they had conscientiously prepared so they were ready when the opportunity arose. The students always enjoyed these sessions, as did the instructors.

I was comfortable with the locations where we had always held the MiG-killer Debrief, the Miramar O-Club or the clubhouse of the Miramar golf course, so I was not excited when Dirty suggested I check on a new venue. I had barely heard of the restaurant and had never been there. But of course I said, "OK, Skipper," and called the barbeque.

I found owner Martin Blair friendly and ready to work with us to accommodate our group. I had to check it out ahead of time, so I went there one evening for dinner to find a busy, very casual bar and restaurant cluttered with photos and memorabilia. In short, perfect! Martin and his wife, Cindy, filled me in on their part of the movie, and how they shut down for a few days while cameras, lights, equipment, actors, and crew filled the place. In that same spirit they said they would be happy to support our modest MiG-killer Debrief, even though Topgun was hardly famous yet. Besides providing a great atmosphere and attitude, they served great barbeque, too.

Several months after filming was complete, I received a call from the San Diego office of the Testor Corporation, an established firm that produced a line of plastic model aircraft, paints, and other hobby supplies. Testors was working with Paramount to bring out three model kits in conjunction with the movie's release: an F-14, an A-4, and an MiG-28 version of the F-5. When they started looking for photos for these projects, they were routed through various offices and phone numbers until they reached me. Their small San Diego office was just a few miles from Miramar, so I drove over to visit them. Having built dozens of model airplanes as a kid, I couldn't resist this opportunity to see how the business operated. I agreed to bring along a few dozen photos.

Located in a small office park, their offices looked like a fun place to work, with unassembled kits, completed models, paints, tools, photos, diagrams, reference books, and other distractions as decorations. It was like a giant hobby room.

My contacts, John Andrews and Gary Cadish, were a few years older than me but showed an enviable enthusiasm for their work. Shortly after I walked in I noticed a new kit for the "Stealth Fighter," the mere existence of which was a topic of speculation at the time. True enthusiasts for aerospace matters and the modeling industry, these gentlemen had tapped every resource and used their own ingenuity to fill in the gaps, developing a model kit for an aircraft that the government didn't even acknowledge. They proudly told me that these Stealth Fighter kits had been big sellers in stores near the Lockheed Skunk Works facilities in Burbank, where work on the project was presumably being done. (Three years later the government publicly announced the Lockheed F-117, but it didn't look anything like the model.)

Our project was at the opposite end of the spectrum from Stealth, with plenty of resources and a big publicity effort in the works. John, Gary, and their coworkers were developing the packaging and instruction sheets for the kits related to the movie. They showed me their work so far and I left my slides with them. When the model kits were released several months later, they gave me a few, which had several of my photos on the boxes. Included in the small print on the back of each box: "Photographs courtesy of Lieutenant David Baranek."

As 1986 arrived, Topgun life continued as before. Five-week classes started in January and March, we gave FAST at Miramar and Oceana, and we continued with the flights, meetings, parties, and other events that made it a great job.

Monday afternoon, April 7, I was working in the training office and got a phone call from a former squadron intelligence officer (like Kodak was at VF-2 before he became a Topgun instructor). I will call him Frank, but that's not his real name. When Frank left the Navy he went to work for the CIA. He asked if I could go to dinner the next night in Huntington Beach, seventy-five miles up the coast from San Diego, to meet someone interesting. When I said I could, he asked me to bring a few other instructors and said we could bring our wives or girlfriends, but we could not tell them who we were going to have dinner with until we got in the car. It sounded intriguing. He said he would call me back in a few minutes and tell me who we were meeting, since he didn't want to say the name in the same phone call. The information wasn't classified, he just wanted to be careful.

(It would've been a security violation to talk about classified information on a regular telephone, and he wouldn't use an illegal work-around such as breaking it into two calls.)

About two minutes later Frank called again and asked if I recognized the name Victor Belenko, which I did. He was the Soviet Air Force pilot who in 1976 delivered the impressive and mysterious MiG-25 Foxbat fighter to the West by breaking away from his training formation and making a daring run, landing at Hakodate airport in Japan where he asked for asylum. The event was front page news, and as a college student absorbed with the prospect of flying fighters, I read everything I could about it. Yes, I knew the name Victor Belenko.

In the years after his departure from the Soviet Union he traveled to U.S. bases and gave classified briefings that helped us get a sense of the enemy, which the Soviet Union most certainly was at the time. I had seen him at one of these briefings when I was in Pensacola, along with two hundred other officers who listened in awe, and now I was going to dinner with him.

Frank gave us the name of a restaurant on the Pacific Coast Highway and said to be there at 8:00 PM. He described Belenko and his group so we could recognize them, as he wasn't going to join us.

Several of us went to dinner. When we arrived we met an attractive female CIA contact who introduced us to Victor and two other pilots who had recently defected from a country that was fighting a Soviet occupation force at the time. The two other gentlemen were young and new to the United States. They didn't speak much English but seemed to enjoy the evening.

Victor also enjoyed the evening. He was gregarious and loved attention, and our group of about ten men and women was just right to keep him occupied. He spoke English with a strong accent and peppered his comments with frequent profanity. We talked openly about airplanes, weapons, the fighter pilot life, the United States, and similar subjects, avoiding detailed discussions about tactics or technical information. The restaurant was busy and loud so our discussions were lost in the noise.

At one point Victor roared, "Don't ask so many f***ing questions!" We all laughed and no one around us reacted, so it was a good environment for our gathering. We kept asking questions, and he kept answering.

The evening was an introduction to another new duty for me. The CIA was going to arrange for Belenko to be available several times a year for formal and classified discussions with the Topgun class, and I became their contact. It was neat to drive to San Diego's Lindbergh Field and pick up a former Soviet fighter pilot. He didn't treat me like one of his new personal friends—he spent time with important and famous people, and I was just another occasional chauffeur—but I enjoyed our spirited discussions on the thirty-minute drives back and forth to Miramar. We were both opinionated fighter guys and found that to be our common language.

MiG killers and MiG pilots were the types of people I thought Topgun instructors met. I didn't expect I would meet Hollywood directors, racing pilots, and model-kit makers, but they were enthusiasts for their craft, too, and I'm sure they sensed my genuine admiration for their various accomplishments.

A week after dinner with Belenko, Dirty and I climbed into an F-5F and took off for Key West. A gaggle of new instructors had reported to Topgun and time in Key West would allow us to focus on instructor-under-training flights to help bring them up to speed.

One of the new instructor pilots was Dennis Broska, call sign Loner, who flew one of the F-14s during filming of the movie. Flying in the movie had nothing to do with him becoming an instructor, as he'd been on the Wish List since he went through the class more than a year before. The fact that his squadron CO picked him to fly in the movie was just another testament to the skill and commitment he showed in everything related to flying. It was an affirmation of the staff's decision to put him on the list.

I put what I needed for Key West in a large bag and dropped it off at the hangar Thursday morning. On Friday a working party of sailors loaded all of these bags on a Navy cargo plane, along with the tools and equipment that maintenance would need to keep our jets going. The cargo plane performed double-duty, providing the forty sailors who joined us on the trip airline-style seats in half of the plane, while the pallets with luggage and equipment filled the other half. They got to Key West Friday afternoon, unloaded, and started preparing the working spaces we would use for the detachment.

I put a few days' worth of casual clothes in my smaller helmet bag, the olive green nylon bag I was issued in Pensacola to carry my helmet, but which all aviators use to carry a weekends worth of clothes whenever we were on the road. Navy aviators hardly ever put their helmet in it, using them instead for everything else. A helmet bag for an aviator is like a briefcase for a lawyer. The F-5F had a roomy cockpit for such a small jet, and I found a place for my helmet bag in a rear corner of the cockpit.

We left Miramar Thursday morning and enjoyed a cross-country flight, climbing to thirty-one thousand feet and flying at 480 knots with the airliners. We only had the range to fly from Miramar to El Paso (705 statute miles), where we refueled at Biggs Army Airfield. We then flew the 570 miles to Bergstrom Air Force Base near Austin, arriving in time for a late lunch. Dirty headed for Houston while I hung out with Darbs and his family, catching up with my good friend from Pensacola and VF-24.

Late Saturday morning, Dirty and I continued east, landing at Pensacola for a quick refuel (gas and go), and arriving at NAS Key West about 4:00 PM on Saturday, April 19.

The advance party was set up and ready. They had told everyone flying over when to arrive, so several other instructors arrived in A-4s and F-5s about the same time we did. Advance party members drove rental cars out to the flight line to meet us, something that would never happen at Miramar but seemed like a nice touch on a detachment. Even further removed from normal operations was their offer of refreshments, cold beers from a cooler in the trunk of one of the cars.

Unusual? Yes. But it was late afternoon, it was warm and breezy, we were done flying for the day, and we were on detachment to Key West. It was easy to rationalize. We left the airfield to change and hit the town.

It was a different Bio on the Key West detachment compared to the new instructor who made the previous trip. Now I had been at Topgun a year and a half and was therefore one of the old guys. As a RIO I was definitely a minority on the staff—around this time we had four or five RIOs out of eighteen or twenty total instructors—but I had established and proven myself. I gave a tactics lecture and a FAST lecture and had become head of the FAST team. I was briefing, leading, and debriefing class flights as well as other training flights. I had learned much and taught much, lost and won arguments, made and corrected mistakes. I knew my facts and mission, the aircraft and weapons, the material and the students.

For me it was a great Key West detachment.

In five days I flew six 1v1 training flights with new instructors, plus a 4vUNK against some fleet Tomcats in town to take advantage of the consistent great weather and operating areas near the field. I also flew one air-to-air gunnery flight, shooting at a six-foot by twenty-foot banner towed on a long cable behind another aircraft. During these detachments shooting the banner was almost equal in priority to training new instructors, as a way of maintaining instructor skill and credibility.

We were busy and enjoying our normal instructor lives, but the movie again became an issue. First, Paramount invited all instructors to a preview at their theater in Hollywood and they needed to know who would attend. This would be the week after we got back from Key West so Rat collected names and sent them to Paramount.

Second, they were having a "West Coast Benefit Premiere" in San Diego in mid-May, and advised us that tickets would cost $50 apiece. You might say we were taken aback. It wasn't even the "world premiere." Weren't we Topgun instructors special? On the practical side, most of us would be taking wives or dates and $100 was pricey just to see a movie, even if it was about us, sort of. The resolution to this micro quandary happened quickly, when Hughes Aircraft Company, manufacturers of the radars in the F-14 and F/A-18, generously offered to cover the cost of two tickets for each Topgun instructor. So Rat once again sent in a list of names.

I left Key West after a week, flying back to Miramar with Player on a Saturday so I could give a FAST course the following week. The busy schedule felt comfortable by this time and kept us from getting bored.

FIFTEEN

Top Gun Becomes a Blockbuster

At 7:00 PM on April 28 I was driving to Paramount's theater in Hollywood with my wife, Laura, for the cast and crew preview of the movie. I had been married for ten months, and . . .

Married?

It would have been impossible to do justice to the story of our relationship in a book about flying, so I left it out to this point. But here's the short version. I met my future wife a few days before Jaws and I started the Topgun class as students, when I was a lieutenant in VF-24 and she was a senior at San Diego State University. I was happy to see that she handled the fighter-squadron lifestyle well. We dated more than two years before we got engaged, and our wedding was a month before the Paramount filming at Topgun. Laura left the VF-24 Christmas party with me when I had my preboard with Sunshine late on a Friday night, kissed Tom Cruise at the cast and crew party at the North Island O-Club pool—on the cheek—and was part of the group at dinner with Victor Belenko.

And now we were driving to Hollywood to watch the movie at Paramount's on-site theater.

When Rat told us about this in Key West (only a week before) he said there were two showings. Most instructors picked the early show, but considering my FAST duties I picked the late one, which started at 9:00 PM.

I had begun this day, a Monday, at 7:30 AM by delivering my Maritime Air Threat lecture to an extra large audience, the officers in four F-14 squadrons and two E-2 squadrons in Air Wing 2 and Air Wing 15. It was unusual to run two air wings through FAST at the same time but was dictated by their schedules and Topgun's schedule. I was the FAST program officer, I had set it all up, so I knew it was the best option.

After my lecture I returned to the squadron to work on other things for a few hours, then went to the simulator building and spent the afternoon training pilots and RIOs to defend their carrier, taking turns with Sobs and Flex running the simulator and debriefing the crew. In the next building a team of E-2 NFOs ran E-2 crews through scenarios in their simulator. Though not Topgun instructors, we closely coordinated with them due to the E-2's importance in carrier defense. I took the last simulator run, which finished at 5:00 PM, conducted a twenty-minute debrief, then went home to change and pick up Laura.

We headed for Hollywood, 120 miles of mostly freeway driving, arriving in time for a quick dinner at the Hard Rock Café on Beverly Boulevard in Los Angeles. We then drove the four miles to Paramount, where the security guard carefully checked my name against his list before waving us through the gate. The fact that I was a Topgun instructor didn't matter: He was checking in movie stars and studio bigwigs, and some military guy was just another random visitor. I knew where the theater was from my visit the previous September to work on dialogue. The first show had ended and people were leaving, so we found a parking spot easily.

In front of the theater we joined a few other Topgun instructors, though most of the crowd consisted of cast and crew who worked on the movie and their significant others. The cast and crew preview is a standard Hollywood event, rewarding those who make a movie with the opportunity to see it before the public does, and it was a professional crowd accustomed to stars, so there was no press or fanfare. The few of us who weren't Hollywood people casually looked around and restrained our enthusiasm over seeing celebrities. In any case, we were here to see the movie. We only waited a few minutes before entering the theater, as plush as I remembered, but this time it was absolutely full.

With no previews of coming attractions, the movie started. The sound was cranked way up—a little too loud in my opinion, but I figured that it supported Tony Scott's vision of the movie as an intense experience.

I was not prepared for what I saw. The opening text provided a concise explanation of Topgun's origin while the rhythmic background music set a cool mood. As the image developed from black into the dramatically lit carrier flight deck action, jet engine sounds and vague announcements punctuated the background audio. And then it all ripped into Tomcats making afterburner cat shots to the sound of Kenny Loggins's "Danger Zone." It started hip, fast, and hot, and kept going. Scott, Bruckheimer, Simpson—the whole crew who put it on film really got it! Though I had seen some of the footage on my trip with Smegs, seeing the final product on the full-size screen was breathtaking. It took a conscious effort not to say "Wow!" every few seconds.

The movie lasted almost two hours, but I was so excited it seemed like minutes. The audience applauded enthusiastically, and everyone sat through the credits. I recalled the last thing I heard on the subject, that the credits were too long and there wasn't room to list the instructors, so I was surprised and thrilled to see our names on the screen as "Top Gun instructors and MiG Pilots." And my name was first! It had been a long day, but that sure added a charge to the evening.

When I looked at all of the credits—Pete Pettigrew as technical adviser, Rat and Bozo listed (by their proper names) as aerial coordinators, Flex Destafney (a former Topgun instructor) as Navy dialogue consultant, to mention just some of the Navy names I knew—I realized how much more work had gone into the film than I had been aware of.

The excited audience swept out of the theater into the cool evening. Things seemed especially quiet after the high volume of the movie, but I was excited and had a huge grin on my face as I talked to Laura and the other instructors and scanned the crowd.

Then, right in front of me, appeared the cute face, iridescent blue eyes, and bright blonde hair of Meg Ryan. I hadn't met her during the filming (I never met Kelly McGillis, either), and my mind went to work. Wow, she is even cuter in real life than on the screen. OK, something helpful would be nice. Oh, yeah, some of the guys were talking about a scene at a house where she was notified of her husband Goose's death and how everyone on the set was crying. It must have been cut because the movie only had a fairly short scene of her and Maverick in Navy quarters.

Those thoughts went through my mind in a flash, and suddenly we were face-to-face. I said, "Hi, Meg. Hey, you're really cute! Your scene after Goose died was so sad. I'm glad they didn't use that other scene, I heard everyone was in tears when it was filmed." I made one or two more goofy comments . . . but did I just tell Meg Ryan, "I'm glad your big scene was cut"?

She looked up at me with a very polite smile, nodded, and we were quickly swept in opposite directions. What a relief. I felt like a star struck fan. I was glad I didn't tell her I was a Topgun instructor! Laura said what she heard didn't sound too bad and that Meg probably hears it all the time.

I didn't see any other celebrities that night, which was probably best for me.

At Topgun the next day we talked about the movie, and instructors were amazed at the superb quality of the aerial photography and how many flying scenes were included. Thanks to Rat reading the script in the ready room we were prepared for the basic storyline as well as the "Hollywood" elements of the plot, such as the romance between Maverick and Charlie, Maverick riding his motorcycle beside the runway, and others. We accepted them as essential for the film to appeal to a large audience, admitting that no one wanted to watch a bunch of guys eating sandwiches in a crowded ready room or coming in on weekends to practice lectures in empty classrooms. But the conversation kept going back to the incredible flying scenes. I would say that as a group we enjoyed the movie and were happy with how it came out.

The next movie-related event would be May 15, 1986, the San Diego premiere. Someone suggested the instructors arrive in limousines, and we all agreed because we were excited about being part of something big. The cast and crew preview helped, for we could see for ourselves that this was a big-league, first-class production.

The "world premiere" was held in the Washington, D.C. area, which disappointed us a little. After all, the story was set in San Diego, Topgun was at Miramar, and it would be cool to attend a world premiere for a movie about us. But holding it in Washington was Paramount's nod to the high-ranking people who agreed to let the Navy support the movie. So our event was called the West Coast Benefit Premiere according to the extra-large tickets delivered to the squadron. With Hughes Aircraft generously covering the $50 per person for our reserved "Gold Circle seating," the limos were easy to swing, even for us poor lieutenants.

The week of the premiere started for me at 7:00 AM Monday, when I gave F-14 Combat Intercepts to the Topgun class. After more than a year with the lecture, giving it caused little stress yet provided a sense of satisfaction. Like all instructors, I constantly made refinements to keep it synchronized with changes in other lectures and reflect developments in the real world, experience with the class, or changes in tactical thought. Incorporating these changes added an element of freshness for me as lecturer. Working in front of a class of fighter pilots and RIOs was enough to prevent complacency, anyway. The class respected the instructors, but the class demanded respect in return, which was a good balance. I was aware that I was representing not only "Bio," but also Topgun's reputation.

It was a full week. After the lecture Monday, I had a 2vUNK. Tuesday I briefed and led a 2vUNK, Wednesday I had two 4vUNK flights on the TACTS Range, Thursday morning I briefed a 2vUNK, and the premiere was Thursday night at seven thirty.

Scheduled events finished a little early Thursday and we all went home to change into our dress uniforms. Our wives and girlfriends dressed formally. We all met at the Town and Country Hotel in San Diego's Mission Valley, in anticipation of the reception we heard would be held there after the premiere. As I pulled into the parking lot I saw the line of six white limousines and a few other instructors with their wives and girlfriends. With the trappings of the premiere, we were even more excited about the movie.

Laura and I walked along the line until we found the car with our names. We were riding with Jaws and his girlfriend (and future wife), Mary, and Kodak and his wife, Mary-Anne. Waiting beside the limos, instructors checked each other to make sure we had our tickets, and inspected our dress uniforms to see that we had the medals and insignia on correctly. We complimented each other's companions and chatted until it was time to go, then climbed into the cars, our anticipation building.

As we approached the theater we saw a lot of other Miramar people, and all of the officers were in their dress uniforms and having a good time. So it wasn't all about us Topgun instructors, it was a movie about everyone who flew fighters. I could accept that.

The theater lobby was crowded and chaotic, but we got through and made it to our seats. The Cinema 21 was one of the largest movie theaters in San Diego, with a capacity of almost one thousand. It was filled with an excited and boisterous crowd, different from the professionals at the preview in Hollywood. For most of us this was our only shot at a movie premiere. Plus, many in the crowd were Miramar aviators, so we knew each other. The atmosphere was, "Party!"

There were some brief introductory remarks and then the movie started. My enjoyment of the dramatic visuals, stunning flying scenes, powerful musical score, and familiar subject matter was only magnified by the energy of the crowd. It was more like a rock concert than a movie. The fact that I had seen the movie before was almost irrelevant, I enjoyed it and again the time passed quickly, and then we were back in the limos.

There was a party a few blocks from the theater at the Stardust Hotel (now the Handlery Hotel and Resort), but we instructors went back to the party at the Town and Country Hotel ballroom. Our limos dropped us a short distance from the crowded entrance, and as we walked up I saw some black limousines that looked more like "real" limos than our white rentals. People said that producers Bruckheimer and Simpson were there. We hadn't planned anything after the movie, so it was great to enter the ballroom and find a complete party setup: a band, food, drinks, and a big crowd.

So this is what a movie premiere is like.

The entire grand evening of celebration was a thrill for me. But even more, I was savoring the realization of this event that had been in my mind for a year. I had felt fortunate to go through the Topgun class as a student, then to return as an instructor, and now I knew that I was extremely lucky to be there when the movie was made and to be a part of it.

After a while several instructors signaled each other to go to one end of the dance floor. It happened quickly and without planning but we all headed to the area, gathering other Topgun instructors as we went. We were going to be photographed as a group.

Soon about eighteen of us were arranged in two rows, all of the current Topgun instructors. A bank of photographers took aim from about twenty feet in front of us. When we were set and standing still, they started shooting. The flashes were like visual popcorn for twenty or thirty seconds. My smile grew and I slapped the back of the guy next to me.

I felt like an astronaut.

This was really cool, a photo of the real Topgun instructors, and I was in it. We all started smiling and laughing, and by the time all of the photographers had taken a few photos it felt like we were somebody.

We instructors stayed at the party awhile longer. Then it faded and we all gradually left, returning to our quiet cars chilling in the San Diego night and driving ourselves home to reality.

The next morning I had a nine forty-five brief for a 2vUNK. No dress uniform, no limos, no photographers, just the stuff I joined the Navy for: jets flying at each other at 900 knots in the clear sky over the dark blue Pacific. Missile shot calls, 6.5 g's, fuel checks, and kneeboard cards provided the atmosphere for this party. The thorough brief and insightful debrief substituted for the storyboards and the reviews. Back to the real world of a Topgun instructor. I never saw that group photo of Topgun instructors in the San Diego paper or anywhere else.

On Sunday afternoon, a dozen "Topgun couples" went to the San Diego Padres baseball game and watched the Beach Boys afterward. It was big fun, as always. But we weren't done with the movie, not by a long shot. The preview and premiere were just the lightning, to be followed by reverberations of thunder.

As I was walking out of the Padres game, three teenage girls yelled to me, "We want to buy your shirt!"

I was wearing a white golf shirt emblazoned with TOPGUN and a silhouette of an F-5. I don't think anyone had ever made a comment in almost two years of wearing it. I'd been in the sun about five hours by this time and the only place this shirt needed to go was the washing machine . . . after dinner at the Old Town Mexican Café, of course. I felt comfortable talking to them because Laura was with me, so I got a name and mailing address and actually sent them three Topgun shirts, in appropriate sizes. They sent me a check for the cost.

In the days after the premiere I took a call at the squadron from Bob Lawson at the Tailhook Association, whose missions are to support aircraft carriers and sea-based aircraft and inform the public of their role in national defense. They are the keepers of the flame for carrier-based aviation. Tailhook was slightly irate that Paramount named the movie *Top Gun* instead of "Topgun." Bob explained that the Navy officially decided that the name was one word, and Paramount clearly used two words in the title of the movie.

I had not given the matter much thought, and it was a little late to fight that battle, so Bob and I just caught up on news related to naval aviation. To be fair, Topgun was written as two words within the Navy plenty of times, too.

The squadron received numerous media requests related to the movie, from a variety of outlets. Almost every instructor got involved, and I did two interviews. The first one was for the regional newspaper, the *North County Times-Advocate*, the second for the *Pacific Flyer*, a widely distributed monthly that catered to aircraft enthusiasts.

Interviews for publications were relatively easy since I had the chance to refine my statements and make points carefully, even more so since these writers were not looking for dirt but rather some elements of interest related to *Top Gun*.

They were weeks apart, but both interviews went about the same. Each time the writer had no trouble getting on the base, and I met him at the gate outside our hangar and escorted him up to the ready room. It was relatively quiet and the background of occasional radio communications between the SDO and an aircrew added to the ambience. As we talked about the movie as well as the real-life Topgun, I answered specific questions and gave some opinions. We walked out to the flight line to look at the jets and take some photos, and that was it. Total time was about thirty minutes for each.

Both writers made a point to mention my name and quote me, and my comments in both articles are similar. From the *Times-Advocate*:

"I'm glad they showed the hard parts," said Lt. David Baranek, radar intercept officer instructor at the Navy Fighter Weapons School. "The movie doesn't glamorize the training. And the students are tense. It's a highly competitive situation."

Baranek said he knows of no one who would have been a character model for either of the male leads. "Maverick is not just a maverick. He does things differently, that's all. The conflict in the movie and his behavior show that he's good."

"The Top Gun instructors' job is to develop, to take off the rough edges," Baranek said.

Reading this now, I think it is obvious that I didn't spend too much time preparing for the interview. (Isn't a definition of a maverick "someone who does things differently"?) Both papers used my photos of the black F-5s from the filming flights, and the *Pacific Flyer* ran a photo of Loner and me, since we did that interview together.

I was happy to give a couple of interviews and see my name in the paper. I saved copies.

There were other print interviews and some for television. The TV interviews were more demanding, partly because of the self-generated pressure of a camera in your face, but also because statements were recorded in real time. These weren't *60 Minutes*-style ambush interviews, but mistakes could be embarrassing. Instructors usually spent some time preparing for the on-camera interviews, and of course we debriefed them afterward.

One afternoon, a reporter and crew were at the squadron and asked if they could interview a pilot getting out of a plane.

It sounded like an interesting setting and got the necessary approval, so the SDO called Jambo and Flex, pilot and RIO in an F-5F, after they landed and asked if they minded being interviewed. They said it would be no problem.

The camera crew ran out to the flight line and set up so the jet would taxi and park next to them. I wasn't there, but I heard it went well—up to a point. The plane captain directed Jambo accurately to the desired spot then gave him a quick engine shutdown, and he and Flex climbed out of the plane. They looked cool in their gear, standing by the sleek F-5F and cradling their helmets. The reporter asked them a couple of easy questions, then referred to one of the tag lines from the movie: "Would you say you are in the top 1 percent of naval aviators?"

Jambo thought for a second and said, "No. There are a lot of talented pilots and RIOs out there." Flex agreed.

"Cut!"

The reporter tried to get them to go along, but they would not agree with the statement. In the end, the reporter completed the interview and didn't ask the "top 1 percent" question again.

Later in the ready room we all thought Jambo and Flex handled it correctly. Topgun instructors took enough heat for being egotistical; we didn't need any video evidence. We didn't feel that way anyway. Really.

The squadron received a small amount of fan mail after the movie came out, which was more than we received before. A few kind people wrote to say thanks for doing a good job. One that got our attention was a long letter from a pilot in Oregon, an instructor who taught aerobatics to pilots of single-engine Cessnas and Pipers. He wrote thoughtfully about how a small amount of aerobatic skill made his students much better pilots by giving them confidence, teaching them how to handle their planes in emergencies, and increasing their knowledge of their aircraft. He asked Topgun's opinion on a few specific questions about maneuvering. It was a great opportunity to establish a dialogue with a talented, enthusiastic professional.

Except we didn't do that. Amazingly, we talked ourselves into the worst-case scenario. What if we reply to this gentleman, and he has an accident, and people say those Topgun guys told him about maneuvers? No one even wrote him a reply.

Then Ron Reagan Jr. (son of the president) filmed a segment for *Good Morning, America* from Topgun, early one morning in an out-of-the-way part of the hangar. No problem, just another nice media story. Except the aerobatic instructor pilot saw that show, and a week later we received a scathing letter from him about how we treated the media like royalty but would not even acknowledge a fellow pilot. We knew we had messed-up with this guy. But no one wrote him back after the second letter, either.

Top Gun was a big hit with the public. It was number one at the box office its first week, got knocked out of that spot by *Cobra* (a Sylvester Stallone movie) and *Poltergeist II*, then returned to number one. It didn't set any one-week records, especially compared to the blockbusters of more recent years, but it had a steady draw. In ten weeks it broke $100 million. Amazingly, in September *Top Gun* again returned to the number one spot almost four months after its release. And when the year ended, *Top Gun* was the top grossing movie of the year, eventually racking up a U.S. box office take of almost $180 million and similar international number for a grand total of more than $350 million.

The movie's title song, Kenny Loggins's "Danger Zone," was another successful result. It was a hit song and an exciting music video that startled me the first time I saw it, with some great flying scenes from the movie. The song perfectly fit producer Don Simpson's description in a *USA Today* interview that the *Top Gun* sound was "kick-butt rock 'n' roll." While working around Tony Scott I heard the phrase, "full-tilt boogie rock 'n' roll in the sky," so I knew the music had to match the flying. "Danger Zone" nailed it.

The soundtrack had other hits, too, including "Take My Breath Away," a ballad by the pop group Berlin, which made it to number one. Echoing the movie's box office success, the *Top Gun* soundtrack album sold nine million copies, making it one of the biggest-selling soundtracks ever.

So all of the work, planning, discussions, energy, commitment, risk, and skill paid off. The movie was seen and enjoyed by millions, and its cultural influence was even wider. Besides the sales numbers, there were newspaper and magazine articles about "*Top Gun* style"—flattop haircuts and leather jackets with patches. Civilians were wearing Navy blue ballcaps embroidered with Top Gun and we started seeing the term "Top Gun" in advertising. It felt good to be even a small part of it.

On June 15, I was again in Oceana. We had planned to spend the week giving FAST lectures and simulators but canceled that when the air wing's schedule changed at the last minute, so we spent the week flying and giving lectures to squadrons that requested them. It was good exposure, because we constantly worked to avoid the appearance that we were focused on Miramar, even though we were based there.

I had been in Oceana for a conference the previous week so I was the detachment coordinator, and Sunday afternoon I went to the flight line to meet Loner, Kraut, Jambo, Pyro, and other instructors arriving in F-5s and A-4s. Of course I had a cooler of beer, but since this wasn't Key West I didn't drive my rental car out to the flight line and I handled the refreshments more discreetly.

Everyone planned to arrive between 4:00 and 5:00 PM, and the tower gave me an update on flight plans so I knew things were on schedule. Two jets flew over from Miramar that day, but others had departed San Diego in the days before and stopped along the way. As the first pilots arrived, we gathered by the camouflaged jets and waited for the rest, swapping stories about quick refueling stops, bad weather, helpful air traffic controllers, and other events that added color to cross-country flights.

Hollywood was one of the last to arrive, so he climbed out of his jet to a small crowd of other instructors. After a few comments he said, "I had lunch with Billy Joel." We thought this was cool, and not hard to believe considering our collective status as minor celebrities. On the trip over he had landed near Long Island to visit some friends, and they went to lunch immediately after his arrival. He was wearing his blue flight suit with Topgun embroidered on the front. When we were away from Navy bases we wore them frequently. And so Hollywood found himself in a blue bag in a small restaurant when a gentleman came over to him and asked if he was really in Topgun. Of course, he said yes. Then the guy invited him over to a quiet booth off to the side to join Billy Joel and his wife, Christie Brinkley, so Hollywood spent a few minutes chatting with them. He told us Billy Joel looked better *in pictures* than he did in person, but Christie Brinkley looked better *in person* than any picture he had seen.

It was the most interesting story of the gathering on the flight line, but it didn't even get a repeat during dinner at The Raven a few hours later. We had a big week ahead of us and a lot of business to talk about, and the local pals who joined us had a lot of catching-up talk about friends, squadrons, and other subjects more enduring than a movie. The movie had been out for a month. For us the wave had crested.

During this trip to Oceana I went to the Navy Exchange— similar to a department store on the base, open only to government employees—wearing a Topgun golf shirt. As I passed a young boy and his mother, I heard the kid say excitedly, "Mommy, look! That man is in Topgun!" I got an inner feeling of satisfaction, something firemen must be very familiar with as the idols of virtually every young boy.

For me it lasted about two seconds because his mother said wearily, "Son, these days everyone's in Topgun."

SIXTEEN

Changing of the Guard

Ranks of Topgun instructors in dress white uniforms stood at "parade rest" in the warm afternoon sun. With our feet apart at roughly shoulder width, hands clasped behind our backs, our formation looked smart and was not as taut as "attention." Parade rest is the position commonly used while waiting, and we were waiting for the change of command ceremony to start.

Some of us started the day early and squeezed in two ACM missions on the Yuma range. This class had some impressive students, RIOs who had the bandit presentation **suitcased** at thirty miles, pilots with the SA to adapt as we presented them challenging threats. And yet, many times several bandits would survive to the merge, to engage. There were always important points to be made in the debrief.

When it was time to come home, Jambo remembered that the rules at Miramar limited formations to four aircraft. We had five jets so he called Dirty and asked for backing if tower personnel complained that we broke this obscure rule. Since the ceremony that afternoon was in honor of Dirty's change of command and his retirement from the Navy, he said, "Sure, you guys can handle it. What are they going to do, fire me?"

We came into the break with five jets, a mix of F-5s and A-4s. I know we looked sharp to ground observers as well as from my vantage point as Dash Three. Miramar tower didn't voice any objections.

We landed and quickly changed from our flight suits into our uniforms, then joined the rest of the squadron forming into ranks on the bright concrete next to Hangar 1. Neat rows of officers, chief petty officers, and sailors in white uniforms stood in front of neat rows of camouflaged A-4s and F-5s. One Air Force officer in his blue uniform punctuated the white array, F-15 pilot Joe Leister, call sign Gozer, who had recently replaced Boa.

A few minutes before the ceremony started a guy in a $1,000 suit walked through the gate, accompanied by two flashy girls. Sailors escorted them to folding chairs where they joined wives, girlfriends, COs and XOs from other squadrons, and other guests. Standing behind the guests, we turned our heads side-to-side to tell each other, "That's Kenny Loggins."

Dirty was being relieved by Commander Rick "Wigs" Ludwig, who had 275 Vietnam combat missions and had flown F-4s and F-14s at Oceana and Miramar. It was a typical fighter squadron change of command ceremony, forty-five minutes long, with speeches by a guest speaker (in this case, a three-star admiral from Washington), then Dirty, and finally Wigs. The speeches were only five to ten minutes each, but ceremonial trappings such as the chaplain's invocation filled out the time.

At the end of the ceremony everyone mingled and I made a point to say hello to Kenny Loggins, telling him I thought "Danger Zone" was a great song. We then went to the O-Club for the traditional party with all of the guests. The next night we had another party where instructors, wives, and girlfriends welcomed Wigs as Topgun CO.

Kenny Loggins's visit was one of the last movie-related events that I recall, and it was incidental to the ceremony. Mirroring the constant demands on the squadron, Skipper Wigs had plenty of substantial concerns to keep him occupied as he began his reign as Topgun One.

- The staff was growing, largely to accommodate those new responsibilities that started during Dirty's tour.
- We were designing (from the ground up) a new building to better support the Navy Fighter Weapons School, with an auditorium, classrooms, briefing facilities, offices, library, locker rooms, and amenities we did not even imagine in our old home in Hangar 1.
- The Navy finally admitted that the A-4 and F-5 were inadequate to simulate some of the threat aircraft faced by Navy and Marine Corps fighter pilots and RIOs, and new enemy fighters soon to enter service (the MiG-29 and Su-27) were more capable. So the Navy was buying

F-16N Fighting Falcons, special versions of a new Air Force fighter, to replace the F-5s and better simulate the coming threat. (Like most aviators we referred to them as Vipers, a reference to the Colonial Viper fighters from the original *Battlestar Galactica* TV series.)

The F-16s and the new building would arrive after I left, but I participated in the planning and preparation, as did most instructors to varying degrees. All of these changes added to the sense that Topgun was redefining itself to be more effective, making milestone improvements in its ability to train.

The normal personnel changes associated with all Navy squadrons reinforced the sense of a new generation. Most instructors who had been there longer than me, and who were in the movie credits, had already left or were about to leave. Tex, Organ, Otter, and more were gone. Jaws, Flex, Jambo, and Hollywood had orders and would depart in the next few months. New instructors had already arrived, including Zone, Tiger, Little Mac, Dirt, Rhino, Mort, Nick, another Tex, Redbone, J.J, and others. There were more new guys coming in than old guys leaving, but the Wish List was full of worthy candidates. Several pilots and a RIO who came through as students during my tenure were now returning as instructors, and they deserved it.

With two years in the squadron I was enjoying the senior status I now held. It's hard to believe that as a twenty-eight-year-old lieutenant I was an "old guy," but that's how it was. I had seen almost everything, was qualified to do almost everything, and had in fact done almost everything. I even got good at flying the F-5F. I had also switched rides, from my faithful '77 Trans Am to a pristine '74 Corvette convertible. Bright yellow, it was like new and looked good beside the other two Corvettes on the staff, Flex's classic gold convertible and Jaws's new black coupe. A couple of Nissan Z-cars, a Prelude, RX-7, and Jambo's Porsche Carrera added interest to the sedans in Topgun's parking lot.

As one of the old guys I carried increased responsibility for things like standardization among lectures and the highest standards of flying operations. But it turned out to be a natural progression; this level of performance had been expected of me since shortly after I arrived, and this expectation was explicitly stated. One of the many things I liked about Topgun was that there was no secret about what constituted acceptable performance, and no shortage of assistance or inspiration in attaining it.

Still, as I thought about my time at Topgun I had feelings that all of my work was walking out the door and that we were performing to meet the expectations of others. I knew this came with the blue suit, but I contemplated how nice it was going to be to return to a Tomcat squadron, where our work was for our own readiness, our own combat effectiveness, and our own squadron reputation. Maybe it was just a case of the grass is always greener, but I was starting to look forward to getting back to the fleet.

But being an old guy at Topgun had advantages. One came in August when I went to Hawaii for a week of flying with Marine Corps F-4 squadrons based at Marine Corps Air Station Kaneohe Bay on Oahu. Along the lines of our regular trips to Oceana, Topgun sent a small team of instructors to Kaneohe every year to give lectures and fly with the Marines and the Navy adversary squadron based at nearby

Naval Air Station Barbers Point. I had seen this trip come up every year, and now I was selected to go, along with two pilots, Circus (Marine Corps Phantom background) and Kraut (Navy Tomcat background). Kraut and I had in-depth experience fighting F-4s in the Topgun class, and the F-4 guys on the staff made sure we were up to speed for the trip. I had also bagged a few flights in the F-4 (having traded with F-4 RIOs and pilots for a hop in the F-5F) so I knew my way around their radar. Topgun's F-5s and A-4s couldn't fly across the Pacific so we flew over on an airliner and flew the local jets once we arrived.

The week in Hawaii was filled with aerial combat, as I gave two lectures and had nine good ACM flights in F-4s and TA-4s. To deal with the withering heat and oppressive humidity, when we landed and popped the canopy to taxi back to the line I guzzled the bottle of water I carried. I enjoyed the spectacular scenery of Oahu's eastern shore, the royal blue sky and brilliant clouds, and the enthusiasm and hospitality all of the squadrons showed us.

And so, despite looking forward to returning to an F-14 squadron, experiences such as the Hawaii trip tipped the balance for me. I wrote the Navy assignment office asking to remain at Topgun an extra six months. I came up with some compelling justification and the CO endorsed my letter.

They quickly denied my request, responding that the fleet needed experienced RIOs. As a small consolation, however, my orders were changed to give me one extra month in compensation for the delays I experienced when leaving VF-24. I would leave Topgun in February at the completion of the "standard thirty month shore duty tour."

An instructor left Topgun about every two months, so having a departure date was a common development. It was actually called a rotation date, signifying the cyclic nature of military tours and military orders. The routine had been the same in VF-24, every other Navy squadron, and every other military unit.

For the ops officer, training officer, and a few other planners, my rotation date was one more of the hundreds of events that affected the schedule. As with all instructors, the effect of my departure rippled through the staff. They would need to qualify more RIOs to fly with new pilots, plan for lecture turnover, pick a new instructor to take over the FAST program, and more.

On a personal level, having a rotation date meant that I knew when I was leaving, and not much more. I remained busy with a lot of great flights, lectures, meetings, parties, and all the other stuff we did. I was giving each of my lectures about once a month and flying an average of eighteen flights a month until my final few weeks. My last six months were similar to any other six-month block at the squadron, with a dash of amusement at turning over my lectures to new instructors. I turned Maritime Air Threat over to an eager new pilot, Zone, and handed over the rest of the FAST program and the F-14 Combat Intercepts lecture to Tiger, a sharp RIO who improved on everything that I did plus added his own touches. I hoped it had seemed like that when I picked up these projects, seemingly ages before.

But the amusement was tempered by the realization that the new guys were anxious for us old guys to get going. They were ready to establish their reps, to "take the stick." No surprise, really—you don't get to be a Topgun instructor by sitting back and waiting for things to happen.

I took my last two F-5 flights on February 12. It was the day before the class ended and the students were doing their big "coordinated strike" event at China Lake, similar to the mission that Jaws and I had flown as students nearly five years earlier, as had every class before us and since. The fighters applied all of their experience, sharpened in the preceding five weeks. In addition, they had real bombers (A-6s and A-7s), jammers, tankers, and other details to coordinate. They faced the challenging surface-to-air threats of the Echo Range as well as a swarm of Topgun bandits arrayed in a layered defense.

I was flying with Zone and we briefed at 6:30 AM with the rest of the bandits. But we were the last priority for an aircraft so we were assigned Topgun Forty-six, which needed some work completed before it could fly. Maintenance finished the job about an hour after everyone else took off so we launched and flew to China Lake alone. Thinking back on my thirty months, hoping for a last big flight, proceeding alone along the route that I had always traveled in a pack, it was almost melancholy. The sky was overcast. Perfect.

After landing at China Lake we refueled as quickly as possible and took off to try to join the fight, but we were a few minutes too late. Zone wanted me to have a good "last flight" so we zoomed around at low altitude. We didn't engage anyone, but there's a lot to be said for flying low and burning gas. We joined up with two other bandits and flew back to Miramar as a flight of three.

When we taxied to the Topgun line after landing, all of the instructors were there with bottles of champagne to spray me down in the traditional last flight celebration. They saved one for me to drink, since my workday was over. A blurry photo shows me with Rat, Nick, and even Jaws, who stopped by on a break from duties at his new squadron. The melancholy long gone, it was a nice finish to a great tour.

The next day the class ended and I started a week of leave, checked out of Topgun, and checked in to the RAG for three months of refresher training. It was Friday, February 20. I had been at Topgun thirty and a half months, so I got two extra weeks.

My Topgun tour was to end as it started.

Zone was going through training to fly the coming F-16s, which were state-of-the-art aircraft, significantly more complex than the F-5s they replaced. Instead of the one-day class and squadron-run syllabus we had for the F-5, the F-16 training program required pilots and RIOs to spend a full month at Luke AFB in Arizona. And that's where Zone was the next time Maritime Air Threat needed to be given. No problem, my schedule at the RAG was very flexible, so I flew to Oceana on a Wednesday, gave the lecture on Thursday, and ran some simulators to help the FAST team. I missed dinner at The Raven, but it was fun to sit at the console one more time.

I went on to give Maritime Air Threat two more times at Miramar before finally hanging up my gold nametag. I gave that lecture before I was attached to Topgun and now had given it after I detached.

The refresher syllabus at the RAG was exactly what I hoped for. Having taught and evaluated them, I was intimately familiar with F-14 tactics and weapons, so lectures on those subjects were optional for me. Since I had not actually flown the F-14 for more than two years, however, I made a point to attend lectures for systems such as fuel and electrical, pleased to find that most of my earlier knowledge was retrievable from its storage space somewhere in my brain.

I knew all of the RAG instructors from being at Miramar for years, and I realized that every time I would pop into the ready room to check on a flight, run through the snack bar where instructors sometimes hung out, or sit in on a class, they would make a point of saying, "Hey, Bio, how's it going?" It reminded me of my first time through the RAG six years before, when Streak got the same treatment as he cycled through for his refresher on the way from Topgun to VF-24. Now I was one of those guys, too.

About nine on a Monday morning in April I once again strapped on leg restraints when I got suited up. I didn't need to carry my parachute out to the jet, it was part of the seat. After giving the jet a good examination from the ground, I climbed the boarding ladder and stood on the broadly curved upper surface of the magnificent gray fighter, looking back at the twin tails and forward at the open cockpit canopy. I felt like I belonged.

The PC helps the pilot and me strap in, we get an ICS check, and I close the canopy as he started the engines.

Methodically sweep the cockpit checking all switches, enter latitude and longitude, start the system checks. A few minutes later, ready to go.

We taxi past dozens of other Tomcats, out of the line and to the hold short, where I call, "Miramar tower, November Juliet 430. F-14 for takeoff."

Glossary

Note: *These definitions refer to how the terms are used in this book, in a U.S. Navy environment.*

Some may differ slightly from how they are used by other services or other countries.

A-4 Skyhawk: Developed in the mid-1950s, the A-4 provided the Navy and Marine Corps with a simple, versatile aircraft that could be operated from aircraft carriers. Built by Douglas Aircraft (which later became McDonnell Douglas), it was used extensively in Vietnam and flown by a half-dozen foreign forces. From 1974 through 1986, the Navy's famous flight demonstration team, the Blue Angels, used A-4s. The TA-4 version included a second seat with complete flight controls, and hundreds were used to train student pilots and NFOs. Topgun flew single-seat A-4s with non-essential equipment removed to save weight and the most powerful engines the

Navy could fit into them. As of 2010, A-4s are still used by several foreign countries.

ACM: Air combat maneuvering, a general term for close-in air-to-air combat training with enemy fighters. Basically, dogfighting. It could involve one friendly fighter against one enemy, known as a one-versus-one or 1v1, or multiple aircraft on each side, such as 2v3. Friendly fighters are always listed before the v.

Afterburner (or burner): Assembly that injects pure fuel into a metal tube that extends aft of the basic engine, and ignites it. Most fighters have them. Increases thrust by fifty percent or more, but fuel consumption goes up ten times or more. The F-14's afterburners had five stages or zones, so Zone 5 was max burner.

Angle of attack: The angle at which an aircraft's wings meet the air stream. Despite the inclusion of the word "attack," the term is not related to weapons, and applies to all aircraft.

Bag: Aviator slang for the Nomex flight suit.

Bandit: An identified enemy aircraft. This is a refinement of the general category of bogey.

Bingo: A fuel state at which the aircraft should stop performing its mission, whether training or combat, and return to its base or head for aerial refueling. Bingo is established before takeoff and varies based on conditions such as weather. It can also be used as a verb to describe when an aircraft has reached the fuel level and bingos to its base.

Bogey: Technically, this is any radar contact. It was sometimes used imprecisely, as in my early years of flying, but later we were better about using "bogey" to indicate an unknown aircraft and "bandit" to indicate an enemy.

Break: A maximum-performance turn, usually in response to a threatening aircraft or missile. Due to aerodynamics (induced drag associated with lift), a break turn caused the aircraft to rapidly lose speed, so could be used to help tactical aircraft return to base faster. They would fly to the airfield at high speed and then perform a break turn overhead the runway, slowing quickly to landing speed.

Call sign: An aviator's nom *de guerre*. Call signs developed because aviators didn't want to use real names on the radio, and there could be multiple people with the same name. Call signs basically replaced given names in squadrons.

CAP: Combat air patrol, a mission in which a fighter patrols assigned airspace using his radar, visual lookout, or other sensors. When Navy carriers operate in the open ocean, fighters were frequently assigned CAP missions, even though there was no enemy and no combat. These flights often became simple training flights with the fighter(s) on other CAP stations.

CO: Commanding officer. The senior officer of a squadron, could be either a pilot or NFO. Had a call sign from his earlier days, but was always called CO or Skipper by those in the squadron.

Deployment: Term for extended overseas operations by aircraft carriers, air wings, and other ships. We usually called one a "cruise." In the 1970s, Navy deployments could last nine months. During peacetime in the early 1980s they were seven and a half months. In the mid-1980s the Navy reduced the standard overseas deployment to six months, and personnel retention improved.

Division: Navy term for four aircraft operating together. Also known as a four-ship.

Echo Range: The electronic warfare range near China Lake, California, officially known as restricted airspace R-2524. Electronic warfare is abbreviated E. W., which in the phonetic alphabet is "Echo Whiskey." The name of the range was shortened to Echo Range.

F-5 Tiger II: Originally developed by Northrop in the 1960s, the F-5 was intended as a lightweight fighter for U.S. allies. The F-5E and F-5F (single-seat and two-seat versions, respectively) were developed in the 1970s and had significant improvements over earlier models. Due to their similarity to the MiG-21, a common threat fighter, in size and many performance aspects, the F-5E and F-5F were used as adversaries by several Navy and Marine Corps squadrons, including Topgun. (The U.S. Air Force used the F-5E.) As of 2010, hundreds of F-5s are still used as operational fighters by countries around the world, and by the Navy and Marine Corps as adversary aircraft.

F-14 Tomcat: A large, sophisticated, maneuverable fighter developed in the late 1960s that served in U.S. Navy fighter squadrons from 1974 through 2006. Manufactured by Grumman Aerospace, the F-14 incorporated many lessons from Vietnam War aerial combat, and had greater maneuverability and better cockpit visibility than its predecessors. It also benefited from decades of radar and missile development, giving it one of the best long-range weapons systems ever deployed on a fighter. As of 2010, F-14s are still in service with Iran, the only other country to operate them.

FAST: Fleet Air Superiority Training, a one-week program run by the Navy Fighter Weapons School to give fighter and E-2 Hawkeye aircrews specialized training in defending an aircraft carrier from a raid by bombers, cruise missiles, and jammers. The concept was to apply Topgun-level training to this challenging problem. FAST included lectures and complex scenarios in simulators.

Furball: Aviator slang for a dogfight, where friendly fighters are engaged with enemy aircraft.

ICS: Intercom system, which allowed the F-14 pilot and RIO to communicate via the microphones built in to their oxygen masks and headphone speakers in their helmets. Virtually all multi person aircraft have ICS.

John Wayne: To do something the hard way or continue doing a task when an automatic system isn't available.

Knots: A measure of speed, nautical miles per hour. A nautical mile is 6,076', which is about 1/6 longer than a statute mile, so speed in knots is roughly 1 1/6 times faster than the miles per hour most people are used to. Here are some common speeds converted to mph:

- 250 knots = 290 mph
- 300 knots = 345 mph
- 450 knots = 520 mph
- 600 knots = 690 mph
- 1,000 knots = 1,150 mph

Merge: The small piece of sky where friendly fighters meet enemy fighters after an intercept.

MiG: Acronym for Mikoyan-Gurevich, a leading builder of fighter aircraft in the Soviet Union and Russia, named after the two founding designers.

Military power: The highest power a fighter's jet engine can produce without using afterburner.

NFO: Naval Flight Officer, a U.S. Navy or Marine Corps aircrew member who is not a pilot. NFOs were referred to by different terms for different aircraft, such as Bombardier/Navigator (BN) in the A-6 Intruder medium bomber, and Tactical Coordinator (TACCO) in the P-3 Orion maritime patrol aircraft. Most Navy aircraft do not have duplicate flight controls for NFOs. NFOs wore gold wings on their uniform similar to pilot wings, except pilot wings had one anchor in the middle, and NFO wings had two crossed anchors.

PC: Plane captain, usually an enlisted person who is responsible for an aircraft. In the U.S. Navy, PCs are usually fairly new to a squadron, but they have broad responsibilities for routine inspection and servicing of aircraft and preparing them for flight.

Phonetic alphabet: The use of a word to represent each letter to ensure clarity of communication over a radio. The U.S. military phonetic alphabet is: Alfa, Bravo, Charlie, Delta, Echo, Foxtrot, Golf, Hotel, India, Juliett, Kilo, Lima, Mike, November, Oscar, Papa, Quebec, Romeo, Sierra, Tango, Uniform, Victor Whiskey, X-Ray, Yankee, Zulu. The pronunciation of numbers is similar to common pronunciation except for "Niner."

RAG: Slang term for squadrons that trained aviators in specific types of aircraft. It came from "replacement air group," a term that had been officially replaced in 1963 by "fleet replacement squadron," but RAG was easier to say than FRS and the nickname survived. The F-14 had two RAGs for a while: VF-124 at NAS Miramar and VF-101 at NAS Oceana in Virginia Beach. There are RAGs for the F/A-18, E-2, EA-6B, and other types, at least one RAG for every major type of aircraft the Navy flies.

Ready 6: The ready room assigned to Fighter Squadron 24 (VF-24) on USS *Constellation* for the 1981–82 deployment. Each squadron had its own ready room.

RIO: Radar intercept officer, a category of Naval Flight Officer who was the second crewman in the F-14 Tomcat. Almost always spoken as "rio," as in Rio Grande. For crew coordination purposes, RIOs were primarily responsible for communication and navigation, as well as operating the F-14 radar. RIOs in the F-14 did not have flight controls (throttles, control stick, and rudder pedals), although Topgun F-5Fs had flight controls in the rear cockpit. In most current fighters, the second crewman is called a weapon systems officer (WSO).

SA: Situational awareness, a broad term encompassing aircrew knowledge of many factors, from minimum essentials such as their own fuel state and weapons load, to more complex subjects such as the requirements of their mission and the number and location of threatening enemy aircraft.

SDO: Squadron duty officer, the junior officer responsible for making the squadron operate effectively and safely during his watch. In a Navy fighter squadron, the SDO was usually a lieutenant or lieutenant (junior grade) who was assigned for twenty four hours and sat behind the duty desk in the ready room while aircraft were flying.

Section: Navy term for two aircraft operating together. Also known as a two-ship.

Suitcase: To have an accurate understanding of the situation; to display great SA.

TACTS Range: Airspace over the desert east of Yuma, Arizona, used in conjunction with the Tactical Aircrew Combat Training System and officially known as restricted airspace R-2301 West. To communicate with the TACTS system aircraft carried a pod that was the size and shape of a Sidewinder missile. The TACTS system gathered and recorded a large amount of data from each aircraft and its weapons system. It could display multiple aircraft real-time and was useful for detailed debriefing.

Tailhook: A strong hook at the end of a steel tube more than seven feet long on an F-14. Most military aircraft have arresting hooks for emergency use, but those on Navy carrier-based aircraft were designed, like the airplanes themselves, for the stress of repeated arrested landings.

TID: Tactical information display, a round display screen, nine inches in diameter, in the F-14's rear cockpit. Symbols showed radar targets and other situation information.

XO: Executive officer. The second-ranking officer in a squadron, under the CO, who could be either a pilot or an NFO. In Navy squadrons, the XO became the CO when the current CO detached for his next duty or if he was lost. Had a call sign from his earlier days, but was always called XO by those in the squadron.

Zone 5: Maximum afterburner in the F-14A. Minimum afterburner was Zone 1.

Acknowledgments

It is very rewarding to finish writing a book, having once committed to the task, and even more rewarding to see it to publication. I am grateful to the people listed below who generously assisted along the way. I apologize to anyone I may have left out.

One of the first people who knew about my project was the late George Hall, an extraordinary aviation photographer, author, businessman, mentor, and friend. George provided accurate criticism, prodding, and inspiration. After we lost him, his wife, Nicky, continued to assist and advise.

The following people provided valuable comments, technical information, links to contacts, or other assistance: Glenn "Monk" McCormick, Marty "Streak" Chanik, Paul "Nick" Nickell, Steve "Sonic" Hejmanowski, Doug Siegfried of the Tailhook Association, Ed Barker of the Naval Education and Training Command, Paul Jarvis, Patrick "M-Dog" Catt, Annie Patenaude, and Diane Tedeschky. I appreciate the comments I received on early drafts of the manuscript from Patrick Morganelli, Kaye Eubank, Makoto Fujisaki, Linda Mars, Carrie Pakroo, Duncan Russell, Paul Danner, Joe Badick, Frank DiPatri, Cathy Richter, Casie Hamman, and Alfredo Maglione. Thanks to photographer David F. Brown, who took a nice set of author photos at the F-14 Tomcat on display at the Veterans of Foreign Wars post in East Berlin, Pennsylvania, and Gary Kopp, who keeps the aircraft and display area in excellent condition.

I found that published authors were generous in discussing the publishing business and patient in answering my novice questions. These include Peter Mersky, Walter Boyne, Robert Dorr, Buzz Williams, Mike Machat, Jay Stout, Ed Ruggero, Jim Farmer, Bob Lawson, Barrett Tillman, Ward Carroll, Duck Auten, James W. Huston, and Jim Hirsch.

I would also like to thank story consultant Dennis Mathis and editor Hillel Black. My editor at Skyhorse Publishing, Mark Weinstein, has been enthusiastic about the book and great to work with—as have the whole crew at Skyhorse.

Finally, I'd like to thank my agent, Robert Astle.

Thank you.

Index